Essays in Literary History and Criticism

✹

TRADITION
AND
POETIC STRUCTURE

✹

J. V. Cunningham

✹

ALAN SWALLOW, *Denver*

Preface

I have attempted in this book to be brief, clear, and cold-blooded, to make a number of positive contributions to the field of literary scholarship, and to present a consistent and no doubt unpoetical attitude toward poetry. I should, perhaps, have practiced more the higher and easier art of literary criticism.

The various essays were written over the years from 1938. Five were presented as a series of public lectures at the University of Chicago in the Spring of 1952, and one at the University of Michigan in the Spring of 1949. A number have been published serially, sometimes in a variant form: the second in *Philological Quarterly,* the third and fourth in *Modern Philology,* the fifth and "The Donatan Tradition, III" in *ELH,* the seventh and "Appendix One" in *Poetry. Woe or Wonder* is reprinted from the original edition (Denver, 1951) with the correction of a howler at the top of page 102 in that book and the addition of two notes, one of which acknowledges an indebtedness I had forgotten by the time of publication.

I have obviously acquired over the years a burden of indebtedness. I shall on this occasion, however, name only the two books that have most deeply influenced me, books whose special value for me doubtless lay in the time at which they were read: W. P. Ker, *Form and Style in Poetry* and Edwin Greenlaw, *The Province of Literary History.* I am grateful to the John Simon Guggenheim Memorial Foundation for the award of a fellowship for the academic year 1959-60 which made the completion of this work possible, and to Brandeis University for, among many other things, the grant of sabbatical leave for the same academic year.

J.V.C.

December 31, 1959
Chicago 37, Ill.

Contents

ESSAYS

Poetry, Structure, and Tradition

This book is about poetry, and particularly about the structure of individual poems and their relationship to a tradition. Consequently, I shall begin with some more general remarks on the nature of poetry, of structure, and of tradition.

To begin with the definition of poetry. It is said that poetry is difficult to define, and the difficulty would seem to be of two sorts. In the first place, there is in different definitions a difference in what is being defined. Poetry is regarded as a kind of literature, a quality of experience, a way of knowing. It is contrasted with verse, with prose, and with science. It is defined in such a way as to favor a special view of experience or to promote the writing or approval of a special kind of poem. The difficulty, then, lies in the fact that the object of definition is not constant. The hesitations, the scruples, the blurring in the act of definition result from this. There remains, however, a constant point, if not of reference at least of departure, in all these formulations, and this is poetry as it is ordinarily understood: the body of linguistic constructions that men usually refer to as poems.

The second difficulty springs from the need to defend and to praise poetry. Very nice things are said of it. In fact, it is felt that one has not only to define poetry but also in so doing to put it in a place of honor, to recover some of the prestige that once accrued to the Muses. A particularly happy definition, one is led to believe, might elicit a donation from some elderly recluse or from a foundation. But these claims for poetry, which invade the description and definition of it, this concern with a higher something, knowledge or feeling, while they might seem designed to improve its estate, have in fact weakened it. They have on the

11

one hand erected pretensions that no linguistic construction, no poem, could ever hope to satisfy. The statements, in brief, are not true. Poets, for example, are not "the unacknowledged legislators of the world," and a good thing it is that they aren't. And the claims have, on the other hand, by qualifying the conception of poetry both limited the kinds of poetry that can be written and the audience that is prepared to receive it. They have exiled most of human experience from the poet's page, and he is left with an image and a mood:

> For all the history of grief
> An empty doorway and a maple leaf[1]

If one glances through the history of criticism it would appear that there are in general three definitions of poetry that have persisted throughout the tradition. The commonest is that which regards it as a quality of experience associated with a special selection and use of language, and the quality of experience is normally one that is thought to command prestige. A representative formulation is offered by one of the standard dictionaries, where poetry is characterised as: "The expression of beautiful or elevated thought, imagination, or feeling, in appropriate language, such language containing a rhythmical element and having usually a metrical form."[2] Of such a definition we may say that it appears to isolate and explore the activity and subject matter of poetry, but that in fact it introduces a principle of value which is prescriptive as to what kinds of poetry should be written or cherished. Furthermore, the principle which arrogates to poetry a higher kind of experience is pretentious. Finally, we may observe that such definitions are fairly reticent about meter, but firmer with respect to rhythm, which is usually regarded as primitive and emotional, and hence, no doubt, higher. Nevertheless, it is true that at different times certain attitudes toward the kinds of experience and certain associated selections of language have been comprised in the idea of poetry. Hence, as a method of defining, not poetry, but the poetry of a given tradition, this is an appropriate and useful method.

12

The second of the definitions that are commonly offered is usually ascribed to Aristotle in the *Poetics*. In that work Aristotle attempts to distinguish a kind of what he calls imitation which had been, he says, up to that time without a name. It is the kind of imitation in which an action is represented by means of language, and he cites as examples the Platonic dialogue and the mimes of Sophron. Of the same kind, with the exception that music as well as language is used as a means of imitation, are epic, comedy, and tragedy. For this more general kind he appropriates the name of poetry, a name which had been more customarily applied, as he points out, to compositions in meter.[3] Aristotle, of course, is simply developing and systematizing a notion already available in the tradition, the notion which Socrates accepts in the *Phaedo* that a poet to be really a poet must employ fiction.[4] It follows, then, that for poetry in this sense meter is not essential; it can be at most a contributory means appropriate to the end. For what is being defined is what we call fiction, and this may be, as it is in Plato's dialogues, in prose, or as in Homer and Sophocles, in verse. However, the use of a common term implies a common object of reference and so the question has arisen again and again since Aristotle's day whether a poem need be written in meter, and whether a poem that is not in some sense an imitation of an action, that is, fiction, is really a poem or rather something else—perhaps rhetoric. But fiction and metrical composition are simply two different things: a work may be both, or either, or neither.

However, though every composition in meter need not have a narrative structure, need not be fiction, it is pretty likely to have some sort of structure analogous to the narrative structure of fiction. If we use *fiction,* then, in a wider sense, if we generalize the notion to extend to the device, whatever it is, that orders the material of the poem in outline, we may regard a metrical composition as having a principle of fiction, and we may discuss what is the fiction of this particular poem, what kinds of fictions various poems exhibit, and perhaps what kinds of fictions are

13

possible or practical in poetry. A fiction in this broader sense is a major principle of order in a work, and I shall discuss a number of such principles in the following chapters.

I prefer with respect to poetry the third, the common or garden variety of definition. I mean by poetry what everyone means by it when he is not in an exalted mood, when he is not being a critic, a visionary, or a philosopher. I mean by poetry what a man means when he goes to a bookstore to buy a book of poems as a graduation gift, or when he is commissioned by a publisher to do an anthology of sixteenth century poems. Poetry is what looks like poetry, what sounds like poetry. It is metrical composition.

To define a poem in this way will seem trivial to some and offensive to others. It will seem to depreciate the importance of poetry. It will seem to signal out what is thought to be an accidental and to ignore the essential quality of poetry. It will be objected to, in addition, as affording no principle of value by which one could distinguish a good poem from a bad, for certainly that distinction will not lie solely or even largely in the meter. But all of these objections, where they are not motivated by a concern to advance the prestige and practice of a special kind of poetry or by the inveteracy of old habit now appalled, spring from a tacit and perhaps unconscious assumption about the nature and function of a definition. It is assumed that the definition is offered in the form and spirit of the Aristotelian tradition. It is assumed that a definition, in marking off an object from all other objects of the more general kind to which it belongs, purports to distinguish the peculiar virtue of the object, and in terms of the point of difference to offer a principle of judgment, a scale of values. And it is assumed that the point of difference is more important than, is important to the detriment of, the general class to which the object is assigned. But there is no need to assume this. The purpose of the definition is simply to mark off the territory and to describe the thing unmistakably.

How these assumptions tacitly operate can be seen in the

14

traditional definition of man as a rational animal. This formulation was preferred to the alternatives, that man is a two-legged or a laughing animal, largely because it was felt that in his rationality lay his peculiar glory and claim to prestige, and that this was a worthy principle of evaluation that could be applied to the rating of particular men. There is not much glory in two-leggedness or laughter, and neither would offer an acceptable scale of values. Again, in the traditional definition, and in the views which grew out of it, the rationality of man was attended to to the depreciation of his animality; the specific took precedence over the generic. But the tacit demands here made on a definition are demands of a different order than the requirements for clarity and accuracy of definition, and the alternative formulations might have served the latter purpose as well or better.

II

To begin, then, with the general class to which poems belong: a poem is a composition; that is, it is a system of propositions. I take *proposition* in a more general sense than is usual; a proposition is a determinate relationship of signs forming an element in a composition consisting of successive elements of this nature. Thus an algebraic equation is a proposition, and that equation subjected to a successive series of transformations would constitute a system of propositions. The syllogism in logic is of the same order, as is a piece of music in so far as the musical signs are grouped into elements, for example, into what are called phrases. Of the same order is a recorded game of chess, in which the elements, of course, are the distinct moves: P-K4, P-K4. But each of these differs from such things as an incident, a statue or picture, a football game or a horse race. We can formulate propositions about these; we can describe the incident, the picture, or the game, and the formulation refers to the object, but it is not the object. The poem, however, is the text; the equation is the equation; and the game of chess is the recorded series of

15

moves. Whatever the source of the propositions and however the man who wrote them down may have arrived at them, once the formulation has been recorded the experience it refers to and the experience it directs are properly confined to the meanings of the terms and the meanings of their relationship and succession.

Consequently, there is an exact analogy between poetry and chess, since they are things of the same kind. The poet in writing a poem has a good many experiences that do not appear in the propositions he puts on paper, the completed poem. The player at chess has a good many experiences that do not appear in the moves he makes on the board, the moves that recorded in the standard notation constitute for him and for anyone who knows chess the game he played. This game is repeatable as the poem is repeatable, and the experiences that properly belong to it are the repeatable experiences. In fact, the game as played and the poem as written constitute a principle of order, a method, for discriminating the relevant from the irrelevant among one's immediate experiences as he plays or reads or writes, and among one's retrospective experiences as he sums up after the game or after the completion of the poem. To be repeatable and to be a method for discriminating relevant from irrelevant experiences are characteristics of all composition.

There is a further characteristic. The player at chess in making each move envisages a variety of alternative moves, and we in replaying the same game must do alike if we are to achieve the recorded experience. Similarly the text of a poem consists of what little is left, out of the wide-strewn wreckage of alternative phrases, lines, and possibilities of development. No one has read a poem who has not constructed and rejected as he read some of the alternative poems whose non-existence gives timbre and resonance to the text.

There is also an inexact analogy between poetry and chess. It is slightly fanciful, but not untrue and not without its applications. The player at chess has an opponent. He makes his moves not only within the rules of the game and the limitation of the

16

board and his pieces, but also within the possibilities afforded by his opponent's moves and by the potentiality of his future moves. The player is not free to erect what structure he pleases within the rules of the game. If he chooses to be whimisical, there are consequences that must be dealt with. If he moves his pieces merely to accomplish a pretty design, an apparent pattern, he moves to disaster. The poet, too, has an opponent. His opponent is experience. The nature and quality of the game the two of them play will depend not only on his own skill but also on the adroitness and resourcefulness of his opposing experience. If experience is simple, unseasoned, without depth, the poet may have an easy time of it but the game suffers; it lacks depth and interest. And if the opponent is dishonest, if he throws away a queen to extricate the poet from a difficult spot, the game will be shoddy and not worth the playing. There are poems that are praised for their order, simplicity, and charm that so far as I can see represent a victory over nothing at all. We must distinguish between the simplicity of a Capablanca against Nimzovitch,[5] of a master of chess against a master of chess, and the simplicity with which one defeats a friend when he negligently forgets to castle. But this is a digression.

To return: it is characteristic of a composition that it is repeatable, that it is a method for discriminating the repeatable from the unique in experience, and that it is the specification of a range of possible compositions. There is a further characteristic which all compositions have. They all conform to the rules of the game, by which is stipulated beforehand what kinds of terms, of propositions and successions of propositions are admissable. For example, the rules of the traditional syllogism of the type *All men are mortal* are fairly simple and fairly easily stated. In brief, there will be three propositions and in this order: all items belonging to a certain general class have a certain property; this item belongs to that general class; therefore, this item has that property. The rules are a method for inventing further syllogisms with the same structure. The rules of chess are more complex, but of the same

17

order. The rules of poetry, or rather the rules of the various traditions of poetry, are of the same order, but even more complex. Nevertheless, they are describable, and to describe the rules of the game is to define a tradition. A tradition is all the ways a particular poem could have been written; it is the potentiality of realized structures, as the rules of chess contain all the games that may be played.

III

But a poem is not only a composition; it is a composition of a special sort. What distinguishes a poem from all other items in its general class is that the propositions are in meter, and hence if poetry has any peculiar province this issues from the fact that it is metrical. There are three possibilities. Since meter is an aspect of language it is possible that certain special meanings can be conveyed by meter that cannot be conveyed by unmetrical language, either different kinds of meaning or more or less refined versions of similar meanings. It is said, for example, that metrical language can deal more subtly and more accurately with feeling. Again, meter may have some special effect on those who use it. Poetry, for example, tends to be more memorable than prose and tends to support a greater extraordinariness of language. The third possibility is this: wherever one finds alternative forms in a language, the existence of a distinction in form tends to beget a distinction in function or purpose, and usually by an unnoticed historical process. In time, then, certain areas of experience will be assigned to metrical and others to unmetrical composition, and this is what has happened in the history of literature. Furthermore, the areas assigned to each medium shift and vary from time to time and place to place. It follows, then, that poetry of a given time and place will tend to deal with those areas of experience which convention and history have assigned to writing in meter. In brief, a poem is the sort of thing that poets write, and what they write is the sort of thing their society has come to regard as poetry. By their society here I mean the larger or smaller group at a given time and place who are concerned with the production and appreciation of poetry. What that society regards as poetry is what I mean by tradition. What it regards as poetry will furnish the rules of the game.

Consequently, though a tradition is historical in that it issues from an historical process, it is not in itself its history. It exists at each moment in completed form. For a tradition is rather, both in the terms in which it must be described and reconstituted by the literary historian and in the actual way in which it is attained and apprehended by a given writer at a given time, a context of notions, often jumbled and sometimes not too consistent with one another, together with the methods and attitudes by which these notions are grasped and applied. A tradition can be located in the body of texts and interpretations current among a given group of writers and readers. Such a description applies equally to the traditions in which Chaucer or Shakespeare wrote and to those which are now current: one must be learned as well as the other, and in the same way.

A tradition, however, is not simply a body of learning. It is a body of learning capable of being applied to the production of what are called original works. It is the method by which the sentences of a poem are discovered: it demarks the field of discovery and orders the succession of sentences. It is the potentiality of any work in the tradition.

Hence, the notions which constitute a tradition are not ideas merely, but principles of order. They are schemes which direct the production of works. For a principle of order is that which directs and determines the selection of the materials that enter into a work, and their succession and importance. Such principles may relate to language as such. Meter and rhyme are of this sort, and so is what we ordinarily call language. A poem in Latin is not a poem in English. But even within a given language there are many sub-languages, and there have been in all periods of the history of poetry special selections of language appropriated to

19

poems, or to certain kinds of poems, or to certain groups of poets.

By selection of language I mean not merely a limited and special vocabulary (the aureate diction of the Scottish Chaucerians, for example) but also certain possibilities of phrasing allowed and others disallowed, certain syntactical patterns predominant and others seldom or never used. The language of Lyly's *Euphues* is an obvious and easily characterised sub-language of this sort.

The principles of order may relate to literature as such, regarded as a separate activity and not as an imitation of life, and of this sort are the numerous literary conventions which both writers and historians have recognised. The conventions of the Petrarchan sonneteer are only partly to be found in the unliterary life of his times; to a considerable extent they exist rather in the experience of literature. The idea of tragedy in a given tradition, though not unrelated to life, is a literary idea. I shall discuss at length in a later essay a principle of order of this sort, the medieval literary convention of the dream vision.

Lastly, principles may be derived from sources external to literature, and may be of the sort that order the material of non-literary experience. Of this nature are the methods of logic, and I shall subsequently discuss such principles at length, or notions proper to theology which I shall take up in connection with the *Phoenix and Turtle*. Principles of a similar nature are common in fiction, those principles, namely, which deal with how men generally act and feel, which have been appropriated by the science of psychology from the ancient art of rhetoric, together with those abstractions as to life and the universe, which belong as abstractions to the province of philosophy and in exemplification to the province of fiction. But all these, though they may be regarded as material or conclusions in other branches of endeavor, are for the man who writes primarily the methods by which he both finds what he has to say and says it in succession and with appropriate emphasis and development.

Consequently, there is a sense in which a work of literature is nothing but an adjustment of a congeries of principles of order.

In another sense, it is only a specification of the potentialities of a tradition. The specification is the structure of the poem. For the poem itself is a structure and it has a structure. By the structure of a poem, then, I mean the principles of order that determine it and their inter-relationships with each other. It should be remarked that no poem could have only a single principle: meter, for example, is always an independent principle. However, to give a full description in every case of the principles that enter into a work would be difficult, certainly clumsy, and largely unnecessary. And so in the following essays I shall in practice discuss only one or two of the leading principles of order in a work and the tradition to which these are related.

IV

If a poem is a system of propositions, and if the propositions are discovered and ordered by a system of principles, then these principles are not extrinsic to the work; they are not merely possible ways of viewing the object, but are intrinsic to it. They are formative elements in the work itself and hence in the experience of the work.

Consequently, it will be relevant to ask at this point, How do we experience a poem? By what process do we apprehend it? And we will find that the question we are raising is really the question, Where and in what way does the poem or work of art exist? What is its mode and locus of existence?[6] It is obvious that the poem is not simply in the text, in the closed book. *Hamlet* as an experience, in fact, is neither in the text, nor, for that matter, on the stage. It can exist as an experience only in the experience of some person, some reader or member of the audience. But there are difficulties in this statement, and not merely the difficulty that the experience of each reader is different, and different at each separate reading, and that some of these experiences, no doubt, are quite far removed from others. There is another difficulty, and one whose resolution will perhaps resolve the difficulty which has just been

21

stated. *Hamlet* is not in the immediate experience of a member of the audience as he is seeing or reading the play. If it were we could never think or speak of the play as a whole. We could only deal with this moment in my experience of the play, and we would have to treat our aesthetic experiences as Rochester treated his erotic, regarding each moment as absolute: "All my past life is mine no more . . . The present moment's all my lot . . ."

The play is rather the experience of having experienced the play. It is the result of a reconstruction in memory and a summing up in judgment after the play is over. The process is described by St. Augustine in one of those passages in the *Confessions* in which his extraordinary genius for introspection is given full scope. He is describing the act of reciting a Psalm:

> I am about to repeat a Psalm that I know. Before I begin, my expectation is extended over the whole; but when I have begun, how much soever of it I shall separate off into the past, is extended along my memory; thus the life of this action of mine is divided between my memory as to what I have repeated, and expectation as to what I am going to repeat; but "consideration" is present with me, that through it what was future may be conveyed over so as to become past. Which the more it is done again and again, so much the more the expectation being shortened, is the memory enlarged; till the whole expectation be at length exhausted, when that whole action being ended shall have passed into memory.
>
> 11.38[7]

So I know a poem or play thoroughly when the beginning, middle and end are comprehended in one synthetic act of recollection, and that synthetic act of recollection is the play.

That is, one leaves the theatre or lays down his book, lights a cigarette, and held within the spell of the experience the experience grows steady; it seems to come together. This is the unity of the work. The process is not wholly intellectual, nor wholly describable in intellectual terms since it is an experience, yet experience never comes together except when ordered by some principles, implicit or explicit, and the principles are describable.

22

Nor is it a matter of indifference what the principles are, for in consolidating the experience they alter it. The difference between the ordinary view of *Hamlet* and the one I shall later urge does not lie primarily in a difference in antecedent experiences, nor in a difference in experiences simultaneous with the experience of the text, since the text is a method of discriminating between the relevant and the irrelevant in those experiences. It does not lie primarily in the varying meaning that various readers impute to the words and constructions of the poem. It lies in the principles allowed and employed in constructing the final experience of the work.

The process is not peculiar to poetry. St. Augustine draws this moral himself in the passage which follows the one just quoted. He says:

> And this which takes place in the whole Psalm, the same takes place in each several portion of it, and each several syllable; the same holds in that larger action, whereof this Psalm may be a part; the same holds in the whole life of man, whereof all the actions of man are parts; the same holds through the whole age of the sons of men, whereof all the lives of men are parts.

It is the process by which each one of us sums up and unifies his life, so far as it can be unified. It is the process by which each constructs his personality. In this precise analogy may be located the moral, or as we now say the emotional or educational, importance of literature: it is an exercise in the recollection, the gathering up, of the elements of personality and in their ordering. And it is moreover true that the kinds of material which we notice, select, and emphasize in this process, together with the principles of order which we elicit from or impose on this material, are—in our society at least—largely derived from the art we favor.

But, though the process here described is not in general peculiar to poetry, there is a feature in the experience of poetry and of similar systems of propositions that is peculiar to it. It is that the object of experience in that case remains steady. In the case of our autobiography, for example, the experience does not remain steady unless we have formulated it and reduced it to a system of propositions. If we sit musing on our past the events shift with the transition of feeling. What was important a moment ago recedes and what was excluded as irrelevant grows large. Images and judgments waver and transform themselves into others, structures dissolve, as in our memory of a dream.

But it is different with a poem. Our experience there derives from and refers to an object that stays steady and persists. The text remains. Our experience is subject to verification and correction, and hence it has an element of externality in it. Futhermore, since it is the peculiar nature of a composition that the experiencing of the work may be repeated, and that we may be assured that this experience refers to the same work as did our previous experience, there is an element not only of externality in each experience, but also of stability, or of what may be called eternality. So in the cumulative re-experience of a given composition, except in so far as habituation ("That monster, custom, who all sense doth eat") deadens the impact, we may hope to come nearer and nearer to the norm of that experience which is ideally implicit in the work. It is the ideal implicit norm of, for example, *Hamlet* that enables us to say that we have seen *Hamlet* five times, though one of the performances was "hardly *Hamlet!*" The ideal implicit norm is the structure of the work; it is the congeries of principles of order that determines the work; it is the work itself. It is a thing external and eternal, a potentiality of experience waiting to be realized. It is the poem.

Classical and Medieval: Statius, On Sleep

There are different kinds of poems. There is, for example, a poem by Statius, the lovely invocation to sleep, which has captured the fancy of many, and especially of the English, critics. They like it so well they call it almost a sonnet, and they would excise three lines in the middle of the poem to make it more sonnet-like. But the poem is not a sonnet and the lines should not be excised, for to do so is to convert a poem of one kind into a poem of another.

The poem reads:

> Crimine quo merui, iuuenis placidissime diuum,
> quoue errore miser, donis ut solus egerem,
> Somne, tuis? Tacet omne pecus uolucresque feraeque
> et simulant fessos curuata cacumina somnos,
> nec trucibus fluuiis idem sonus, occidit horror
> aequoris et terris maria adclinata quiescunt.
> Septima iam rediens Phoebe mihi respicit aegras
> stare genas; totidem Oetaeae Paphiaeque reuisunt
> lampades et totiens nostros Tithonia questus
> praeterit et gelido spargit miserata flagello.
> Unde ego sufficiam? non si mihi lumina mille,
> quae sacer alterna tantum statione tenebat
> Argus et haud umquam uigilabat corpore toto.
> At nunc heu! si aliquis longa sub nocte puellae
> brachia nexa tenens ultro te, Somne, repellit,
> inde veni, nec te totas infundere pennas
> luminibus compello meis—hoc turba precatur
> laetior—: extremo me tange cacumine virgae,
> sufficit, aut leuiter suspenso poplite transi.[1]

25

I have translated this as literally as possible, taking care at the same time to represent those formal aspects of the poem which will come under discussion so that the reader whose English is better than his Latin may be at ease in the argument:

> What was my crime, youthful most gentle god,
> What folly was it that I alone should lack,
> Sweet Sleep, thy gifts? All herds, birds, beasts are still,
> The curved mountains seem wearily asleep,
> Streams rage with muted noise, the sea-wave falls,
> And the still-nodding deep rests on the shore.
> Seven times now returning Phoebe sees
> My sick eyes stare, and so the morning star
> And evening, so Tithonia glides by
> My tears, sprinkling sad dew from her cool whip.
> How, then, may I endure? Not though were mine
> The thousand eyes wherewith good Argus kept
> But shifting watch, nor all his flesh awake.
> But now, alas! If this long night some lover
> In his girl's arms should willingly repel thee,
> Thence come, sweet Sleep! Nor with all thy power
> Pour through my eyes—so may they ask, the many,
> More happy—: touch me with thy wand's last tip,
> Enough, or lightly pass with hovering step.

The conventional opinion of this poem is based on Mackail's comments. "Perhaps the finest, certainly the most remarkable," he says of Statius' occasional verses, "is the short poem (one might almost call it a sonnet) addressed to Sleep." He then quotes the text and remarks:

> Were the three lines beginning *Unde ego sufficiam* struck out— and one might almost fancy them to have been inserted later by an unhappy second thought—the remainder of this poem would be as perfect as it is unique. The famous sonnet of Wordsworth on the same subject must at once occur to an English reader; but the poem in its manner, especially in the dying cadence of the last two lines, recalls even more strongly some of the finest sonnets of Keats.[2]

26

This judgment has been accepted, extended, and hardened by English critics and literary historians. Tyrrell says: "This beautiful and pathetic little poem seems to have (more than any other ancient poem except, perhaps, the *Sirmio* of Catullus) the effect of a sonnet." Slater speaks of Statius' "short poem on sleep, which is admitted to be a masterpiece," paraphrases Mackail's comments, and quotes Fyfe's translation of the poem in the form of a sonnet (published 1903), remarking that the translator "has excised what Mackail considers a blemish in the original, the allusion to Argus of the thousand eyes." Garrod in the *Oxford Book of Latin Verse* quotes Fyfe's translation in the appendix of "Translations and Imitations," and follows it with six sonnets to sleep by Sidney, Daniel, Drummond, Wordsworth, Keats, and Hartley Coleridge. E. E. Sikes preserves the comparison with the English sonnet— the poem "is deservedly famous and may well take rank with the sonnets to Sleep by Wordsworth and Keats"—but translates the poem himself in three six-line stanzas and defends the Argus passage. In this he is a lone dissenter. Mozley in the introduction to the Loeb translation comments: "Best known of all the *Silvae*, probably, is the little sonnet-like poem addressed to the god Sleep." Duff quotes Mackail's "one might almost call it a sonnet," and adds that "if certain mythological lines are dropped, it can be reduced to the requisite proportions." He then prints his own early translation (published 1906) of the poem in the form of a sonnet. Finally, Philip Schuyler Allen says in introducing an English rendering by Howard Mumford Jones: "the translation has been designedly cast into a form suited to display to English readers the virtues of its original: a verse scheme after Sir Philip Sidney's hexameter sonnet."[3]

It is time now to examine Mackail's judgment. One must admit there is a nice sensitiveness in the comparison between the "dying cadence" in Statius' last lines and a similar effect in the last lines of some of Keats' sonnets, though not particularly, as the later critics have assumed, of the sonnet to Sleep. But the close of the sonnet on the Sea:

> Sit ye near some old cavern's mouth, and brood
> Until ye start, as if the sea-nymphs quired!

and especially of the sonnet "On a Leander Gem":

> see how his body dips
> Dead-heavy; arms and shoulders gleam awhile:
> He's gone: up bubbles all his amorous breath![4]

have a close similarity of effect to the close of Statius' poem. The similarity, however, is not mysterious; it is not the result of some affinity of spirit that can only be intuited by the literary tact of the critic. It resides in, and wholly in, the use of precisely the same technical devices by both poets, with such differences only as are required by the difference in language and in poetic tradition. In both the Leander sonnet and Statius' poem there is a kind of semi-dramatic colloquialness ("He's gone" and "sufficit"), and the use of a more specialized statement for the direct statement it implies ("up bubbles all his amorous breath," which implies "He is drowned," and "leviter suspenso poplite transi," which implies "May I be even the least bit asleep.")

But these similarities only support and limit the kind of similarity Mackail points to. This is the similarity in the movement of the verse. One may ask, What determines the movement of a verse line? It is determined by the metrical principles of the line itself, and by the relation of syntactical units to the ends of lines. In these terms there is a distinction between two traditions of verse movement, and this will ultimately turn out to be a distinction between two kinds of poetry. To one of these traditions both the passage from Statius and those from Keats belong.

It will be well to make this distinction clear by citing two other passages, both in English. The first is the invocation at the beginning of Gascoigne's *The Steele Glas,* the earliest non-dramatic poem of any length in blank verse; the second is Milton's invocation at the beginning of *Paradise Lost.* That the one is universally conceded to be better than the other is for the present beside the point—we are interested in making a distinction.

The Nighingale, whose happy noble hart,
No dole can daunt, nor fearful force affright,
Whose chereful voice, doth comfort saddest wights,
When she hir self, hath little cause to sing . .

Of Mans First Disobedience, and the Fruit
Of that Forbidden Tree, whose mortal tast
Brought Death into the World, and all our woe . . [5]

The differences are obvious. The meter of the one, though
not without certain discreet variations, displays and enforces in
every line the simple metrical pattern. Every line conforms strictly
to type: a regular alternation of unaccented and accented syllables
with a pause after the fourth syllable.[6] The lines in the second
passage also conform to a metrical type, but they conform in a
different sense. They conform in the sense that the type can be
inferred from a collection of lines; it is implicit in them. In the
first passage the type is apparent and, as it were, explicit in any
single line. Milton, as he himself says, observes "apt Numbers"
and "fit quantity of Syllables";[7] that is, his metrical practice is
based on the concept of decorum, or the reasonable adherence to
an implicit norm. Gascoigne's practice is based on the concept of
law, or the rational adherence to an explicit norm.

The passages differ also with respect to the relation of syntax
to the metrical structure. In Gascoigne each line is end-stopped,
and the internal pause occurs at precisely the same point in each
line. The thought is apprehended in units of alternately four and
six syllables. But it is a principle of Milton's prosody that the
sense should be "variously drawn out from one Verse into another," that the thought should be apprehended in units that cut
across the metrical structure. The difference is not simply one of
merit or skill, a question of monotony and variety; it is a difference
in kind. For the first passage, though not distinguished, is not
without merit. What it needs is rhyme, and for two reasons.
Rhyme would sustain the verse line, which tends as it is to dis-

appoint the ear, and would impart, if not a singing quality, at
least a kind of conviction to the rhetoric—for example:

> The nightingale whose happy noble heart
> No dole can daunt, no fearful force can start . . .

Secondly, since conformity to an external pattern is the guiding
principle in this tradition of poetry, the articulation of rhyme
in a fixed stanza would impose on the poem that order and articulation of thought, the lack of which is here more offensive than
is the apparent monotony of the verse line. For the poem is conceived in couplets, but not written in couplets.

Clearly the method of Milton is that of Keats and of Statius.
The metrical line in each, though it conforms to the patterns of
their respective traditions, yet exhibits considerable variety in
the permissible substitution of feet, in the placing of the pause,
and in the playing of accent against quantity in the quantitative
metre[8] and of quantity against accent in the accentual metre. In
each the syntactical structure of thought deviates from and plays
against the verse line. These formal elements carry with them a
disposition of feeling which is inherent in the method and which
is of the same general nature in each poem. But the agreement
between the close of the Leander sonnet and the close of Statius'
poem is much more particular; it is almost coincidental:

> see how his body dips
> Dead-heavy; arms and shoulders gleam awhile:
> He's gone: up bubbles all his amorous breath!

> hoc turba precatur
> laetior—: extremo me tange cacumine virgae,
> sufficit, aut leviter suspenso poplite transi.

> so may they ask, the many,
> More happy—: touch me with thy wand's last tip,
> Enough, or lightly pass with hovering step.

The types of syntactical structure and their placing relative to
the metrical line are almost identical in the two passages. There

30

could hardly be found for one ignorant of Latin a better illustration of the formal effect of Statius' lines than this passage from Keats.

Thus far I have approved of Mackail's remarks, and have even extended them. There remain now the two propositions, that the poem is sonnet-like and that the Argus passage should be excised. It is clear what Mackail and his successors have in mind. If you excise the three lines on Argus the poem falls into two parts of ten and six lines, which is close enough to the proportions of a sonnet. Furthermore, you may consider that the four lines (7-10) which precede the Argus passage (11-13) and which relate with four mythological references how the poet has been sleepless for a full week could be reduced to two lines at the most and could at the same time be improved by being disencumbered of mythological adornment.[9] What the modern reader fails to see, it may be remarked in passing, is that myth for the Latin poet is a field of poetic details parallel to and comparable with the field of natural landscape, as is illustrated in this poem. However, in this way a poem is begotten that corresponds precisely to the eight and six lines of the sonnet. Moreover, the octave can be conceived to present the situation, and the sestet the reflection upon the situation, and thus the poem could be said to exhibit perhaps the commonest type of internal form to be found in the sonnet. But this is not Statius' poem; it is one the critic has written himself in a form familiar to him.

The form of the original can be studied by comparing it with the famous sonnet by Wordsworth on the same subject to which Mackail and his successors allude:

> A flock of sheep that leisurely pass by,
> One after one; the sound of rain, and bees
> Murmuring; the fall of rivers, winds and seas,
> Smooth fields, white sheets of water, and pure sky;
> I have thought of all by turns, and yet do lie
> Sleepless! and soon the small birds' melodies
> Must hear, first uttered from my orchard trees;

31

And the first cuckoo's melancholy cry.
Even thus last night, and two nights more, I lay,
And could not win thee, Sleep, by any stealth:
So do not let me wear to-night away:
Without Thee what is all the morning's wealth?
Come, blessed barrier between day and day,
Dear mother of fresh thoughts and joyous health![10]

The resemblance of the two poems is quite close—the parallels in the third and fifth lines are particularly striking. This similarity in subject will consequently afford a surer basis than might otherwise have been for the comparison of formal qualities.

The sonnet has in common with Statius those elements that have already been discussed, a complex meter and the run-over line. In fact, if the run-over lines are scrutinized more closely they will be seen to be in both of a special type: in both the phrase halts early in the subsequent line:

> the sound of rain, and bees
> Murmuring . . .

> I have thought of all by turns, and yet do lie
> Sleepless . . .

> donis ut solus egerem,
> Somne, tuis?

In the first and third instances, at least, and less obviously in the second, the grammatical construction could be considered completed at the end of the line: "the sound of rain, and bees" and "donis ut solus egerem" are phrases sufficient in themselves. Yet the additional word or phrase at the beginning of the next line is by no means otiose: what it does is to extend the construction from one recognized syntactical pattern to another so that the addition, though it is not required, nevertheless affords when it has been made that effect of inevitability which arises from a completed pattern. Hence the resolution of the latter carries with it the special effect that it is the resolution of a pattern which emerged out of a former one.

In these respects, then, the poems are similar. But the respects in which they differ are more numerous, more obvious, and more important. The most obvious is that Wordsworth's poem is a sonnet, a fixed form, whereas Statius' could have been of any length. There was nothing in the ancient poet's tradition that prescribed the exact number of lines. In fact, it is a characteristic of Latin antiquity that even poems with a fixed refrain have an irregular number of verses between the refrains: for example, Vergil's Eighth Eclogue and Catullus lxii. Consequently, the particular length of this poem could only have been determined by chance, as Coleridge tells us the length of *Kubla Khan* was determined, or, as seems rather to be the case here, by what may be called an internal necessity: that is, the length was determined by the law of decorum or tact, by the fitness and aptness of the external form to the internal form of what was to be said. But the law of the sonnet is law in the strict sense: it is fixed, eternal, and given. It has the characteristics of Jehovah's pronouncements.

Thus the form of a sonnet does not emerge like the more modern God and take shape in the process of writing; it is an Idea and prior to the specific poem. The case is not that the poet has an inspiration in the sense of having a subject that moves him to write and that the poem turns out when he is finished to be a sonnet of exactly fourteen lines. If this were so, there would be few sonnets. The case is quite otherwise: he who would write a sonnet must begin with the idea of the form, and one can almost say, for paradox is sometimes an instrument of truth, that he hopes it will turn out to have a subject.

Of course, it is possible, and I have done it myself, for a poet relatively late in the process of writing to expand or reduce to the compass of a sonnet what was originally conceived as a poem, say, in quatrains, though scarcely one in blank verse. He may even begin scribbling lines, poetically exploring some subject, with no defined notion of its ultimate form apart from the metre, and even that may be changed at an early stage in the process of composition. Finally, when a certain number of lines and approximate formulations are scattered on the page, pages, or backs of envelopes, he may suddenly realize that the whole can best be redacted in the form of a sonnet. But at what point was the poem as it finally exists in the text first conceived? It was conceived when its potential realization was envisioned, when the poet saw that it would make a sonnet. But the kind of form which is envisioned alters essentially both the experience of writing and the final text so that a distinction in kinds of form is a distinction in kinds of experience and in kinds of poetry: in the one the external form is fixed and given in the tradition; in the other the external form presents at least the illusion of being a free determination.

But a sonnet is not only a poem of a given length; it is also a poem that conforms to one of a very few patterns, and patterns that are for the most part established in the tradition. The pattern of Wordsworth's sonnet is the familiar one in which two units of expression of four lines each comprise the first major division, and three units of two lines each comprise the second. Furthermore, the divisions are marked by an obvious device of external form, the arrangement of rhymes, and the divisions of thought correspond point for point with the external divisions. An outline of the rhyme-scheme and an outline of the thought of the poem would coincide. Even the relation of the two major divisions is an accepted one; the first is an exposition of the situation, the second a reflection on it.

But Statius' poem falls into two, or three, divisions, and the uncertainty on this point is characteristic of his kind of poetry. The first division comprises the first ten lines, in which are presented, as in Wordsworth's poem, the fact of the poet's sleeplessness and the contrast with the peace and quiet of external nature. But the passage is not subdivided into equal parts. The opening question, "Why do I alone lack sleep?" occupies two

34

and one-third lines. The illustration of the uniqueness of the poet's experience by contrast with the due and proper rest after exertion which external nature enjoys is expressed in three and two-thirds lines. And the return to his own situation, the complaint that he has been sleepless for a full week so that the gods pitied him, is expressed in four lines. Here is no point for point correspondence of the internal to the external form, no units of expression that bear a simple mathematical ratio, one to the other.

So it is with the rest of the poem, whether the Argus pasage is taken as a separate major division or as a part of the concluding section of nine lines. The passage itself occupies three lines: "I could not endure to lie thus open-eyed"—an aspect of sleeplessness—"even though I had the thousand eyes of Argus and could open and close ones by turn." Then in two lines: "But, taking the situation as it is, if there are those who can sleep, being happy in love, and will not since they would enjoy their love"—and now in one-third of a line: "transfer their rights in sleep to me." The paraphrase may be halted at this point since the second point of difference between the two poems is now sufficiently clear; the one conforms to an established pattern, the other establishes its own.

There is a third point of difference. If the above paraphrase is compared with the actual text, it will be found that little of what is made, and must be made, explicit in the paraphrase is explicit in the poem. It is true that the opening proposition is relatively explicit, yet it is given a rhetorical treatment that removes it from the bluntness of plain statement. The poet does not say directly that he alone has been sleepless; rather he asks why he alone has lacked thy gifts, Sleep. And the whole is framed in a rhetorical question as to the ᴄauses why sleep has been denied him, which by the gravity of the causes suggested (*crimen, error*) implies the gravity of the effect. Thus something else is said by indirection than could have been said in the same compass by direct statement, and this something else requires the active participation of the reader in finding it out. The reader must actively assist in constructing the poem.

For example, Statius does not say as one translator has him
say:

> But my sad eyes their nightly vigil keep.

He does not say that he has been sleepless a full week, though
this is clearly what he means. He says:

> Septima iam rediens Phoebe mihi respicit aegras
> stare genas; totidem Oetaeae Paphiaeque reuisunt
> lampades et totiens nostros Tithonia questus
> praeterit et gelido spargit miserata flagello.

> Seven times now returning Phoebe sees
> My sick eyes stare, and so the morning star
> And evening, so Tithonia glides by
> My tears, sprinkling sad dew from her cool whip.

Is this nothing but rhetorical amplification? It is that, of course,
but with a purpose. The sad plight of the poet is essential to the
poem, and there is required a certain bulk of language to give it
due importance. Such is the primary function of amplification.
But the passage in its precise wording has further purposes. The
succession of the moon, the morning star, and then the evening
star, and finally dawn again indicates by its very succession the
continuity and duration of time. It is the implying of a process
by a kind of poetic imitation of the process.

There are other types of implication in the poem. In the
last line of this passage the poet says that Tithonia sprinkles from
her cool whip. There seemed no way of excluding the word dew
from the translation; English style will hardly permit the omission.
In the original, however, the reader is not told what the dawn
goddess sprinkles but must himself complete the inference from
the material furnished by the poet, and the completion of the
inference is an integral part of the experience of the poem. Furthermore, in the same line there is involved another process of
completing the inference, the process that has come to be called
fusion in modern criticism. For Tithonia who sprinkles dew also

takes pity on the poet. But to take pity on someone is to shed a tear for him, and that tears are the dew of the eyes has been established by generations of poets.[11] Consequently, the reader must not only elicit both dew and tears from a passage that makes no mention of either; he must also through a feeling for literary tradition fuse or identify the image of dew and of tears.

Of the four kinds of poetic implication which have been analyzed so far—implication by rhetorical figure, by a kind of imitation of a process, implication in the proper logical sense, and implication by fusion—the two latter may be discussed a little more fully. Why is it that the poet cannot sleep? Is it, as Vollmer conjectures, because the poem was written during a spell of illness? Certainly insomnia accompanies some illnesses, and from another poem we learn that the poet was once quite ill.[12] But when we ask why the poet asserts that he cannot sleep, we must answer in terms of the particular poem. He cannot sleep in this poem because he is that conventional figure, the unhappy lover. For this reason Tithonia, rising from the bed of her senile husband, pities his condition; and for the same reason he begs of Sleep that if some happy lover willingly gives up his sleep, since being happy in love he could sleep if he would, some portion of that rejected sleep should be transferred to him. But the request is strictly qualified. He disclaims any petition for full and contented sleep, for it would be impious of the unhappy lover to pray for what is not his due. In the ancient erotic tradition sleeplessness is an inseparable accident of the unrequited lover; hence he asks only for the least bit of sleep. Thus the reader construes what is said in the poem in the light of the literary tradition, and infers what the situation of the poet is. The process is similar to, though not quite the same as, the construction of a hypothesis that saves the phenomena. It is different in that a poem is a closed system, and that tradition furnishes the lines of construction.

Implication by fusion will account for the Argus passage. The poet asks only for a little sleep, in fact, only for so much as Argus had who could close some of his thousand eyes while the others kept vigil. In this lies the function of the passage which Mackail would excise; it is the turning point in the poem, the hinge upon which the whole swings. It announces for the first time the conceptual basis of the poem, for this is not the contrast between no sleep and full sleep, but between a lack of sleep and the least degree of it. The Argus passage, then, foreshadows the final prayer, and being held in memory fuses with the last lines. The reader sees at that moment that the poet wishes to be Argus with respect to sleep.

To sum up, the paraphrasable meaning of Statius' poem is implicit in the text rather than explicit. But in Wordsworth's sonnet, on the contrary, the paraphrasable meaning is quite explicit. "I have thought of all by turns," he says, and by *all* he means the images of external nature which constitute the opening lines, "and yet do lie Sleepless." The poet himself gives in explicit statement the paraphrasable content of the octave; the wording of a paraphrase would be the wording of the text. This is clear also in the sestet:

> Even thus last night, and two nights more, I lay,
> And could not win thee, Sleep!   .   .   .
> So do not let me wear to-night away   .   .   .

The fourth and final point of difference between the two poems emerges from what has already been said. The conceptual basis of Statius' poem is not the contrast between sleeplessness and its logical contrary, but between degrees of sleeplessness. But Wordsworth's sonnet takes no note of such humanistic quibbling. The contrast there is plainly between one state and its logical opposite: the poet is either A or Not-A with respect to sleep, and there is in the text no middle ground.

In the course of this paper six characteristics of one kind of poetry have been discriminated and opposed to six characteristics of another kind. The one employs a complex and modulated metre; the other an obvious metre conforming to a simple mathematical scheme. The one plays the syntactical structure against

38

the metrical line; the other shows a marked coincidence of the two. In the one tradition the length of the poem tends to be a free determination; in the other it tends to be fixed and given. The outline of thought in the one tends not to correspond to the units of the external form; in the other it tends to correspond. The paraphrasable meaning of the one is largely implicit and to be inferred from the text; with the other it is explicit. Finally, the conceptual basis of the first kind of poetry will tend to be one of continuity and degree; in the second kind it will tend to be one of discontinuity, identity, and contradiction. The first kind is exemplified by the poetry of Horace, Vergil, and Statius, by Milton's *Lycidas* and most of his sonnets, and by a great deal of more modern poetry. The second kind is exemplified in most medieval and Tudor lyric. The first may be called the classical method, the second the medieval, and the history of the English lyric may be construed in terms of the transition from the second to the first.

Logic and Lyric:
Marvell, Dunbar, and Nashe

The discussion in the previous chapter raises the question, May the principal structure of a poem be of a logical rather than an alogical sort? For example, to confine ourselves to the Old Logic, May a lyric be solely or predominantly the exposition of a syllogism? and may the propositions of the lyric, one by one, be of the sort to be found in a logical syllogism?

The incautious romantic will deny the possibility, and with a repugnance of feeling that would preclude any further discussion. For logic and lyric are generally regarded as opposites, if not as contradictory terms. "It is a commonplace," says a recent writer on logic, "that poetry and logic have nothing to do with each other, that they are even opposed to one another."[1] You will find this explicitly stated, sometimes with the substitution of 'science' for 'logic', in most of the school handbooks on the study of literature, in most of the introductions to poetry. "The peculiar quality of poetry," we read in one of these:

> can be distinguished from that of prose if one thinks of the creative mind as normally expressing itself in a variety of literary forms ranged along a graduated scale between the two contrasted extremes of scientific exposition and lyrical verse.

And, a little later:

> [Poetry] strives for a conviction begotten of the emotions rather than of reason.

Consequently, we are told:

> The approach of poetry is indirect. It proceeds by means of sug-

40

gestion, implication, reflection. Its method is largely symbolical.
It is more interested in conotations than in denotations.[2]

This is common doctrine. Poetry is in some way concerned with emotion rather than reason, and its method is imaginative, indirect, implicit rather than explicit, symbolical rather than discursive, concerned with what its terms suggest rather than with what they state. The kind of poetry which most fully possesses and exhibits these concerns, methods, and qualities is generally thought to be the lyric, and hence it, of all poetry, is regarded as the most antithetical to reason, logic, and science.

This was not always the case. In the eighth century, for example, a scholiast of the school of Alcuin regarded not only grammar and rhetoric but dialectic or logic also as the disciplines that nourish and form a poet. In the medieval and renaissance traditions of commentary on Aristotle's logic, poetic is sometimes regarded as a part, a sub-division, of logic—as, indeed, I consider it myself. So late as the eighteenth century David Hume writes in an essay *Of the Standard of Taste*:

> Besides, every kind of compostion, even the most poetical, is nothing but a chain of propositions and reasonings; not always indeed the justest and most exact, but still plausible and specious, however disguised by the coloring of the imagination.

And even today the writer on logic whom I quoted earlier asserts, in denial of the commonplace: "Every poem, except in rare extreme cases, contains judgments and implicit propositions, and thus becomes subject to logical analysis."[3]

But may the chain of propositions and reasonings be not merely plausible and specious but even sufficiently just and exact? May the poem be not merely subject to logical analysis but logical in form? May, to return to our point, the subject and structure of a poem be conceived and expressed syllogistically? Anyone at all acquainted with modern criticism and the poems that are currently in fashion will think in this connection of Marvell's *To His Coy Mistress*. The apparent structure of that poem is an

41

argumentative syllogism, explicitly stated. "Had we but world enough and time," the poet says,

> This coyness, lady, were no crime . . .

> But at my back I always hear
> Time's winged chariot hurrying near . . .

> Now, therefore . . .
> . . . let us sport us while we may . . .

If we had all the time and space in the world we could delay consummation. But we do not. Therefore. The structure is formal. The poet offers to the lady a practical syllogism, and if she assents to it the appropriate consequence, he hopes, will follow:

> Had we but world enough, and time,
> This coyness, Lady, were no crime;
> We would sit down and think which way
> To walk and pass our long love's day.
> Thou by the Indian Ganges side
> Shouldst rubies find: I by the tide
> Of Humber would complain. I would
> Love you ten years before the Flood,
> And you should, if you please, refuse
> Till the conversion of the Jews.
> My vegetable love should grow
> Vaster than empires, and more slow;
> An hundred years should go to praise
> Thine eyes and on thy forehead gaze;
> Two hundred to adore each breast;
> But thirty thousand to the rest;
> An age at least to every part,
> And the last age should show your heart;
> For, Lady, you deserve this state,
> Nor would I love at lower rate.

> But at my back I always hear
> Time's winged chariot hurrying near;

And yonder all before us lie
Deserts of vast eternity.
Thy beauty shall no more be found,
Nor in thy marble vault shall sound
My echoing song: then worms shall try
That long preserved virginity,
And your quaint honor turn to dust,
And into ashes all my lust:
The grave's a fine and private place,
But none, I think, do there embrace.

Now, therefore, while the youthful hue
Sits on thy skin like morning lew,
And while thy willing soul transpires
At every pore with instant fires,
Now let us sport us while we may,
And now, like amorous birds of prey,
Rather at once our time devour
Than languish in his slow-chapt power.
Let us roll all our strength and all
Our sweetness up into one ball,
And tear our pleasures with rough strife
Thorough the iron gates of life:
Thus, though we cannot make our sun
Stand still, yet we will make him run.[4]

The logical nature of the argument here has been generally recognised, though often with a certain timidity. Mr. Eliot hazards: "the three strophes of Marvell's poem have something like a syllogistic relation to each other." And in a recent scholarly work we read: "The dialectic of the poem lies not only or chiefly in the formal demonstration explicit in its three stanzas, but in all the contrasts evoked by its images and in the play between the immediately sensed and the intellectually apprehended."[5] That is, the logic is recognised, but minimized, and our attention is quickly distracted to something more reputable in a poem, the images or the characteristic tension of metaphysical poetry. For

Mr. Eliot the more important element in this case is a principle of order common in modern poetry and often employed in his own poems. He points out that the theme of Marvell's poem is "one of the great traditional commonplaces of European literature . . . the theme of . . . *Gather ye rosebuds,* of *Go, lovely rose."* "Where the wit of Marvell," he continues, "renews the theme is in the variety and order of the images." The dominant principle of order in the poem, then, is an implicit one rather than the explicit principle of the syllogism, and implicit in the succession of images.

Mr. Eliot explains the implicit principle of order in this fashion:

> In the first of the three paragraphs Marvell plays with a fancy that begins by pleasing and leads to astonishment. . . We notice the high speed, the succession of concentrated images, each magnifying the original fancy. When this process has been carried to the end and summed up, the poem turns suddenly with that surprise which has been one of the most important means of poetic effect since Homer:

> > But at my back I always hear
> > Time's winged chariot hurrying near,
> > And yonder all before us lie
> > Deserts of vast eternity.

> A whole civilization resides in these lines:

> > Pallida Mors aequo pulsat pede pauperum tabernas
> > Regumque turres . . .

> A modern poet, had he reached the height, would very likely have closed on this moral reflection.

What is meant by this last observation becomes clear a little later where it is said that the wit of the poem "forms the crescendo and diminuendo of a scale of great imaginative power." The structure of the poem, then, is this: it consists of a succession of images increasing in imaginative power to the sudden turn and surprise of the image of time, and then decreasing to the conclusion. But is there any sudden turn and surprise in the image of time? and does the poem consist of a succession of images?

This talk of images is a little odd since there seem to be relatively few in the poem if one means by image what people usually do—a descriptive phrase that invites the reader to project a sensory construction. The looming imminence of Time's winged chariot is, no doubt, an image, though not a full-blown one since there is nothing in the phrasing that properly invites any elaboration of sensory detail. But when Mr. Eliot refers to "successive images" and cites "my *vegetable* love," with *vegetable* italicised, and "Till the conversion of the Jews," one suspects that he is provoking images where they do not textually exist. There is about as much of an image in "Till the conversion of the Jews" as there would be in "till the cows come home," and it would be a psychiatrically sensitive reader who would immediately visualize the lowing herd winding slowly o'er the lea. But "my *vegetable* love" will make the point. I have no doubt that Mr. Eliot and subsequent readers do find an image here. They envisage some monstrous and expanding cabbage, but they do so in mere ignorance. *Vegetable* is no vegetable but an abstract and philosophical term, known as such to every educated man of Marvell's day. Its context is the doctrine of the three souls: the rational, which in man subsumes the other two; the sensitive, which men and animals have in common and which is the principle of motion and perception; and, finally, the lowest of the three, the vegetable soul, which is the only one that plants possess, and which is the principle of generation and corruption, of augmentation and decay. Marvell says, then, my love, denied the exercise of sense, but possessing the power of augmentation, will increase "Vaster than empires." It is an intellectual image, and hence no image at all but a conceit. For if one calls any sort of particularity or detail in a poem an image, the use of the wrong word will invite the reader to misconstrue his experience in terms of images, to invent sensory constructions and to project them on the poem.

45

A conceit is not an image. It is a piece of wit. It is in the tradition in which Marvell was writing, among other possibilities, the discovery of a proposition referring to one field of experience in terms of an intellectual structure derived from another field, and often enough a field of learning, as is the case in "my vegetable love." This tradition, though it goes back to the poetry of John Donne, and years before that, was current in Marvell's day. The fashionable poetry at the time he was writing this poem, the poetry comparable to that of Eliot or of Auden in the past two decades, was the poetry of John Cleveland, and the fashionable manner was generally known as Clevelandising. It consisted in the invention of a series of witty hyperbolical conceits, sometimes interspersed with images, and containing a certain amount of roughage in the form of conventional erotic statements:

> Thy beauty shall no more be found,
> Nor in thy marble vault shall sound
> My echoing song   .   .   .

It was commonly expressed in the octosyllabic couplet. Cleveland, for example, writes *Upon Phillis Walking in a Morning before Sun-rising*:

> The trees, like yeomen of the guard,
> Serving her more for pomp than ward   .   .   .

The comparison here does not invite visualization. It would be inappropriate to summon up the colors and serried ranks of the guard. The comparison is made solely with respect to the idea: the trees like the guard serve more for pomp than ward. Again:

> The flowers, called out of their beds,
> Start and raise up their drowsy heads,
> And he that for their color seeks
> May see it vaulting to her cheeks,
> Where roses mix—no civil war
> Divides her York and Lancaster.[6]

46

One does not here picture in panorama the Wars of the Roses One sees rather the aptness and the wit of York and Lancaster, the white rose and the red, reconciled in her cheeks, or one rejects it as forced and far-fetched. This is a matter of taste.

But if the poem is not a succession of images, does it exhibit that other principle which Mr. Eliot ascribes to it, the turn and surprise which he finds in the abrupt introduction of time's chariot and which forms a sort of fulcrum on which the poem turns. Subsequent critics have certainly felt that it has. In a current textbook we read:

> The poem begins as a conventional love poem in which the lover tries to persuade his mistress to give in to his entreaties. But with the introduction of the image of the chariot in l. 21, the poet becomes obsessed by the terrible onrush of time, and the love theme becomes scarcely more than an illustration of the effect which time has upon human life.

And the leading scholar in the field, a man who is generally quite unhappy with Mr. Eliot's criticism, nevertheless says:

> the poet sees the whole world of space and time as the setting for two lovers. But wit cannot sustain the pretence that youth and beauty and love are immortal, and with a quick change of tone—like Catullus' *nobis cum semel occidit brevis lux* or Horace's *sed Timor et Minae*—the theme of time and death is developed with serious and soaring directness . . .[7]

These, I believe, are not so much accounts of the poem as accounts of Mr. Eliot's reading of the poem. Let us question the fact. Does the idea of time and death come as any surprise in this context? The poem began, "Had we but world enough and time." That is, it began with an explicit condition contrary to fact, which by all grammatical rules amounts to the assertion that we do not have world enough and time. There is no surprise whatever when the proposition is explicitly made in line 21. It would rather have been surprising if it had not been made. Indeed, the only question we have in this respect, after we have read the first line, is, How many couplets will the poet expend on the ornamental re-iteration of the initial proposition before he comes to the expected *but*. The only turn in the poem is the turn which the structure of the syllogism had led us to await.

Mr. Eliot compares the turn and surprise which he finds in this poem to a similar turn in an ode of Horace's, and the scholars seem to corroborate the comparison. This is the fourth ode of the first book:

> Solvitur acris hiems grata vice veris et Favoni,
> trahuntque siccas machinae carinas . . .

The poem begins with a picture of spring and proceeds by a succession of images, images of the external world and mythological images:

> Sharp winter relaxes with the welcome change to Spring and the west wind, and the cables haul the dry keels of ships. The herd no longer takes pleasure in its stalls or the farmer in his fire, and the pastures no longer whiten with hoar frost. Cytherean Venus leads her dancers beneath the overhanging moon, and the beautiful graces and nymphs strike the ground with alternate foot, while blazing Vulcan visits the grim forges of the Cyclops. Now is the time to wind your bright hair with green myrtle or with the flowers that the thawed earth yields. Now is the time to sacrifice to Faunus in the shadowed woods, whether it be a lamb he asks or a kid:

> > Pallida mors aequo pulsat pede pauperum tabernas
> > regumque turres.

> Pallid death with indifferent foot strikes the poor man's hut and the palaces of kings. Now, fortunate Sestius, the brief sum of life forbids our opening a long account with hope. Night will soon hem you in, and the fabled ghosts, and Pluto's meagre house.[8]

Death occurs in this poem with that suddenness and lack of preparation with which it sometimes occurs in life. The structure of the poem is an imitation of the structure of such experiences in

48

life. And as we draw from such experiences often a generalization, so Horace from the sudden realization of the abruptness and
impartiality of death, reflects

vitae summa brevis spem nos vetat incohare longam.

The brief sum of life forbids our opening a long account with
hope.

But the proposition is subsequent to the experience; it does not
rule and direct the poem from the outset. And the experience in
Horace *is* surprising and furnishes the fulcrum on which the poem
turns. It has, in fact, the characteristics which are ascribed to
Marvell's poem but which Marvell's poem does not have. The
two are two distinct kinds of poetry, located in distinct and almost antithetical traditions; both are valuable and valid methods,
but one is not to be construed in terms of the other.

In brief, the general structure of Marvell's poem is syllogistic,
and it is located in the Renaissance tradition of formal logic and of
rhetoric. The structure exists in its own right and as a kind of
expandable filing system. It is a way of disposing of, of making
a place for, elements of a different order: in this case, Cleveland-
izing conceits and erotic propositions in the tradition of Jonson
and Herrick. These re-iterate the propositions of the syllogism.
They do not develop the syllogism, and they are not required by
the syllogism; they are free and extra. There could be more or
less of them since there is nothing in the structure that determines
the number of interpolated couplets. It is a matter of tact, and a
matter of the appetite of the writer and the reader.

The notion of a structure as a kind of expandable filing
system may deserve a few sentences. The narrative structure of
a Shakespearean play can be regarded as a structure of this order.
It exists in its own right, of course, but it is also a method for
disposing various kinds of material of other orders, a set speech
or passion here, an interpolated comic routine in another place.
The structure offers a series of hooks upon which different things
can be hung. Whether the totality will then form a whole, a

unity, is a question of interpretation and a question of value. It is a question, for example, of what sort of unity is demanded, and whether there are various sorts.

In Marvell's poem, only the general structure is syllogistic; the detail and development are of another order, and critics have been diligent in assigning the poetic quality of the whole to the non-syllogistic elements. Is it possible, then, to write a lyric that will be wholly or almost wholly syllogistic? It is. There is such a lyric in the *Oxford Book of English Verse,* a lyric of somewhat lesser repute than Marvell's, but still universally praised and universally conceded to possess the true lyrical power. It is Dunbar's *Lament for the Makaris.*

The structure of Dunbar's poem is the structure of the traditional syllogism with which everyone is acquainted: *All men are mortal, I am a man;* together with a concluding practical syllogism, *What must be, must be accepted, but I must die.* The syllogism is developed in two ways, both characteristic methods in the logical tradition of the later Middle Ages. It begins with the immediate induction from experience of the leading principle, the major premise:

> I that in heill wes and gladnes,
> Am trublit now with gret seiknes,
> And feblit with infermite;
> *Timor mortis conturbat me.*

The experience, then, is the sudden alteration from health to illness, and this yields the generalization:

> Our plesance heir is all vane glory,
> This fals warld is bot transitory,
> The flesche is brukle, the Fend is sle:
> *Timor mortis conturbat me.*

The premise, then, is: this false world is but transitory; and it is presently expressed in more restricted terms:

The stait of man dois change and vary,
Now sound, now seik, now blith, now sary,
Now dansand mery, now like to dee:
    Timor mortis conturbat me.

The syllogism is now developed by another form of induction, and this development accounts for the remainder of the poem, except for the last stanza. It is developed through induction by simple enumeration in support and explication of the major premise, but with this special feature, that the induction proceeds by a hierarchical method. Nothing could be more characteristic of medieval logic. The argument is: if everything sublunary changes and varies, is mortal, then every estate of man is mortal, and the poet enumerates the estates:

On to the ded gois all Estatis,
Princis, Prelotis, and Potestatis,
Baith riche and pur of al degre:
    Timor mortis conturbat me . . .

He takis the campion in the stour,
The capitane closit in the tour,
The lady in bour full of bewte:
    Timor mortis conturbat me.

He sparis no lord for his piscence,
Na clerk for his intelligence;
His awfull strak may no man fle:
    Timor mortis conturbat me.

Art, magicianis, and astrologgis,
Rhetoris, logicianis, and theologgis,
Thame helpis no conclusionis sle:
    Timor mortis conturbat me.

In medicyne the most practicianis,
Lechis, surrigianis, and phisicianis,
Thame self fra ded may not supple:
    Timor mortis conturbat me.

If all estates must die, then poets too must die. And now Dunbar proceeds by a simple enumeration, a roll-call, of poets.

> He has done petuously devour
> The noble Chaucer, of makaris flour,
> The Monk of Bery, and Gower, all thre:
> *Timor mortis conturbat me.*

> The gude Syr Hew of Eglintoun,
> And eik Heryot, and Wyntoun,
> He has tane out of this cuntre:
> *Timor mortis conturbat me.*

He continues to enumerate poet after poet whom death has taken, until he comes finally to his friendly enemy, the poet, Kennedy, and to himself:

> Gud Maister Walter Kennedy
> In point of dede lyis veraly,
> Gret reuth it were that so suld be:
> *Timor mortis conturbat me.*

> Sen he has all my brether tane,
> He wil nocht lat me lif alane,
> Of forse I man his nyxt pray be:
> *Timor mortis conturbat me.*

Therefore, I must die, concludes the syllogism. And now follows the practical syllogism, the act of resignation:

> Sen for the deid remeid is none,
> Best is that we for dede dispone,
> Eftir our deid that lif may we.
> *Timor mortis conturbat me.*[9]

Almost every proposition in the poem is strictly controlled by the syllogistic structure. The exceptions are the refrain and a certain number of affective phrases and affective sentences: "He has done petuously devour / The noble Chaucer" and "Gret reuth it wer that so suld be." These direct the feeling of the poem.

Yet though the poem is so completely determined by logical method and logical structure it has seemed, and justly, to generations of readers to be a moving poem and properly poetical.

I shall conclude with another poem of the same sort, a lyric of even greater renown in modern criticism. This is the song from *Summer's Last Will and Testament* by Thomas Nashe, "Adieu, farewell, earth's bliss." It too has a refrain, though in English, a response from the Litany of Saints, which was customarily recited through the streets of London in time of plague. The poem, like Dunbar's, consists of a series of discrete, self-enclosed stanzas, in which each line is end-stopped. The structure of the poem is, like Dunbar's and Marvell's, a practical syllogism explicitly propounded, though not quite so formally as in the preceding poem. It opens with the rejection of earthly happiness. The argument is, to begin with the suppressed premise: true happiness is certain, but the world is uncertain; therefore worldly happiness is not true happiness. The world is uncertain since it is subject to the certainty of death and change. Nor can the goods of this world buy continued life, nor the art of medicine procure it: the plague increases. What is best in this life—and here we have the structure of the next three stanzas—beauty, prowess, and wit, all fade:

> Haste therefore each degree
> To welcome destiny . . .

For the world after death is certain, and its happiness true happiness:

> Adieu, farewell, earth's bliss!
> This world uncertain is:
> Fond are life's lustful joys,
> Death proves them all but toys.
> None from his darts can fly;
> I am sick, I must die—
>   Lord, have mercy on us.

Rich men, trust not in wealth,
Gold cannot buy you health;
Physic himself must fade;
All things to end are made;
The plague full swift goes by;
I am sick, I must die—
    Lord, have mercy on us.

Beauty is but a flower
Which wrinkles will devour;
Brightness falls from the air;
Queens have died young and fair;
Dust hath closed Helen's eye;
I am sick, I must die—
    Lord, have mercy on us.

Strength stoops unto the grave,
Worms feed on Hector brave;
Swords may not fight with fate;
Earth still holds ope her gate;
Come, come! the bells do cry—
I am sick, I must die—
    Lord, have mercy on us.

Wit with his wantonness
Tasteth death's bitterness;
Hell's excutioner
Hath no ears for to hear
What vain art can reply;
I am sick, I must die—
    Lord have mercy on us.

Haste therefore each degree
To welcome destiny;
Heaven is our heritage;
Earth but a player's stage;
Mount we unto the sky;
I am sick, I must die—
    Lord, have mercy on us.[10]

The poem is a series of fairly literal propositions, some exactly in logical form: *This world uncertain is. All things to end are made, Queens have died young and fair, Haste therefore each degree.* They are such propositions as might have been translated from the *Summa Contra Gentiles* of Thomas Aquinas, and they are located in that general tradition. Thomas, for instance, discusses the following questions: That human happiness does not consist in carnal pleasures; that man's happiness does not consist in glory; that man's happiness does not consist in wealth; that happiness does not consist in worldly power; that happiness does not consist in the practice of art; that man's ultimate happiness is not in this life, "for if there is ultimate happiness in this life, it will certainly be lost, at least by death."[11] But these are the propositions of Nashe's lyric, some literally, some more figuratively put.

Of the propositions in the poem perhaps the most figurative is *Strength stoops unto the grave,* which yet is fairly literal, as we see the suggestion of an aged figure bent over more and more until he is almost prone. And there are, of course, affective elements in the poem, as in *death's bitterness* and *Hell's executioner.* But the special distinction of the poem and the source of an unusual quality of feeling perhaps lies in the meter as much as in anything else. The six-syllable line glides from a regular iambic pattern into a triple movement—accented, unaccented, accented—and back again as if both were its mode of being and neither had precedence over the other:

> Beauty is but a flower
> Which wrinkles will devour;
> Brightness falls from the air;
> Queens have died young and fair .   .   .

The poem in this respect belongs to a curious episode in the history of English meter; for this phenomenon appears only to my knowledge in the songs written within a fairly short period, of perhaps ten or twenty years, in the 1590's and early 1600's. Of a similar sort is Shakespeare's:

> Come away, come away, death,
>   And in sad cypress let me be laid;
> Fly away, fly away, breath;
>   I am slain by a fair cruel maid.

But the special distinction of the poem has usually been found in the line, *Brightness falls from the air.* This is certainly a proposition of a different order from those we have discussed, and one that has excited the sensibilities of innumerable modern readers. It is a line in the symbolist tradition. One remembers how Stephen Dedalus in the *Portrait of the Artist as a Young Man* recalls the line, though at first in an altered form:

> She had passed through the dusk. And therefore the air was silent save for one soft hiss that fell. And therefore the tongues about him had ceased their babble. Darkness was falling.
>
> *Darkness falls from the air.*
>
> A trembling joy, lambent as a faint light, played like a fairy host around him. But why? Her passage through the darkening air or the verse with its black vowels and its opening sound, rich and lutelike?
>
> He walked away slowly towards the deeper shadows at the end of the colonnade, beating the stone softly with his stick to hide his revery from the students whom he had left: and allowed his mind to summon back to itself the age of Dowland and Byrd and Nash.
>
> Eyes, opening from the darkness of desire, eyes that dimmed the breaking east. What was their languid grace but the softness of chambering? And what was their shimmer but the shimmer of

the scum that mantled the cesspool of the court of a slobbering Stuart. And he tasted in the language of memory ambered vines, dying failings of sweet airs, the proud pavan . . .

The images he had summoned gave him no pleasure. They were secret and enflaming but her image was not entangled by them . . .

Yes; and it was not darkness that fell from the air. It was brightness.

Brightness falls from the air.

He had not even remembered rightly Nash's line. All the images it had awakened were false.[12]

But all the images it had awakened were false for still another reason. The line as Joyce quotes it is certainly an evocative line, a line in the symbolist tradition, and hence apt and fitted to entangle itself in revery. But it seems out of place in the poem. It is so much a line in the symbolist tradition that the historical scholar grows wary and suspicious. He turns to the text. He looks in the great modern edition of Nashe, the edition of Mc-Kerrow, and he finds that the editor records with a sigh: "It is to be hoped that Nashe meant 'ayre,' but I cannot help strongly suspecting that the true reading is 'hayre,' which gives a more obvious, but far inferior, sense."[13] So we have the alternatives: *Brightness falls from the air* or *Brightness falls from the hair.* But the latter is a literal account of the effect of age and death. The proposition so read is of the same order as all the other propositions in the poem, of the same order as *Queens have died young and fair.* There is no doubt, then, as to the correct reading. In fact, the symbolist line, however good, is a bad line in context since it is out of keeping. And so the poem loses its last claim to modernity. It becomes a Renaissance poem. It returns to the park of logic from the forest of revery. The experience of the poem is the experience of syllogistic thinking with its consequences for feeling, attitude, and action. It is a mode of experience that the Renaissance practiced and cherished, and expressed with power, dignity, and precision. It is a poetical experience and a logical, and it is both at once.[14]

Convention as Structure:
The Prologue to the Canterbury Tales

A literary convention is obviously a principle of order in poetry. I shall maintain in this essay, against the concensus of scholarly opinion, that Chaucer derives the structure of the Prologue to the *Canterbury Tales* from one of the most common of the literary conventions of his time.

The Prologue is the only one of Chaucer's major works for which there is said to be no model, no genuine antecedents in the tradition. The *Book of the Duchess,* the *House of Fame,* the *Parliament of Fowls,* and the Prologue to the *Legend of Good Women,* for example, all belong to the well-recognized tradition of the dream vision, whose history and peculiar features have been described at length in a number of standard monographs. The antecedents of the *Troilus* are well known, and Chaucer himself assigns it to the medieval category of tragedy. The shorter complaints belong to a common literary type. But the most familiar of Chaucer's works and the one generally thought to be the best seems, as a whole, to be without literary predecessors, though there are, of course, sources for particular aspects and details. This circumstance has been construed by the literary historians in Chaucer's favor. They have seen in it the triumph of originality over convention and of realism over artifice. They have pictured Chaucer going directly to reality and reporting what he found. And so the defect of literary history becomes the glory of literary criticism.

The state of the question is summarized by one scholar: "For the *Prologue,* as for the general device of the Canterbury pilgrimage, no real model has been found." Another remarks: "There had

never before . . . been the like of that singularly *modern* thing—
to use our most complacent term of approbation—the Prologue."
And a third: "no source for" the Prologue, "the most distinctive
of Chaucer's works, has ever been discovered."[1] The features
which scholarship has particularly distinguished as unprecedented
are the series of portraits in the Prologue and the device of a
journey, and especially of a pilgrimage, as the frame for a series
of stories. For example, the scholar continues in the passage just
alluded to, "No such series of descriptions [of characters] is to be
found in any work of ancient or medieval literature which could
have come to Chaucer's attention."[2] It is recognized, of course,
that "individual sketches of knights or priests or peasants are
common enough," that the "allegorical writings of the age, both
sacred and secular, abound in personified types . . . some of which
Chaucer clearly imitates." But the general conclusion is that "in
none of his predecessors has there been found a gallery of portraits like that in the *Prologue,* and there is very little that is com
parable in later English poetry except in Chaucer's avowed imita-
tors."[3]

For the second feature—the general idea of a frame story—
it is agreed that no particular model need be sought. Chaucer had
already used it in the *Legend of Good Women,* and the idea was
common in the tradition. For the device of a journey, and
especially of a pilgrimage, there is a distant analogue in Boccaccio's
Decameron and a closer one in a contemporary Italian work in
which the tales are actually told by a single figure in the course of
a journey. But the difficulty here has been that, though Chaucer
could have been acquainted with these works, we have no evidence that he was. Furthermore, what has seemed to modern
scholarship the special merit of Chaucer's device—the interplay
of personalities on the journey—is only rudimentary in these
possible models. The conclusion has been, as the latest writer on
the subject puts it: "There is really no necessity to search for the
'source' of Chaucer's pilgrimage. It would, indeed, have been
strange had there been no reflections in imaginative literature of

the common medieval custom of going on a journey with a party of travellers."[4] This is the general opinion. "For his particular device of a group of persons on a pilgrimage to Canterbury on horseback," we are told in the standard work, "he needed only to draw on life about him . . . Thus the device of a pilgrimage as a narrative framework was repeatedly presented to him in actual life, and he was at liberty to adopt it for his literary purpose with whatever degree of realism he found convenient."[5]

It is noteworthy that this flight to reality on the part of eminent scholars is always subsequent to a search for an antecedent of the motif and a failure to find it. This is almost too obviously making a virtue of necessity and suggests that perhaps the search for antecedents has been misconducted. It has been a search for the prior appearance of the particular motif. And when this search fails, it has been felt that the only alternative is the recourse to reality. But the alternative is as unsatisfactory as the original undertaking, for it does not explain what it pretends to explain.

The pilgrimage was undoubtedly a common occurrence in Chaucer's day, and he had in all likelihood seen a good many groups of pilgrims among whom were to be found close analogues to the characters in the Prologue. Scholars have been concerned to establish that he lived in Greenwich on the Canterbury road, where he could have seen groups of pilgrims passing before his window, perhaps while he was writing the *Canterbury Tales.* Kittredge is willing to wager he had undertaken a Canterbury pilgrimage himself.[6] The argument is that what he found day after day in real life he needed no literary precedent to invent. But this is not so. It is not the direct observation of murders and of the process of detection that leads to the construction of a detective story. Nor was it the perception of violent death in high places that prompted the Elizabethan dramatist to compose a tragedy. What a writer finds in real life is to a large extent what his literary tradition enables him to see and to handle.

It may be conceded that experience is sometimes obtrusively

61

at odds with tradition. We can see that it is, for we can see how tradition has been modified to render it more supple to experience. But the one term is always tradition, not unalterable but never abandoned, as, of course, the other term is always experience. The one is form, method, a way of apprehending; the other is matter, realization, and what is apprehended. What we should be concerned with, then, is to discover, if possible, a literary form extant in Chaucer's tradition of which the Prologue to the *Canterbury Tales* is a realization. It must be a form that will account not only for particular motifs, for the device of the journey or the series of portraits, but also for the other elements of the work and for their order and succession.

A literary form exists only in what I call a tradition. I use that word in the sense in which we speak of the tradition of the hard-boiled detective story or say that Shakespeare's sonnets are in the tradition of the *Astrophel and Stella* sequence or, more generally, in the Petrarchan tradition. A tradition is the body of texts and interpretations current among a group of writers at a given time and place. The description of literary traditions is a principal subject of literary history, and the nature of a tradition can be reconstructed only by the methods of literary history. If one were to construct, for example, the tradition of a number of contemporary poets in America, it could be described in terms of the poetry of Eliot, of Pound, Hopkins, Auden, and some fragments of Donne and Marvell, together with the associated body of commentary, the "new criticism." When a poet in this tradition undertakes what he has learned to distinguish as a metaphysical poem, the principles that determine the realization of what he regards as a particular literary form—the appropriate subject, devices, and structure—are principles located in that tradition.

It follows from this that a literary form is not simply an external principle of classification of literary works, as is the Dewey Decimal System in the public library, nor is it an Idea. It is rather a principle operative in the production of works. It is a scheme of experience recognized in the tradition and derived from prior works and from the descriptions of those works extant in the tradition. It is, moreover, a scheme that directs the discovery of material and detail and that orders the disposition of the whole. If a literary form is an Idea, it is an idea only in the sense that it is the idea that the writer and reader have of the form. Thus a literary form may vary somewhat from work to work, since it is only a summary description of those elements of the tradition that entered into the conception and realization as into the appreciation by a qualified reader of the particular work.

I come now to my thesis, which may as well be stated clearly and simply at the start. The literary form to which the Prologue to the *Canterbury Tales* belongs and of which it is a special realization is the form of the dream-vision prologue in the tradition of the *Romance of the Rose* and of the associated French and English poems of the subsequent century and a half. This is certainly to find the answer in the most obvious place, to find it, like the purloined letter, in plain sight. For if one were to look for the source of anything in Chaucer, the first place an experienced scholar would look is in the *Romance of the Rose* and its tradition. The *Romance,* it has been said, "probably exerted on Chaucer a more lasting and more important influence than any other work in the vernacular literature of either France or England."[7] There are throughout Chaucer innumerable borrowings in detail from that work, and four of Chaucer's most extended poems are clearly in the form of the dream vision: one of them, indeed, is explicitly a prologue framing a series of tales, as is the masterwork of Chaucer's contemporary and friend, John Gower. If one asks why the similarity of the Canterbury Prologue to this well-known type has not been seen before, the answer lies in the method by which the form has been described in the scholarship on the subject. It has been described in terms of particular motifs, but the motifs have not been generalized and regarded as functional in a structure. One scholar, for example, enumerates "the regular features of the love-vision": "the introductory device of reading a book, the discussion of sleeplessness and dreams, the setting on May-day or in the springtime, the vision itself, the guide (who in many poems takes the form of a helpful animal), and personified abstractions, Love, Fortune, Nature, and the like."[8] There is only one element in this description that is also to be found in the Canterbury Prologue, and that is the setting in spring, an element which is common to many other literary forms in the Middle Ages.

But if we describe the Canterbury Prologue in terms of the scheme of experience which orders it, in terms of its elements and their succession, we will find a striking similarity to—in fact, an identity with—the scheme of the dream vision. The Prologue can be described accurately enough in this fashion: at a certain time of the year—and the season is then described—the author comes to a place, to the "Tabard" in Southwark. He there meets a company, who are then depicted, one after the other in panel fashion. After a brief digression, one of the company, not described so far (our host, Harry Bailly), is singled out as a master of ceremonies and proposes the device that orders the remainder of the poem, the telling of tales on the journey.

I shall now describe in the same fashion the opening of the *Romance of the Rose* and of a number of English poems in the same tradition. The *Romance* begins with some expository remarks on the truth of dreams, illustrated by the dream related in this book whose name is the *Romance of the Rose* and whose subject is an autobiographical account—for everything fell out just as this dream relates—containing the art of love. After a brief prayer and praise of the lady, the dream begins. It is May, and there is an extended description of the season. The author walks out into the fields, crosses a stream, and comes to a garden inclosed by a wall. He then describes, one after the other, a series of allegorical portraits painted on the wall, ten in number. He wants to enter the garden but can find no way in. Walking around the wall, he comes finally to a wicket gate and pounds on it. The porter Idleness opens the door, "whose hair was as

64

yellow of hue as any basin newly scoured," and leads him into the garden, which is described at length. He finds Sir Mirth dancing and singing there in company and depicts the company in a series of set portraits, fifteen in number. He then walks in the garden, followed by the God of Love with his arrows ready. The garden is leisurely described, including the well where Narcissus died, which leads to the interpolated tale of Narcissus. In the well he sees a rose bush full of roses; there is one bud in especial which he has a great longing to pluck. At this point the God of Love, who has been stalking him, looses an arrow, and the author is committed to the sentimental enterprise which directs the remainder of the poem.

These are the elements and their order: after the preliminary matter and the dream, at a given time of the year—and there is a description of the season—the author comes to a place where he sees a number of allegorical characters painted on a wall and describes them; a guide then appears and leads him to another place, where he sees a company in action, though the characters are personifications, and describes them in the same manner. There follows a framed tale, and then one of the characters initiates the action which leads to the remainder of the poem. This character is not strictly a master of ceremonies, but he might in another poem and in other hands develop into one. The form is clearly not too unlike the form of the Canterbury Prologue, particularly if we collapse into one movement the two instances of an author's coming to a place and substitute for allegorical characters and personifications realistic portraits of representative members of society.

In other poems of this tradition the dream-vision prologue appears now as a separable and independent form, now as an element and sometimes a repeatable element in a work of larger scope, and most commonly as an introduction to a poem that continues now in one way, now in another. It is so used in the *Confessio Amantis.* In this poem, after a discursive and sententious preface, similar to, but more extensive than, the one in the

Romance of the Rose, the author comes to his *matere.* He walks out in May and comes to a wood, where he begins to complain of his woe and falls into a swoon. On recovering, he utters a prayer to Cupid and Venus, whereupon he sees both of them come by. The King of Love, as he passes, throws an arrow through his heart, but the Queen pauses and speaks to him. On hearing what he has to say, she proposes the device: he shall confess to her priest, Genius. The essential structure of the Romance is here preserved, though in summary fashion. The nature description is quite brief, as are the descriptions of the characters. A swoon supplants the dream, and the interpolated prayer, an element in the opening of the *Romance,* occasions the appearance of the figures. Nevertheless, the author goes out at a certain time of the year and comes to a place where he sees figures riding by, one of whom proposes the device that directs the remainder of the poem.

The scheme of the vision is repeated, this time without the dream, in the course of one of the tales that form the bulk of Gower's work. This is the tale of Rosiphelee.[9] Before dawn on a May morning she walks out in a park through which runs a great river. She bids her women withdraw. She sees the flowers blooming, hears the birds singing, and sees all the animals, male paired with the female. As she looks around, she sees a company of ladies riding by, whose dress is then described. She wonders who they are and then sees a woman on a horse, who is described at length. She questions her about the company of ladies and receives the answer which changes the course of her life. Here is the typical nature description, the character who comes to a place where he sees a company, and, finally, the master of ceremonies, who disposes the particular device of this poem. And in this case it is no dream.

So much for Gower. Chaucer himself had written, if we allow the accepted chronology of his work, four dream visions by the time he undertook the Prologue to the *Canterbury Tales;* indeed, while he was engaged in the composition of the *Tales,* he rewrote

66

with considerable thoroughness the last of these, the Prologue to the *Legend*. The earliest, the *Book of the Duchess,* begins with preliminary matter on the melancholy and sleeplessness of the author, who reads a book to pass the time, the tale of Ceyx and Alcyone. At one point in the tale Alcyone prays Juno for sleep and a dream, and the author decides to try the same method, whereupon he falls asleep and dreams. It is a May morning, with birds singing. He finds himself in a room with glass windows and full of pictures depicting the whole story of Troy and the whole *Romance of the Rose,* both text and gloss. He hears the sound of hunters, rises, takes his horse, and comes to a field, where he overtakes a great company of hunters. He inquires of one of them, "Who is hunting here?" and is told the Emperor Octavian. He follows the chase. When the hunt ends, he walks from a tree and follows a whelp into a field full of flowers, where he becomes aware of a man in black. This is the figure that introduces the device of the poem.

The *House of Fame* is a poem in the same tradition. It begins with preliminary matter similar to that in the *Romance* and the *Book of the Duchess,* a proem on dreams and an invocation. It continues with the dream. Exactly on the tenth of December— there is in this case no description of the season—the author falls asleep and in a dream finds himself in a temple made of glass. There are many images there, finely wrought portraits, among them one of Venus, "naked fleeting in a sea," of Cupid, and of Vulcan, "that in his face was full brown." As the dreamer walks about, he sees on the wall the story of the *Aeneid,* portrayed in a series of panels. These are described at length, one after the other—"There saw I," "There saw I"—in a manner and in a position in the scheme of the poem analogous to the portraits on the wall in the *Romance* or the portraits of the pilgrims at the Tabard. The author then leaves the temple, finds himself in a barren desert, looks up to heaven in prayer, and becomes aware of an eagle larger than any he has ever seen. The eagle is the figure who disposes the device which accounts for the remainder of the poem.

I come now to the Prologue to the *Legend of Good Women*. The later of the two versions is more relevant to our purpose, since it is closer in form to the scheme of the Canterbury Prologue, though the differences between the versions are not sufficient to call for separate treatment. The poem begins with preliminary matter, in this case of exceptional distinction, and then the poet late in the month of May falls asleep and dreams. He finds himself in a field—"With floures sote embrouded was it al"—where "The smale foules, of the seson fayn" sing a hymn to St. Valentine. There appear the God of Love and his Queen, Alceste, whose dress in particular is described at some length. Behind the god the author sees nineteen ladies in royal dress, and after them an extraordinary number of women. There follows the action which leads to the device: the King and especially the Queen as masters of ceremonies impose on the author the task of writing a series of tales of true lovers as penance for his heresy in love.

The underlying scheme of the dream-vision prologue should now be clear. If we set aside the preliminary matter as not relevant to the form of the Canterbury Prologue and begin, as it does, after the dream, we will find the following elements in this order. The poem is set at a given time of the year, generally in May, but perhaps exactly on the tenth of December, or sometime in the latter part of April, as the astrology of the Canterbury Prologue indicates. The time of the year leads in many cases to a description of the season, which may be brief or leisurely, simple or, as in the case of the Canterbury Prologue, ornate, with elements drawn from the introductory nature descriptions of other literary forms. The author, usually as the dreamer, is a character in his own poem, though when the scheme is used in a narrative, as in the tale of Rosiphelee, the principal character takes the place of the author. He comes to a place, usually a field, but sometimes a chamber or temple of glass, and in one case the Tabard in

68

Southwark. He sees there a company, or occasionally one or two persons, and sometimes some birds who are treateed as characters. Or he sees a number of portraits depicted on a wall, or incidents in a famous story, and then, after another journey, comes to a company. These may be described at length, one after another, in panel fashion, or they may, especially if the material is common in the tradition, be briefly and summarily denominated. At this point, or after another journey, or, as in the case of the Canterbury Prologue, after a brief digression, one of the company or another character who is now met, the man in black or Harry Bailly, initiates the action of the poem. This may consist, as in the Prologue to the *Legend* and the Prologue to the *Canterbury Tales,* in proposing the relation of a series of tales.

But the *Canterbury Tales* extend beyond the Prologue. Is there any precedent in the tradition for the particular way in which Chaucer proceeds to develop the poem? Of course, there is precedent in the *Legend* and in Gower for the framed tales, but I have in mind something more definite and limited than this. I have in mind the problem of the principles of order in the work as a whole, of which the idea of the frame story is only one. I have in mind a very restricted question: Is there in the tradition or in those realizations of the tradition that Chaucer had already accomplished any scheme of development from the dream-vision prologue that is similar to the development in the *Canterbury Tales?*

The whole problem of the construction of the *Canterbury Tales* is a vexed and difficult one. The work as it has come down to us consists of a number of fragments, each disjoined from the others and each consisting of several tales and of the prologues to and links between the tales. The general Prologue, for instance, is followed by three tales with the links between them and breaks off abruptly, shortly after the beginning of a fourth tale. This section is usually called the "A Fragment." I will concern myself only with this.

It is clear from the state of the manuscripts, then, that the project was never one that was complete in design though in-complete in execution. The design itself was in a fluid state. The general outlines of the framework were perhaps clear: it would involve a pilgrimage, and the completion of the journey would coincide with the completion of the design. The characters of most of the pilgrims, at least, were determined. There was to be a leader of the party, the Host, whose word was law. Each pilgrim was to tell a given number of tales, and the tales he told were to accord with his rank and nature according to the ancient principles of decorum. But within what was already determined there was much that was indeterminate, especially the principle or congeries of principles that would determine the succession of speakers and tales.

What principles had Chaucer? He begins with the principle of lots which could have served to order the whole, but he uses it only to determine the first speaker. Again, the principle of lots, whether by chance or by Providence guiding chance or by the manipulation of the Host, serves to pick out the man of highest rank in the company as the first to speak. This again would have served as a sufficient principle; the order of precedence in society could have determined the order of precedence in the telling of tales, and the Host, who was a proper man to be a marshal in a hall, could easily have settled the questions of etiquette. But this principle breaks down immediately after the Knight's tale. The Host calls on the Monk, who would probably be considered next in social rank, to relate something that will fit in with the Knight's tale. But the Miller, who is a churl and will abide no man for courtesy, cries out in Pilate's voice, "I know a noble tale with which I will repay the Knight's." His tale, of course, is just the opposite: it is an ignoble tale of churls and obscenity rather than a noble tale of princes and high love.

Is there any precedent for this in the tradition? There is, in the scheme of experience of a dream vision which Chaucer wrote some years before this, the *Parliament of Fowls*.[10] In that poem, after the customary preliminary matter, the author falls asleep

70

and dreams. A guide leads him to a spring scene, a garden full of birds and trees, where he sees Cupid and Will, his daughter, and many other allegorical figures and a temple of brass with more figures inside it and the story of many famous lovers painted on the wall. He walks forth again from this place and comes on the figure who disposes the device that orders the rest of the poem. This is Nature, who is holding a parliament of birds on St. Valentine's Day. The birds are then summarily described. Nature opens the parliament and stipulates that the birds shall speak in order of rank; and so they do until suddenly the lower orders break out, crying, "Have don, and lat us wende! . . . Whan shal youre cursede pletying have an ende?" The subject has been high courtly love, and now the vulgar point of view is urged by a vigorous churlish personality amid a certain amount of general uproar.

Obviously, the scheme of progression at the beginning of the *Canterbury Tales* is similar in these general respects to the scheme of the *Parliament of Fowls*. It is not only the form of the Prologue that derives from the dream vision, but from the particular scheme of a particular dream vision which Chaucer had written some time before derives the underlying principle of order of the A Fragment as a whole. In both, the master of ceremonies, by stipulation and by lot, appoints the highest in rank to speak first. The discourse is on high courtly love. It is interrupted by the lower orders of society who urge a vulgar point of view, and there follows strife among the churls. This is developed in the A Fragment by a new principle, the principle of retaliation. The Miller tells a tale about a carpenter, and the Reeve, who had been a carpenter, answers with a tale about a miller. The Cook offers to go on in this vein, begins, and the fragment breaks off. It is open to question whether or not in this instance the form of the dream vision itself broke down, whether or not it was inadequate to handle the material which Chaucer wished to explore by its means. But it does not seem to me open to question that the form of the Prologue and indeed of the A Fragment is, if we

71

understand by a "literary form" the method by which material is discovered and ordered, the form of the dream vision in whose terms Chaucer himself had learned to feel and think through many years of love and apprenticeship.

The identity of the literary form of the Prologue to the *Canterbury Tales* with the conventional form of the dream-vision prologue can be regarded as established. It may be felt, however, that the distinctive feature of the Canterbury Prologue—the series of portraits—has not adequately been accounted for. No one, I trust, will ask one to account for the greatness of Chaucer's portraits, for his peculiar skill in writing. If such matters can be explained, certainly they lie outside the scope and method of this chapter. The question is rather, I should say, Is the technique of portraiture in the dream-vision convention of the same kind as Chaucer's technique in the Prologue? It is. The model in the tradition—and the model to which Chaucer recurred here—is the double series of portraits at the opening of the *Romance of the Rose,* the portraits that occupy the same place in the scheme of that poem as Chaucer's do in the scheme of his.[11]

I would distinguish several points of similarity of technique in the portraits themselves and two further points in their connection with the remainder of the poem. The portraits are given in succession in both poems, without transition or with the most summary form of transition: "And next was peynted Covetise," "Elde was paynted after this," "And alderlast of everychon / Was peynted Povert al aloon," "And next hir wente, on hir other side," "Love hadde with hym a bacheler." Chaucer's technique is similar: "With hym there was his sone, a yong squier, / A lovyere and a lusty bacheler," "A Monk ther was." There are a number of such portraits, a group of ten and of fifteen in the *Romance* and twenty-one in the Prologue, plus the five guildsmen who are treated as a unit and several others who are just named. The portraits are of varying length, but they vary roughly within the same range: in the *Romance* they run from four to ninety-six lines, averaging around thirty-two; in the Prologue they run from nine

to sixty-two lines, averaging around thirty-one. The peculiar coincidence in the averages, of course, is of no significance. The
portraits in each are introduced by brief critical remarks in which
the terms derive from the medieval arts of poetry. The second
series in the *Romance* begins (I quote the medieval translation of
the poem which is often ascribed to Chaucer):

> Then gan I loken ofte sithe
> The shap, the bodies, and the cheres,
> The countenaunce and the maneres
> Of alle the folk that daunced there,
> And I shal telle you what they were.[12]

Chaucer begins with an explicit remark, "Me thynketh it ac-
cordaunt to resoun," that is, *secundum rationem,* in accordance
with the law of the kind. He begins the *Complaint of Mars* with
a similar remark, indicating an awareness of the requirements of
a literary kind:

> The ordre of compleynt requireth shylfully.

He proceeds:

> Me thynketh it accordaunt to resoun
> To telle you al the condicioun
> Of ech of hem, so as it semed me,
> And which they weren, and of what degree,
> And eek in what array that they were inne . . .

These are the principal technical correspondences. But one
might observe further that the method in both poems is one that
allows not only objective presentation and analysis but also
author's comment and that the portraits in both contain a good
deal of sharp realistic detail of the same type. For example, of
Hate:

> Hir heed ywrithen was, iwis,
> Full grimly with a greet towayle . . .

Avarice is clad

> Al in an old torn courtepy
> As she were all with doggis torn.[13]

There are two further points that concern the relation of the portraits to the remainder of the poem. The first is that some at least of the characters described act and interact as the poem goes on—this is obvious in the *Canterbury Tales* but is also true in some measure of the *Romance*. The second is that the author who describes these characters as an external observer becomes involved in action with them.

In brief, the technical features of the portraits in the Canterbury Prologue have exact analogues in the portraits of the *Romance*. There are in each a number of portraits of moderate length, containing realistic detail, introduced by critical remarks, described by the author in his own person, and presented one after another with the minimum of transition, as in the description of a panel of portraits on a wall. If a composition instructor were to assign the portraits in the *Romance* as a model for imitation and stipulate that the method there exhibited be applied to a range of figures from contemporary society, his better students would produce a series of characters not too unlike the series in the Prologue. And if he should extend his assignment to the whole scheme of the opening portion of the *Romance* and of the associated poems in the tradition, the result could well be the Prologue to the *Canterbury Tales*.

In these terms the development of Chaucer's career becomes intelligible. We must give up the naive conclusion of literary criticism and literary scholarship that in his earlier work Chaucer had yielded "with docility to medieval schematism" and then suddenly broke "with all such rigid notions of order." We can no longer say, as the latest writer on the subject does, that "one of the most astonishing things about the *Canterbury Tales* is that Chaucer, a courtly artist, steeped in French, Latin, and Italian models, chose as a framework a direct departure from them. He

74

did not have to go to sleep and dream in order to get started . . ."[14] For Chaucer did not simply go to reality; he apprehended reality by the means he had learned and cultivated. He was original and traditional at the same time, and his originality lay in the application to fresh material of the old method—new wine in the old bottle. He brought to life a tradition that had grown, perhaps, too contrived, though the Prologue to the *Legend* is an exquisite thing of its kind. But he brought it to life within the framework of the tradition. He was an artist, and he worked by artifice, for he knew that realism is artifice.

Idea as Structure:
The Phoenix and Turtle

I am concerned in this chapter with another of the principles of order that determine the structure and detail of a poem. This is the use of some field or system of ideas in the writer's tradition which serves as a scheme or paradigm by which material of another order is apprehended and expounded. I have already appropriated in an earlier essay the term *conceit* for this procedure. Here I shall show how the material of courtly love in Shakespeare's *Phoenix and Turtle* is treated in terms of scholastic theology.

I

The characteristic feature of scholasticism for our purpose is its terminology. The whole system, in fact, may be said to be implicit in the definition of its terms, as in our own times the systems of clinical psychology are implicit in such terms as "regression," "libido," "flight from reality," and "inferiority complex." Consequently, if we find that Shakespeare uses such a scholastic term as "essence" in its technical sense and in a technical context we may presume not only that he was acquainted with scholastic notions but also that he was capable of thinking and feeling in those terms.

Essence occurs three times in Shakespeare. It appears in a well-known passage in *Measure for Measure*:

> Merciful heaven,
> Thou rather with thy sharp and sulphurous bolt
> Split'st the unwedgeable and gnarled oak
> Than the soft myrtle. But man, proud man,

> Drest in a little brief authority,
> Most ignorant of what he's most assur'd
> (His glassy essence), like an angry ape,
> Plays such fantastic tricks before high heaven
> As make the angels weep . . . 2.2.114-22[1]

This is the scholastic notion in a scholastic context: man's essence is his intellectual soul, which is an image of God, and hence is *glassy* for it mirrors God. *Glassy* is used in this sense in *Hamlet*:

> There is a willow grows aslant a brook,
> That shows his hoar leaves in the glassy stream.
> 4.7.168-9

and in 1 *Henry VI*:

> As plays the sun upon the glassy streams,
> Twinkling another counterfeited beam . . .
> 5.3.62-3

The full context of the notion here involved is given in the following passage from Ralegh's *History of the World*:

> But man, to cover his own ignorance in the least things . . . that is ignorant of the essence of his own soul, and which the wisest of the naturalists (if Aristotle be he) could never so much as define, but by the action and effect, telling us what it works, (which all men know as well as he,) but not what it is, which neither he nor anyone else doth know, but God that created it, (*For though I were perfect, yet I know not my soul,* saith Job:) man, I say, that is but an idiot in the next cause of his own life, and in the cause of all the actions of his life, will, notwithstanding, examine the art of God in creating the world . . . [2]

His glassy essence is, of course, a sharp poetic phrase. But there is no need to fuse the denotation of the adjective, *glassy*, with connotations which are not exacted by the noun it qualifies in order to render it poetic. "Brittleness," "clarity," and "pellucidness" may be charming notions but they are inaccurate in context and beside the point. It is not irrelevance that makes a phrase poetic. Shakespeare's is poetic in that it initiates a moment's reflection and invites the energy of a linguistic inference by which one sees that the phrase means "image of God" through the ascending aspect of imaging rather than through the more customary descending aspect of being imaged.

Essence is also used technically in Valentine's speech about Silvia in the *Two Gentlemen of Verona*:

> And why not death rather than living torment?
> To die is to be banish'd from myself;
> And Silvia is myself. Banish'd from her
> Is self from self—a deadly banishment!
> What light is light, if Silvia be not seen?
> What joy is joy, if Silvia be not by?
> Unless it be to think that she is by
> And feed upon the shadow of perfection.
> Except I be by Silvia in the night,
> There is no music in the nightingale.
> Unless I look on Silvia in the day,
> There is no day for me to look upon.
> She is my essence, and I leave to be
> If I be not by her fair influence
> Foster'd, illumin'd, cherish'd, kept alive.

3.1.170-84

The speech begins on a relatively human level, for the assertion that Silvia is myself and the question, "What light is light, if Silvia be not seen?" may both be taken sufficiently metaphorically. Nevertheless, Silvia is designated as perfection, for to imagine her present when she is absent is to feed upon the shadow, the image, of perfection. If she were here one would be in the presence of perfection. However, when a Christian of Elizabeth's time comes right down to it, there is only one true perfection, God, and only one set of terms in which to discuss it, the theological language of the Schools. And it is precisely in these terms that Valentine speaks. His language and thought are those, for example, of Hooker, except that Silvia is substituted for God:

78

God hath his influence into the very essence of all things, without which influence of Deity supporting them their utter annihilation could not choose but follow. Of him all things have both received their first being and their continuance to be that which they are. All things are therefore partakers of God, they are his offspring, his influence is in them . . . Otherwise, how should the same wisdom be that which supporteth, beareth up, and sustaineth all . . .

So that all things which God hath made are in that respect the offspring of God, they are *in him* as effects in their highest cause, he likewise actually is *in them,* the assistance and influence of his Deity is *their life.* 5.56.5[3]

Silvia, consequently, is regarded as perfection, as Love in the absolute sense, as the ultimate principle of the lover's being, as that by which he is fostered, illumined, cherished, sustained. She is God. She is immanent and transcendent, and the lover's relation to her is that of scholastic creature to scholastic Creator. Apart from the blasphemy involved, there is only one difficulty in the passage: this resides in the proposition, *She is my essence.* The proposition is technically incorrect with regard to the relation of creature and Creator in the scholastic system, for it is manifestly false to say that the soul is of the substance of God. Although the soul is a simple form in its essence, it is not its own being but is a being by participation. Therefore, it is not pure act like God (ST, 1.90.1.c. and ad 2).[4] For man is made to the image and likeness of God, but "the preposition *to* signifies only a certain approach, as of something at a distance" (ST, 1.93.1).

Valentine's relation to Silvia, it is true, conforms in general to the centuries-old scheme of courtly love; the lover is to the beloved as vassal to lord, or if the scheme be construed in Neo-Platonic terms, as it often was, as shadow to substance or as image to archetype. But the commonest and most available source of Neo-Platonic ideas in the sixteenth century was the scholastic doctrine of the Christian God, who is only protected from utter Neo-Platonism by an unceasing vigilance in qualification. If one

79

abandons the qualification, locates the infinite Idea in the finite beloved, maintains the theological language of the Schools regarding God's immanence and ceaseless providence and yet ascribes all reality to the Idea to the extent that the lover's essence is the Idea, he arrives at this passage. It is wordly Neo-Platonism, precipitated out of the latent Neo-Platonism of Christian dogma. However, there remain two difficulties for anyone familiar with these schemes of thought: 1) the analogical relationship of the derived and Underived is contradicted by the predication of identity of essence, and 2) the identity of essence takes the special form that the essence of the derived *is* the Underived.

II

The difficulties can be understood and their source located in the light of the third passage in Shakespeare in which *essence* occurs. The passage is found in his "poetical essay" on "the former subject, viz., the Turtle and Phoenix," one of a group of poems on this theme "by the best and chiefest of our modern writers"[5] which was appended to Robert Chester's *Loves Martyr* (1601). The poem represents a memorial service for the Phoenix and Turtle, the beloved and lover, and is divided into three parts. In the first part the poet appoints "the bird of loudest lay" as Herald, the swan as Celebrant, and the "treble-dated crow" as one of the mourners, and interposes an interdict against the presence of certain others. There follows the anthem, with which we will be concerned, in which is stated the relationship of the lovers:

> So they lov'd as love in twain
> Had the essence but in one.

Reason concludes the poem by pronouncing a threne over the urn where their cinders lie, to the effect that Beauty and Truth, Love and Constancy, in their ideal forms are now dead:

Leaving no posterity:
'Twas not their infirmity,
It was married chastity.

There are a number of problems here, some integral to the
text and some only associated with it, but nevertheless troublesome.
The characters in the poem, for example, are birds, and the
ordinary Elizabethan expectation would be that they represent
persons in the situation the poem derives from and refers to,
but who they are is unknown, and the situation can only be inferred from the text. It is apparently a poem with a key, and the
key has been lost. Read with a certain literal-mindedness, and
this is generally a good way to read poetry, it would appear to
commemorate the more or less simultaneous deaths of a married
couple who had taken and kept vows of marital chastity, and
hence in all likelihood were Recusants.[6] But Time and Chance
have destroyed or mislaid the evidence, with the consequence that
the uncertainty of reference imputes, illegitimately perhaps, a kind
of uncertainty to the poem as a whole.

And a similar uncertainty arises from the literary context of
the poem. It is one of a series of poems, signed by Vatum Chorus,
Ignoto, Shakespeare, Marston, Chapman, and Jonson, and dedi-
cated to the recently knighted Sir John Salusbury of Lleweni. What
is clear from the text is that the poems were severally written on
a theme propounded to the poets and do not refer to a common
situation. Both Marston and Jonson make this clear. In Shakespeare's, the first of the poems on the theme, the birds die without
issue. Marston in the poem that follows Shakespeare's begins with
a direct comment: "O 'twas a moving epicedium!" and then
proceeds by inquiring, "can blackest Fate consume / So rare
creation? No . . . Then look. For see what glorious issue . . . now
springs from yonder flame." In brief, his poem is on a different
situation, has another reference: in this case there is posterity.
Jonson in his turn begins: "We must sing too? What subject
shall we choose?" That is, clearly it is a command performance.
And characteristically he asserts that there could not be:

81

A beauty of that merit that should take

Our Muse up by commission. No, we bring
Our own true fire. Now our thought takes wing,
And now an Epode to deep ears we sing.[7]

And he copies out a poem he had had around the house for some time.[8] But beyond this it is difficult to go, though there is enough partial evidence available on the literary situation in 1601 so that a patient and divining spirit may some day make it all clear, particularly if he finds more evidence.

We are concerned, however, only with the central part of the poem, which states clearly, technically, and reiteratively the relationship of the lovers, and here there is no uncertainty:

Here the anthem doth commence:
Love and constancy is dead,
Phoenix and the turtle fled
In a mutual flame from hence.

So they lov'd as love in twain
Had the essence but in one;
Two distincts, division none:
Number there in love was slain.

Hearts remote, yet not asunder;
Distance, and no space was seen
'Twixt this turtle and his queen;
But in them it were a wonder.

So between them love did shine
That the turtle saw his right
Flaming in the phoenix's sight:
Either was the other's mine.

Property was thus appalled,
That the self was not the same;
Single nature's double name
Neither two nor one was called.

Reason, in itself confounded,
Saw division grow together,
To themselves yet either neither,
Simple were so well compounded;

That it cried, 'How true a twain
Seemeth this concordant one!
Love hath reason, reason none,
If what parts can so remain.

Here is stated in exact, technical, scholastic language the relationship of the lovers. They are Love and Constancy, Beauty and Truth, Phoenix and Turtle. The nature of their love was such that love in each had the essence (the defining principle by which anything that is, is what it is) only in one. Obviously, then, the effect of their love was unitive. But in what way? in terms of what scheme of ideas is this union conceived? Let us examine the possibilities. It is not unlike, of course, the Neo-Platonic union, in which the soul, being reduced to the trace of the One which constitutes its resemblance to it, is absorbed, submerged, and lost in the presence of the One. There is no more distance, no doubleness, the two fuse in one.[9]

But the language here is Latin and has passed, as had the doctrine of Plotinus, through the disputations of the Schoolmen: *essence, distincts, division, property, single nature's double name, simple, compounded.* Furthermore, the chief point of Shakespeare's poem is lost in the Plotinan formulation: for the central part of the poem consists wholly in the reiteration—line after line as if the poet would have you understand even to exhaustion—of the paradox that though identical the two are distinct; they are both truly one and truly two. Thus, for example, in the Plotinan union there is no interval between the two—*And no space was seen*—but the contrary element of the paradox—*distance*—is lacking.

The language and the ideas of the poem, then, are technical and scholastic. But is this the scholastic doctrine of love? Is the

83

scheme of thought here of the same order as the material of the poem? The doctrine of Thomas Aquinas on this point is sufficiently representative of the scholastic position. Love, he tells us (he is quoting the Neo-Platonist, the Pseudo-Dionysius) is a unitive force. The manner of this union, the way in which the beloved can be said to be in the lover, can be comprehended by an analogy. For just as when someone understands something there is a certain notion of the thing in the man who understands, so when someone loves something there is a certain impress, so to speak, of what is loved in the feeling of the lover, and with reference to this one can say that what is loved is in the lover as what is understood is in him who understands (ST, 1. 37.1). But union in this sense by no means amounts to absolute identification; it is not possible to say according to this account that she is my essence.

Thomas in another place distinguishes a three-fold sense in which union is related to love. There is the union which is the cause of love, and this is a genuine and substantial union with respect to one's love of himself; it is a union based on similitude with respect to one's love of others. Secondly, there is that union which is essentially love itself, and which involves a certain conformation of feeling toward the object (see ST, 1-2, 28. 5). If this is the love of friendship, the nature of the relationship is similar to the substantial union spoken of above, for the lover loves the other as himself; if it is the love of desire, he loves the other as something that belongs to him. There is, finally, a third kind of union which is an effect of love, and that is that union of the parties involved which the lover seeks of the loved. This union is in accordance with the demands of love, for, as Aristotle says in the *Politics* (2. 4. 1262 b 11), "Aristophanes said that lovers desire from being two to become one," but since "the result of this would be to destroy either one of them or both," they seek a suitable and proper union, namely to live and speak together and to be joined in other ways of this nature (ST, 1-2. 28. 1 ad 2).

From this much it is clear how carefully Thomas distinguishes and how painstakingly he points out that the effect of union in love, together with those other related effects which he goes on to discuss—a mutual inherence of one in the other, an ecstatic going out of oneself, and a zealousness in appropriating the good which one loves (1-2. 28. 2-4)—only take place in a certain sense. The love of desire, it is true, does not rest with attaining any external or surface enjoyment of what it loves, but seeks to possess it absolutely, penetrating as if to the very heart of the beloved (1-2.28.2). But it is only *as if*. For human love admits of no real identification. Though we desire it, if it were attained, one or both would be destroyed.

In Shakespeare's poem, however, the lover is identified with the beloved; the beloved is his essence; they become one and yet neither is annihilated. The lovers are of course destroyed in that they have passed in a mutual flame from this life, but clearly they have only passed into the real life of Ideas from the unreal life of materiality.

It might be suspected, looking back on the passage in the *Two Gentlemen of Verona,* that the relation implied here is that of the Beatific Vision, in which our love of God and God's love for us finds its ultimate fulfilment. If this were so it would certainly offer us what we are looking for. It would offer us a model or paradigm by means of which the relationship of the lovers in this poem is constructed and construed. But though the doctrine of the Beatific Vision be thorny and difficult to understand, nevertheless one thing is clear: even in that last eternal embrace, in which, no longer through a glass darkly, we see the essence of God face to face (ST, 1. 12. 1: "We shall see Him as He is." 1 Jn. 3. 2.), there is no absolute identification of essence. Thomas makes this clear in the following passage, which I translate paraphrastically in order to render it as easy as possible to the uninitiated (the italics are mine):

Since some form is required in any cognition by which the object can be cognised or seen, there is required for the cognition of separated substances nothing less than the separated substance itself which is conjoined to our intellect as the form, being both the object and the means of understanding. In fact, whether this apply or not to other separated substances, it behooves us to accept that mode of understanding as applying to the vision of God through His essence, because in no other way could we be conducted to the divine essence. *But this explanation is not to be taken in the sense that the divine essence is really the form of our intellect, or that there results an absolute unity from the fusion of the divine essence and our intellect,* as is the case with form and matter in natural, as distinguished from supernatural, things. Rather, there is a proportion of the divine essence to our intellect on the analogy of form to matter. For, whenever there are two things in the same receptacle, of which one is more perfect than the other, they maintain a proportionate relationship of the more perfect to the less perfect, like that of form to matter.

3. 92. 1. c. sub fin.

III

But anything is forgiven a lover, the reader may exclaim at this point, even the grossest hyperbole. Perhaps this is so; our present business, however, is simply with interpreting a text. Now, if anything be clear in the history of the lyric, it is that *The Phoenix and Turtle,* whatever its merits, is not a gracious and charming trifle, and could not have been intended as such. One half of the poem consists of a grimly reiterated paradox, stated with the minimum of decoration and the maximum of technical exactitude. The inference is that the poet was trying to say something precisely, and this lays on us the obligation, if we wish to read the poem at all, of trying to find out precisely what he was saying.

The doctrine of the poem is not sanctioned by the scholastic doctrine of human love, nor indeed, so far as I know, by the facts of nature. It is not sanctioned by the doctrine of the Beatific Vision. Is there a source in the tradition from which is derived the structure of thought and the technical terms by which it is displayed? There is, in fact, only one model in the tradition for the notion that distinct persons may have only one essence, and that is the doctrine of the Trinity. Not, of course, the Incarnation, for the two Natures (or Essences) of Christ are distinct (ST, 3. 2). The relation of lover and beloved in Shakespeare's poem is that of the Persons of the Trinity, and the technical language employed is that of scholastic discussion on the subject. With this clue, all the difficulties of the expository part of the poem are resolved, and if it still remains difficult to understand, it is no more difficult than the Trinity.

The principal point of the doctrine of the Trinity in this connection is summed up in Hooker's *Laws of Ecclesiastical Polity*:

> The Persons of the Godhead, by reason of the unity of their substance, do as necessarily remain one within another, as they are of necessity to be distinguished one from another . . . And sith they all are but one God in number, one indivisible essence or substance, their distinction cannot possibly admit separation . . . Again, sith all things accordingly love their offspring as themselves are more or less contained in it, he which is thus the only-begotten, must needs be in this degree the only-beloved of the Father. He therefore which is in the Father by eternal derivation of being and life from him, must needs be in him through an eternal affection of love.   5. 56. 2-3

The Father and Son are distinct persons, yet one essence. Furthermore, as the learned Doctors tell us, the Son proceeds from the Father by way of the intellect in that he is the Father's understanding of Himself; and the Holy Ghost proceeds from both by way of the will in that He is the mutual love of both. But when anyone understands and loves himself, he is in himself not only through the identity of the subject, but also in the way in which what is understood is in the one who understands, and what is loved is in the lover. Thus the Holy Ghost, who proceeeds from the reciprocal relation of the Father and Son, is a distinct person, but is at the same time the bond between Them, inasmuch as He is Love (ST, 1. 37. 1. c and ad 3):

> So they lov'd as love in twain
> Had the essence but in one . . .

In the next line—*Two distincts, division none*—the terminology is obviously scholastic, and its context is the doctrine of the Trinity. "To avoid the Arian heresy," Thomas says, "we must avoid the terms *diversity* and *difference* so as not to take away the unity of essence; we can, however, use the term *distinction* . . . So also to avoid taking away the simplicity of the divine essence we must avoid the terms *separation* and *division,* which apply to parts of a whole . . . " (ST, 1. 31. 2.).

Number there in love was slain, for plurality is always the consequence of a division, as Thomas points out; but the division of a continuum from which springs number, which is a species of quantity, is found only in material things. But number in this sense cannot be applied to God. When numerical terms are used they signify only the things of which they are said, and so we may say one essence, signifying only the essence undivided, and many persons, signifying only those persons and the undividedness of each. (ST, 1. 30. 3). *Hearts remote, yet not asunder* repeats the central paradox. *Distance, and no space was seen*; the Son is co-eternal with the Father in order of time (1. 42. 2) and hence in order of space (1. 42. 1., and see 1. 81. ad 3.). *But in them* (and in God!) *it were a wonder.*

The next stanzas are based on the scholastic distinction of *proprium* and *alienum*: what is proper is what belongs to the one, but not to the other; what is alien is what belongs to the other, but not to the one. The terms are contraries, and exclude each other. But in the Trinity the relations which constitute the three Persons are their several Properties. Though property is the same as person, yet in the Father and the Son, as there is one essence in the two persons, so also there is one property in the two persons (ST, 1.40.1.), So also in the Phoenix and Turtle: love so shone between them (and Love is the relationship of the Father and the Son in the Holy Ghost—1.37.2) that the one saw what belonged to him ("his right": *suum proprium*) in the sight of the other; but the other's sight was the instrument by which the second saw reciprocally what belonged to him in the sight of the first. Each was the other's "mine": *meum*. No wonder *Property was thus appalled*: for *property* is the personification of *proprium*.

Single nature's double name: Each of the Persons of the Trinity has His proper name, yet they are all of one nature, one essence (1.13; 1.33.2; 1.34.1-2; 1.36.1; and especially 1.39.2-7), and the name *God* stands of itself for the common nature—hence, *Neither two nor one was called.*

Reason, in itself confounded,—for reason is the principle of distinction and its method is division—*Saw division grow together;* each of the two was distinct (*To themselves*), yet neither one of them was one or the other (*yet either neither*). And the last line of this stanza repeats again the same paradox, and again by one of the common scholastic dichotomies: *Simple were so well compounded.* Any separated substance is simple; thus the Phoenix and the Turtle are simples, but are so compounded as to form a simple. Hence, at the final recapitulation of the paradox, Reason confesses its inadequacy to deal with the mystery of love: *Love has reason, reason none | If what parts* can remain unparted (*can so remain*).

The relation of the Phoenix to the Turtle is now clear. It is conceived and expressed in terms of the scholastic doctrine of the Trinity, which forms in this sense the principle of order of the poem. The Phoenix and Turtle are distinct persons, yet one in love, on the analogy of the Father and the Son in the Holy Ghost. If the reader does not immediately understand this mystery, the point of the poem is that it is a mystery at which Reason is confounded and confesses that true Reason is above it and is Love.

Plots and Errors:
Hamlet and King Lear

We read some works, even literary ones, coldly for what they are, as we read a menu or a casual novel. But not works of prestige. These we approach differently, under one of two kinds of context. Some we read possessively; they are the favorites of a group, whether socially broad or narrow. They are Works of Fashion. We come to them, either initially or in time, with a prepared attitude and verify that attitude in rehearsing the text. There is, for example, within the academic community that consistent and repetitive attitude toward the more popular works of Chaucer which may be called the Chuckle School of Criticism, or "Good old Chaucer." There is, more narrowly, the attitude toward Statius *On Sleep* illustrated in an earlier essay, or the dominance of the Eliot gloss in our experience of Marvell's *To his Coy Mistress.* In each case there is a possessiveness of the group toward the text and a limitation of the experience of the text to the form of the prevailing gloss. It is a fixed point from which raids are made on the detail of the work.

But with such texts as *Hamlet* and *King Lear,* though antecedent glosses do in part direct our experience, as it is only human they should, there is something else involved. These are texts of a special sort in our society. They are not simply works of prestige: they are Scripture. They are much more than works; they are iron magnets for innumerable filings. And they must, in our society at least, be serious, if not solemn; they must engage our humanity. When we come to interpretation we do not simply interpret a text but rather attempt to order a massed experience of discussion, quotation, and concern that has a ghostly yet substantial existence

90

distinct from the page. This constitutes a field, comparable to, or almost of the same kind as, the field out of which in one of the current modes of composition a poem is precipitated. There is involved a process of divination and emotional accomodation. The result must come together; it must satisfy. In the case of Scripture it must satisfy by attaining a unity ordered by the modes of our own emotional life and by alluding to those deeper concerns set loose by the autonomy of religion: human destiny, the human heart, tragedy and the plight of modern man. We write our own poems in the form of literary criticism, and what we divine are our own forms.

Consequently, for many years we have tended to regard the greater Shakespearean tragedies as primarily concerned with the psychological or spiritual nature and development of the main character, to regard character, routinely said to be indistinguishable from action, as the guiding principle of order that directs the construction of the plays. In this way we get rid of the action. Bradley, for example, says of *Hamlet*: "the whole story turns upon the peculiar nature of the hero." And Allardyce Nicoll, to choose one more example among many, speaks of "that which forms the very core of the tragedy, the mental and spiritual Hamlet."[1] Again, almost everyone assumes that the spiritual development of Lear is the principle of that play, and that all that is not directly concerned with Lear is nevertheless related. The story of Gloucester, it is said, repeats the design of the main plot; it forms a second, a sub- or echo-plot, and in the repetition emphasises, intensifies, and even universalises, the significance of the main plot, the development of Lear's character. Hence we regard the political and local circumstances of the story as of little consequence; it is a universal and a domestic tragedy. Finally we view the internal method of construction according to the familiar analysis of high-school lore: it consists of the initial exposition, followed by the rising action which culminates in the emotional climax or crisis, and then falls away to the resolution. It is a curve of feeling which rises and falls, and the only problem is to

91

locate the point of highest tension, whether in the storm scenes on the heath, or later in the reconciliation with Cordelia.

Such ways of viewing experience and its reflections in fiction are familiar to us; they are common in the modern novel, but they are not necessarily the principles of all fiction. Indeed, we may distinguish for our present purposes broadly two kinds of fiction, corresponding roughly to the two kinds of lyric previously distinguished.[2] The one exhibits—to use our commonplace—artificial or mechanical form; the other aims at organic form. The former is found in Roman comedy, in Jonson, in many of the comedies and some of the greater tragedies of Shakespeare. It is differentiated by having as a major principle of order a plot in the old sense, a contrivance, a sequence of actions moved by scheming and mistakes. The latter would appear uncontrived. In it character is indeed indistinguishable from action, action from character, and in fact the parts subsist only in the impression of the whole. In the former things are brought about. In the latter they happen. Toward the end of Henry James' *Ambassadors,* for example, the principal character remarks: "I don't think there is anything I have done in such a calculated way as you describe. Everything has come as a sort of indistinguishable part of everything else."[3] This is not the sort of thing that Davos or Mosca, Iago or Edmund, or indeed Claudius or Laertes could with any accuracy say.

For what is missing in the modern accounts of Shakespearean tragedy is precisely the plot of the play, the series of intrigues and mistakes by which the situation as initially expounded comes to the catastrophe. For this reason the modern critic has always had special difficulties with *King Lear.* He wonders at the disappearance of the Fool, as if the Fool had some bearing on the issue of the action. And he finds that the play falls off after the storm scenes. It falls off after the storm scenes because the poet has action to deal with, a story to tell, a plot to unfold, and the modern critic is not interested in this. He would like to leave out the plot.

He would like to leave it out because in the modern view it is a good thing to be rid of. Mark Twain threatened to shoot anyone attempting to find a plot in his narrative of Huckleberry Finn. Sherwood Anderson: "The plot notion did seem to me to poison all story-telling. What was wanted, I thought, was form. not plot." André Gide resolves in the *Journal* to the *Counterfeiters* "to avoid the 'artificiality' of a 'plot'." And E. M. Forster commenting on that novel, apparently with approval, describes Gide's attitude in these terms: "As for plot—to pot with the plot, break it up, boil it down. Let there be those 'formidable erosions of contour' of which Nietzsche speaks. All that is prearranged is false." Elizabeth Bowen asks, "What about the idea that plot should be ingenious, complicated—a display of ingenuity remarkable enough to command attention?" gives no answer, and passes on. The distinguished poet and critic, Edwin Muir, says, "It was Thackeray who first made a clear break with the plot both as a literary and a popular convention . . ." so that in *Vanity Fair* "All the plot that remains is the series of incidents which widen and diversify the picture, and set the characters in different relations . . . What we ask [of the incidents] is that they should arise as naturally as possible, that the plot should not appear to be a plot." And again: "There is no external framework, no merely mechanical plot; all is character, and all is at the same time action." "This spontaneous and progressive logic is the real distinguishing feature of the dramatic novel."[4]

But "spontaneous and progressive logic" is not a characteristic of Shakespearean tragedy, and indeed was not a notion available at that time. I suggest in this essay a return from the concerns of modern fiction and modern life to the commonplaces of Shakespeare's own tradition, commonplaces that fit his works with a remarkably unsubtle obviousness. If this method of interpretation seems not to enrich our experience of the works but rather to limit and simplify that experience, I can only confess that this is my intention. Interpretation, I feel, should sharpen and define, subtract, not add. One does not make progress in this field; the trick is to go back, to recover.

If in the process of recovery we ask what traditions were available to Shakespeare, from what sources could he draw those structures and schemes of language, person, scene, and action which he used, and in what context would his audience perceive and feel them, we shall find that with respect to the theater there were, among others, three important traditions. The first, which will not concern us here, is the tradition of pageantry and court entertainment, of hermits, allegorical and supernatural characters, of special scenery, dance, song and "the study of magnificence."[5] It is a tradition relevant to many of Shakespeare's comedies, and one that receives its final realization in the masques of Jonson.

The second is the tradition of show business, of the professional actor and the popular stage. It is a tradition of juggling, tumbling, comic beatings, of Tom o' Bedlam and "Exit, pursued by a bear," of fencing matches and vaudeville skits. In this tradition a narrative is only partly useful for its own sake; it is at the same time a device for disposing and arranging a series of theatrical routines, just as the story of the modern musical play is largely an occasion for songs, dances, comedy acts, and what not. It forms, as was earlier maintained, a sort of expandable filing system. Hence the story or plot of an Elizabethan play has in this sense a double function. It is presented for its own sake, and at the same time it forms a sort of framwork or outline allowing a number of independent acts or routines. It is a way of plotting out, of arranging, a wide variety of theatrical material—comic scenes, songs, and exhibitions of odd characters, such as Osric in *Hamlet* or Clove and Orange in Jonson's *Everyman Out of His Humor*:

Mitis.   What be these two, signior?
Cordatus. Marry, a couple, sir, that are mere stranges to the
          whole scope of our play; only come to walk a turn or
          two in this scene of Paul's, by chance.

                                                    3.1.16-19

94

It allows for soliloquies or passions, and scenes of the same sort, such as the scenes on the heath, expressing the feeling attached to the story. It leaves room, as Jonson says in discussing unity of action, "for digression and art."[6] The critical rule that pertains to these is not that they should blend together and be integrated into a single and organic effect, that they should exhibit some kind of qualitative progression. It is rather the rule of decorum, the negative rule that they should be not inappropriate. Plot in this sense, then, is a method for disposing and arranging the heterogeneous material of the play. And the difference in aesthetic effect between two plays with approximately the same quantity of plot but with greater and less digression and episode will be, as Coleridge noted of *Hamlet* and *Macbeth*: "the one proceeds with the utmost slowness, the other with a crowded and breathless rapidity."[7] Or, to put it less perceptively: the one in a school text I have at hand runs to fifty pages, the other to thirty.

The third tradition is academic, the tradition of literary criticism and analysis employed in the reading and discussion of Roman comedy in the schools. We shall find that Shakespeare constructs the plots of *Hamlet* and *King Lear* consciously and deliberately according to the rubrics of this tradition. The basic texts are the classics of ancient rhetoric and Donatus on Terence, and the general context is elementary school learning, rehearsed and repeated with the singlemindedness of a Freudian interpreter. We could assume that Shakespeare knew this tradition, knew it by heart, even without the work of the many scholars who in recent years have firmly established the fact,[8] for it was the tradition of prestige in his time. But how well he understood and how easily he handled the basic terms and distinctions of that tradition can be illustrated by the exegesis of a phrase in Polonius' speech about the players in which the councilor displays his familiarity with current literary and dramatic terms:

The best actors in the world, either for tragedy, comedy, history, pastoral, pastoral-comical, historical-pastoral, tragical-historical, tragical-comical-historical-pastoral; scene individable, or poem unlimited.   2. 2. 415-19

The enumeration of dramatic genres begins like the enumeration in a patent for a company of players, and then introduces that contamination of genres which was being currently discussed and explicitly practised, as in Guarini's *Il Pastor Fido* (1590), a pastoral tragicomedy, or in the comical satires of Jonson. The last two phrases in the enumeration, culminating in the quadrate contamination of "tragical-comical-historical-pastoral," are not in the text of 1604 (the second quarto) but appear for the first time in the folio text of 1623. They may represent an addition, gagging up the passage. However, the phrases we are specially concerned with are "scene individable" and "poem unlimited." The commentators do not know what is meant, and have settled on the guess that it is a reference "to dramas that observe the unities of time and place and also those that give no heed to such limitation."[9] It is a distant guess. A better guess and a more obvious one would be that "scene individable" refers to the question, which was receiving some attention at the time, of whether the acts of a play should be divided into scenes. Muretus in his notes to Terence (1550), which were incorporated in the later editions of that author, comments, "As to dividing the acts of a play into scenes, designating scene one, scene two, and so on, how skillfully and intelligently it is done is, I think, questionable. For my own part I take it that this distinction comes from the teachers of literature and not from the poets;" and he advises a friend whose tragedy he had read "to remove entirely the useless and superfluous and dreamed up by teachers division of acts into scenes."[10] Jonson may well have had such comment in mind in the following passage from *Every man Out of His Humor* (1599, published 1600), in which Shakespeare was a principal actor:

Mitis.   Does he observe all the laws of comedy in it?

96

Cordatus.   What laws mean you?

Mitis.   Why, the equal division of it into acts and scenes, according to the Terentian manner .   .   .

Cordatus.   O no, these are too nice observations.

Induction, 235-42

But there is no need to guess what "poem unlimited" means. All that is needed is an elementary Elizabethan education, a familiarity with the basic distinctions of Cicero and Quintilian, and a willingness to countenance the persistent Renaissance habit of using rhetorical concepts in the discussion of poetry. Let us translate the phrase, as an Elizabethan would naturally do, into Latin: *poema infinitum*. Of course. He had learned from rhetoric that there are two kinds of topics one could write or speak on: "quaestiones esse aut infinitas aut finitas."[11] They are unlimited or limited; either general, without reference to persons, time, or place, or they are implicated in circumstance. "Should men marry?" is unlimited; "Should Antony marry Octavia?" is limited. An unlimited poem, then, is an expository poem on a general topic, such as *De Rerum Natura* or John Davies' *Nosce Teipsum* (1599).

The concepts of this tradition enter into the structure of Shakespeare's drama in various ways. The principle of social rank, for example, that tragedy involves heads of state and comedy the affairs of the citizen class, is retained and modified. It serves, to use our own terms, to distinguish domestic from true tragedy, and romantic from realistic comedy. One of the most interesting consequences of this principle in Shakespearean comedy is the implicit stipulation that romantic love is only possible to the well-born, so that to introduce this element into the citizen comedy of the *Merry Wives of Windsor* the author must introduce a well-born lover, a Mr. Fenton who is a courtier and so of necessity a Throckmorton, a Knyvett, or a Blount.

There is another principle relating to comedy that Shakespeare sometimes scrupulously observes and sometimes deliberately violates. It seems to have had a fascination for him. This is

97

the stipulation that comedy should be *sine periculo vitae,* "without the threat of death." The action in one of his earliest comedies, the *Comedy of Errors,* is deliberately set in the frame of a violation of this law. Indeed, the observance of the law in the *Merry Wives of Windsor* is sufficient to distinguish that play absolutely in kind from *Much Ado about Nothing* and *Measure for Measure.* The knot of error in *Much Ado* is tied by a supposed death, and *Measure for Measure* exploits to the full the tragic attitudes of fear and resignation to death: "Be absolute for death." The former is simply comedy; the latter are tragicomedy in the form in which it was being developed at this time in practise and theory. For "he who composes tragicomedy," says Guarini, "takes from tragedy its great persons but not its great action . . . its danger but not its death."[12]

In brief, Cicero and Donatus, Quintilian and Diomedes furnish Shakespeare and his interpreter with the relevant notions. Consequently, when Viola exclaims in *Twelfth Night*:

> O Time, thou must entangle this, not I;
> It is too hard a knot for me t'untie!

> 2.2.41-2

we recognize the allusion to the Donatan tradition of analysis, and we perceive that the plot of *Twelfth Night* is constructed precisely according to that tradition. In general Donatus describes the structure of Terence's comedies in terms of the error that furnishes the problem of the play, and the plots and errors that complicate and lead to the tying of the knot whose resolution yields the catastrophe. He comments, for example, on *Andria* 2.4: "This scene ties the knot of error of the play, and the difficulty proper to comedy; it also sets in motion the schemes." On 2.6: "This scene contains the plots of both characters, by which each marvellously takes, and is taken, in." On 5.4: "And here the error of the play is wholly revealed." Again, on *Hecyra,* 4.4: "In this scene is the final error before the catastrophe."[13] So in *Twelfth Night*, after the situation is expounded in a series of

98

scenes, the plot begins with the initial error, an error like that in the *Silent Woman,* "error personae":[14] Olivia falls in love with the disguised Viola, thinking her a man, and there follow later the subsequent errors springing from the twinness of Sebastian. Immediately after the initial error the first plot begins, Maria against Malvolio. This is a separate plot that has its own issue and has no bearing on the catastrophe. The next plot, however, does. Sir Toby and Fabian's practice on Sir Andrew, leading to the duels, precipitates the catastrophe. In brief, the action of the play develops simply and solely through plots and errors; they constitute the engine that runs the show.

Likewise in *Hamlet,* when Horatio after the catastrophe of that play proposes to "speak to th' yet unknowing world /How these things came about" and goes on after Fortinbras' assent to say:

> But let this same be presently perform'd,
> Even while men's minds are wild, lest more mischance
> On plots and errors happen.

> 5.2. 404-6

one who knows that tradition understands the terms and perceives that it is being authoritatively stated that the catastrophe resulted from a series of plots and errors. As it does. It would not particularly bother him that the mechanisms of comedy are employed in tragedy, for he would know with Jonson and many others who wrote on the subject that "the parts of a comedy are the same with a tragedy."[15]

The action of *Hamlet,* the busy part of the play, begins with Hamlet's assumption of madness, an alteration that amounts to a disguise. The subsequent scenes are produced by the plots of the King and Polonius through Rosencrantz and Guildenstern, Ophelia, and the Queen to find out "The very cause of Hamlet's lunacy," and of Hamlet against the King to discover his guilt. This movement culminates in the killing by error of Polonius as an accidental consequence of his plot to use the Queen in discovering Hamlet's secret. Hamlet is immediately packed off to England—this is the King's plot; and Rosencrantz and Guildenstern "go to 't" by a plotted error:

> O 'tis most sweet
> When in one line two crafts directly meet.
>
> 3.4 209-10

In the final scene of the play the carefully contrived scheme to murder Hamlet, as it were accidentally, goes awry:

> purposes mistook
> Fall'n on th' inventors' heads.

In error the foils are exchanged; in error the Queen drinks the poisoned cup.

This is a plot of intrigue, a tale of "mischance that on plots and errors happen," enriched by scenes and speeches of comedy, passion, satire, hung on the framework of the plot and not inappropriate to the whole. To our modern question, What is Hamlet's tragic flaw? or, In what way are we to construe his final death as issuing out of the depths of his personality? we answer: His tragic flaw is Claudius and Laertes. He was cold-bloodedly murdered by means of a contrived diabolical plot. One need not assume, therefore, that he was in our current jargon "murder-prone."

Lear, too, is a play of mischance that on plots and errors happen. There is in it also the spiritual story of Lear and the spiritual story of Gloucester, of course, but neither of these nor both together furnish the structure of the whole. It is not these that bring about the catastrophe.

The action begins with the first plot at the end of the scene of state that opens the play. Goneril and Regan, fearful of the threat to their new eminence from the King's character and his very kingness, as also from his hundred knights who with their retainers constitute a sizeable army, begin to scheme:

100

if our father carry authority with such dispositions
as he bears, this last surrender of his will but
offend us.

1.1. 308-10

Regan says, "We shall further think on't," but Goneril fiercely
replies, "We must do something, and in the heat." What she
proposes to do becomes clear in a later scene. The second strand
of the play is now introduced with the soliloquy of Edmund, who
expounds his plot:

> Legitimate Edgar, I must have your land . . .
> Well, my legitimate, if this letter speed
> And my invention thrive, Edmund the base
> Shall top the legitimate.

1.2. 16, 19-21

And with the entrance, first of Gloucester, then of Edgar, he
immediately puts it into execution. The next scene shows Goneril's
plot in operation: Lear is to be treated with such disrespect,
offensive to the name of King as well as father, that, given his
character which she knows, he will leave in a huff. "And let his
knights have colder looks among you," she tells little Oswald.

> What grows of it, no matter; advise your fellows so:
> I would breed from hence occasions, and I shall
> That I may speak; I'll write straight to my sister
> To hold my course.

1.3.23-5

The difficulty between Lear and Goneril is not the spontaneous
consequence of differing temperaments, nor is it the result of the
offensive and riotous senility of an old man. These are merely
Goneril's allegations, and have no standing against the claim of
duty to a King and father. Rather, the difficulty between Lear
and Goneril is coldly and explicitly provoked. It is the consequence
of a plot.

The next scene shows Kent in disguise taking service with

101

Lear, and Oswald furthering Goneril's plot, though he is tripped up for his pains in a comic routine. Up to this point, from the conclusion of the exposition, all has been plots on the part of Goneril and Edmund, and in the case of Kent's disguise an error. There follows an interlude, the Fool's routine with Lear, which, however important it may be to our feeling about the play, is irrelevant to the plot. Its primary purpose is to drive home the wrongness of Lear's initial mistake, and to display some wit. The plot resumes with the entrance of Goneril who has, as she planned, bred occasions to insult Lear. He hurries off in a rage to the other daughter, and she sends Oswald with a message urging Regan to a similar course of action. This plot comes to a head when Lear, rejected by Regan, goes out into the storm. Meanwhile, Edmund's plot against Edgar has been successful; Edgar flees, is proclaimed, and assumes the disguise of Tom of Bedlam. Kent in the storm discloses his political plot against the Dukes, the alliance with France which culminates in the battle. But this leads to the furtherance of Edmund's second plot, the plot against Gloucester, who has been approached by Kent's party and confides this to Edmund. By revealing the intrigue to Cornwall he destroys his father and attains his title and lands. This is the culmination of his original plot.

Gloucester is blinded, Cornwall slain, the French Army landed at Dover, Goneril and Regan vie for Edmund's favor, and Albany comes to the side of the good. Oswald, carrying a letter from Goneril to Edmund, runs across Gloucester, is slain by the disguised Edgar, and the crucial error of the plot occurs—Edgar finds on Oswald's body Goneril's letter. This leads to the unloosing of the knot of the play. For, with the defeat of Cordelia, Edmund is at the height of his power. He plots by way of the Captain the death of Cordelia and Lear. Meanwhile, Albany has been shown Goneril's letter and has consented to Edgar's scheme of a trial by combat. In the quarrel for pre-eminence between Albany and Edmund, Regan openly espouses Edmund; it is a marriage ceremony:

102

> Witness the world, that I create thee here
> My lord and master.
>
> 5.3.77-8

And Albany, on the evidence of the letter that went astray, forbids the banns:

> For your claim, fair sister,
> I bar it in the interest of my wife;
> 'Tis she is sub-contracted to this lord,
> And I, her husband, contradict your banns.
>
> 5.3.84-7

Regan has been poisoned by Goneril, and is led off. The trial by combat ensues, with Edgar triumphant and Edmund mortally wounded. Goneril is exposed, exits, and commits suicide. The death of Gloucester is announced, and then on the repentance of Edmund, who discloses his plot against Lear and Cordelia, his orders are recalled. But it is too late. Cordelia is dead,and Lear soon dies. This is hardly the story of the psychological development of Lear and Gloucester.

We have left out much, and much that conduces to the richness and deep feeling of the play—the scenes on the heath, the mighty passions of Lear corresponding to the soliloquies of Hamlet, the regeneration of Lear and of Gloucester—but we have left out none of the action, nothing that is necessary to the plot. In *Lear,* this is the plot of Goneril and Regan against Lear, of Edmund against Edgar and Gloucester, of Kent against the Dukes, of Goneril against Regan, of Edmund against Lear and Cordelia, and the counter-action stemming from the errors of Edgar's disguise and the letter gone astray.

Nor is there in the modern sense a double plot in the play, though there is in a Renaissance sense. A prominent Italian critic, for example, writing in the 1540's says:

> I call that plot double which has in its action diverse kinds of persons of the same station in life, as two lovers of different character, two old men of varied nature . . . and other such

things, as they may be seen in the *Andria* and in the other plots of the same poet, where it is clear that these like persons of unlike habits make the knot and solution of the plot very pleasing. And I believe that if this should be well imitated in tragedy by a good poet, and the knot so arranged that its solution will not bring confusion, double structure in tragedy will be no less pleasing (always remembering the reverence due to Aristotle) than it is in comedy. . .[16]

Obviously, in these term *King Lear* has a double plot, for Lear and Gloucester are two old men, though in this case of similar rather than of varied nature, and Edgar and Edmund, Cordelia on the one hand and Goneril and Regan on the other yield further doublings. But this is not what the modern critic has in mind when he speaks of the main and sub- or echo-plot of that play. Rather, a plot in this tradition consists of several lines of action, separately developed at the beginning, but impinging on each other to form the complication, and each necessary to the final solution or catastrophe. It follows in this tradition that a line of action necessary to the complication and solution does not constitute a separate or sub-plot but is an integral part of the plot itself. There is, consequently, on this view no double, no main-and sub-plot, in *King Lear,* for Edmund and Edgar are the principal agents in the catastrophe.

The method and intention of such doubling in Renaissance drama is illuminated by a later critic, Guarini. "It now remains to defend this grafting in of subordinate stories," he says, and we recall that Shakespeare grafted the Gloucester story from Sidney's *Arcadia* on to the old story of Lear:

> In order to do this I shall consider four agents indispensable to the plot of the *Andria* . . . : Pamphilus the first, Glycerium the second, Philumena the third, and Charinus the fourth . . . the principal subject is nothing else than the love of Pamphilus and Glycerium, not interrupted by that of Charinus, but greatly aided. And if that love alone had been represented, with the pregnancy of Glycerium and the displeasure of Simo, the father of Pamphilus,

how insipid the story would have been! A young man fallen under the displeasure of the father because he had married a woman of no standing, who at last, when she is discovered to be a free woman, is given to him as his wife—what is there in that to make a plot? The plot might indeed have been pathetic and have displayed character, but there would have been no activity, which is the strength of the dramatic art. How would the plot have come to a crisis? From the indignation of the father and the love of the son strong feelings could have resulted, but not intrigues.[17]

The author's exclamation, "What is there in that to make a plot?" is clearly applicable to the plot of *Lear* as it is ordinarily summarized for us. An old man acts foolishly, estranges the child who loves him, is brutally rejected by his other children, goes into a feverish delirium, is finally reconciled to the good child, and then by a trick of fate she is killed and he dies broken-hearted. The story is repeated about another old man. One could say with our Renaissance author: "The plot might indeed have been pathetic and displayed character, but there would have been no activity, which is the strength of the dramatic art. How would the plot have come to a crisis? . . . strong feelings could have resulted, but not intrigues."

Tradition and Modernity:
Wallace Stevens

I have defined tradition in such a way that every poem necessarily has a tradition, but this is not the common meaning of the
term. For we distinguish between what is traditional and what is
not, and in the latter case the principle is a negative one. This
is a concern for tradition that is a modern concern, and provoked
by something so simple as a sense of alienation from the past, a
feeling for history as distinct. It is motivated by the persuasion
that tradition has been lost and is only recoverable in novelty.
From this arises a corollary concern with modernity in poetry, for
which the poetry of Wallace Stevens will serve as an illustration.
He himself writes in the poem entitled "Of Modern Poetry":

> The poem of the mind in the act of finding
> What will suffice. It has not always had
> To find: the scene was set; it repeated what
> Was in the script.
> > Then the theatre was changed
> To something else. Its past was a souvenir.[1]

To be modern in this sense is not the same thing as to be
contemporary, to be living and writing in our time, or to have
lived and written within our normal life span. There are many
contemporary poets who are not modern. The modern poet writes
the new poetry, as it was called some years ago. His poetry is
modern in that it is different from the old, the traditional, the
expected; it is new. This is the sense in which *modern* has always
been used in these contexts: the modern poets in Roman antiquity
were Calvus and Catullus who wrote in new and untraditional

poetic forms, in forms borrowed from another language and regarded by the traditionalists of the times as effete and decadent; whose subjects were novel and daring; and whose attitudes were in conscious distinction from those of the old morality. Again, the *moderni,* the modern thinkers in the late Middle Ages, were those who advocated and embraced the new logic of that time and whose attitudes were thought to be dangerous to the established order; it was later said that they caused the Reformation.

The modern poet, then, is modern only in the light of tradition, only as distinguished from the old. His forms, his models, his subjects, and his attitudes are different from and in opposition to the customary and expected forms, models, subjects, and attitudes of his own youth and of his readers. Consequently to be modern depends on a tradition to be different from, upon the firm existence of customary expectations to be disappointed. The new is parasitic upon the old. But when the new has itself become the old, it has lost its quality of newness and modernity and must shift for itself.

This is the situation with respect to what is still called modern poetry; it is rapidly becoming the old and the traditional. There appeared some years ago a number of articles in the leading conventional journals of this country in defense of modern poetry. Had the poetry still needed defense, the articles would never have been accepted by the editors of those journals. But modern poetry is, in fact, in secure possession of the field, and its heroes are aged men with a long public career behind them. Wallace Stevens, in fact, died recently at the age of seventy-six after a public career of forty years. Yet the attitude of modernity still persists. These poets still represent to the young writer of today the new, the adventurous, the advance-guard, the untried. Their names are still sacred to the initiate.

For it is the condition of modernity in art that it appeal to the initiate, that it provoke the opposition of the ordinary reader who has the customary and old expectations which it is the purpose of modern art to foil. Hence it lives in an attitude of defense; is close and secret, not open and hearty; has its private ritual and its air of priesthood—*odi profanum vulgus et arceo,* "I despise the uninitiated crowd, and I keep them at a distance." It is obscure, and its obscurities are largely calculated; it is intended to be impenetrable to the vulgar. More than this, it is intended to exasperate them.

There is something of this in all art that is genuine. For the genuine in art is that which attains distinction, and the distinguished is uncommon and not accessible to the many. It is different, it must be different, and as such provokes the hostility of the many, and provokes it the more in that its difference is a claim to distinction, to prestige, and to exclusion. This claim is diminished by time. Wordsworth is now regarded as quite traditional, quite stuffy and conventional. For the particular qualities of difference in an older body of poetry that has been absorbed into the tradition become part of that tradition, and so something that the reader actually need not see since he does not know it is different. He may then in his early years and through his school days develop a set of social responses to the received body of poetry; he may enjoy that poetry without effort, be pleased by his conditioned responses, and think of himself as a lover and judge of poetry. When the audience for poetry becomes satisfied with a customary response to a customary poem, when they demand of the poet that he write to their expectations, when distinction is lost in commonness, there is need for the modern in art, for a poetry that is consciously different, even if it often mistakes difference for distinction. The poet must exasperate his reader, or succumb to him.

Such was the situation out of which Stevens wrote, at least as it seemed to him and to those of his contemporaries who have become the aged fathers of modern poetry. They sought to appear different, and hence distinguished, and they succeeded perhaps too well. The first thing that strikes the reader of Wallace Stevens, and the quality for which he was for a long time best known, is

108

the piquant, brilliant, and odd surface of his poems. They are full of nonsense cries, full of virtuoso lines, such as

> Chieftain Iffucan of Azcan in caftan
> Of tan with henna hackles, halt![2]

which unexpectedly make grammar and sense if you read them slowly with closed ears. They are thronged with exotic place-names, but not the customary ones of late romantic poetry; instead of "Quinquereme of Nineveh from distant Ophir" there is "a woman of Lhassa," there is Yucatan. Rare birds fly, "the green toucan," and tropical fruits abound, especially the pineapple. Odd characters appear—Crispin, Redwood Roamer, Babroulbadour, black Sly, Nanzia Nunzio—and are addressed in various languages —my semblables, Nino, ephebi, o iuventes, o filii. And they wear strange hats.

A good deal of this, of course, is simply the unexpected in place of the expected; a new and different collection of proper names, for example, instead of the old collection, but used largely for the same purpose while seeming to deny this by being designedly different.

> Canaries in the morning, orchestras
> In the afternoon, balloons at night. That is
> A difference, at least, from nightingales,
> Jehovah, and the great sea-worm.[3]

The process is common in Stevens, and can be seen neatly in one of his most engaging stanzas. The theme of the stanza is the traditional one of Tom Nashe's

> Brightness falls from the hair,
> Queens have died young and fair.

But instead of Helen and Iseult there are references to the beauties in Utamaro's drawings and to the eighteenth century belles of Bath:

109

> Is it for nothing, then, that old Chinese
> Sat titivating by their mountain pools
> Or in the Yangtse studied out their beards?
> I shall not play the flat historic scale.
> You know how Utamaro's beauties sought
> The end of love in their all-speaking braids.
> You know the mountainous coiffures of Bath.
> Alas! Have all the barbers lived in vain
> That not one curl in nature has survived?[4]

A woman's hair is here used as a synecdoche for her beauty. Have all those who have cared for and cherished her hair, have all the barbers, lived in vain, that though much has survived in art, none has survived in nature? The poet concludes then, expressing the sense of the couplet of a Shakespearean sonnet:

> This thought is as a death, which cannot choose
> But weep to have that which it fears to lose.

in the more specialized terms of his synecdoche, but almost as movingly:

> Why, without pity on these studious ghosts
> Do you come dripping in your hair from sleep?

Much of this is rather amusing, and even, as we say now, intriguing. Sometimes, indeed, it is much more than that, as in the stanza just quoted which is poetry of a rare though too precious kind. But Wallace Stevens had a public career in poetry for forty years, and forty years is a little too long for this sort of pepper to retain its sharpness and piquancy. We have to ask, then, what is the motive and purpose in this?

It is usually said that these aspects of Stevens' work derive from a study of the French poets of the latter nineteenth century, the Symbolists and Parnassians, and this explanation no doubt is true enough. But it is not a sufficient explanation. The prestige of that poetry was not so high in Stevens' youth as to serve as a motive, though it might be sufficient now. The motive is rather

110

a more human one. It is disdain—disdain of the society and of the literary tradition in which he grew up, of himself as a part of that society, and of his readers so far as they belonged to it. He sought, he tells us:

> when all is said, to drive away
> The shadow of his fellows from the skies,
> And, from their stale intelligence released,
> To make a new intelligence prevail.

How did he go about it? He celebrated the rankest trivia in the choicest diction. He was a master of the traditional splendors of poetry and refused to exercise his mastery in the traditional way; he displayed it in the perverse, the odd:

> he humbly served
> Grotesque apprenticeship to chance event . . .

He became "a clown" though "an aspiring clown." In his own summary, in the passage that immediately follows the lines quoted above, he explains:

> Hence the reverberations in the words
> Of his first central hymns, the celebrants
> Of rankest trivia, tests of the strength
> Of his aesthetic, his philosophy,
> The more invidious, the more desired.
> The florist asking aid from cabbages,
> The rich man going bare, the paladin
> Afraid, the blind man as astronomer,
> The appointed power unwielded from disdain.[5]

He possessed "the appointed power"—the Miltonic and Scriptural phrasing is blasephemous in this context, and deliberately so—but would not wield it from disdain. The question then is: Why should he have felt such disdain? The answer can be collected from various of his poems but is given full and detailed exposition in the one from which I have just quoted. This is "The Comedian as the Letter C," the show-piece and longest

111

poem in his first book. The poem is sufficiently complex to have several centers of concern. I shall interpret it, however, in terms of our question, and we shall find that this will turn out to be a primary concern of the poem.

The poem consists of six sections, each .of a little under a hundred lines of blank verse. It is in form and subject a poem that depicts the growth of a poet's mind, and though the main character is given the fictitious name of Crispin, he may be taken as an aspect of the author, a mask for Wallace Stevens the poet, so that the poem in effect is autobiographical. It belongs, then, to that literary form of which the model and prototype is Words-worth's *Prelude*. It is not a wholly easy poem to read, partly because much of it is written in Stevens' fastidious and disdainful manner, partly because its structure is not adequately adjusted to its theme. The hero of the poem makes a sea voyage to a strange and exotic country, in this case Yucatan, and back to his own land. The motive for the voyage is explicitly given late in the poem in the passage already quoted:

> What was the purpose of his pilgrimage,
> Whatever shape it took in Crispin's mind,
> If not, when all is said, to drive away
> The shadow of his fellows from the skies,
> And, from their stale intelligence released,
> To make a new intelligence prevail?

His voyage is a rejection of his society as banal and trite, of its intelligence as stale, and his quest is the quest of a new intelligence. His problem was the problem that every teacher of freshman composition sets his better students, the problem of striking through routine phrasing and syntax to the genuine, the honest, the possibly distinguished.

The hero is portrayed as having been before this trip a man who was master of his environment, but he was a little man, "the Socrates of snails," "this nincompated pedagogue," and the environment itself was trivial; it was a land "of simple salad-beds, of

112

honest quilts." It was, in fact, to quote Stevens' own summary of his early environment in an essay of later date, "the comfortable American state of life of the 'eighties, the 'nineties, and the first ten years of the present century."[6] It was the time and place when the sun

> shone
> With bland complaisance on pale parasols,
> Beetled, in chapels, on the chaste bouquets.

It was that middle class culture of business, public chastity, and official Christianity which we often call, with some historical injustice, Victorianism. In this world Crispin wrote the conventional poetry of the times. He was one

> that saw
> The stride of vanishing autumn in a park
> By way of decorous melancholy . . .
> That wrote his couplet yearly to the spring,
> As dissertation of profound delight . . .

However, he found that

> He could not be content with counterfeit . . .

It was this dissatisfaction with the conventional—in society and in poetry—"That first drove Crispin to his wandering." He alludes to it as "The drenching of stale lives," a life of "ruses" that was shattered by the experience of his voyage.

He found the sea overwhelming; he "was washed away by magnitude." "Here was no help before reality." It was not so much that he was cut off from the snug land; he was cut off from his old self:

> What counted was mythology of self,
> Blotched out beyond unblotching.

and hence from his environment. He was destitute and bare:

113

> The salt hung on his spirit like a frost,
> The dead brine melted in him like a dew
> Of winter, until nothing of himself
> Remained, except some starker, barer self
> In a starker, barer world . . .

From this experience he came to Yucatan. The poetasters of that land, like the poetasters at home, in spite of the vividness of experience around them

> In spite of hawk and falcon, green toucan
> And jay . . .

still wrote conventional verses about the nightingale, as if their environment were uncivilized. But Crispin's conversion at sea—for it was obviously a conversion—had enlarged him, made him complicated

> and difficult and strange
> In all desires . . .

until he could reduce his tension only by writing an original and personal poetry, different and unconventional.

The experience at sea is now reinforced by another experience in Yucatan, of the same elemental, overwhelming sort:

> one
> Of many proclamations of the kind,
> Proclaiming something harsher than he learned

from the commonplace realism of home:

> From hearing signboards whimper in cold nights.

It was rather "the span / Of force, the quintessential fact,"

> The thing that makes him envious in a phrase.

It was the experience that altered and reinvigorated his poetry, the source from which he drew that distinction of style that marks off his published work from the sentimental verses he had printed in the college magazine some twenty years before. The experience was of the type of a religious experience:

114

                    His mind was free
          And more than free, elate, intent, profound
          And studious of a self possessing him,
          That was not in him in the crusty town
          From which he sailed.

The poetry he now wrote issued from this context. It was conditioned by the kind of dissatisfaction that drove Crispin to his wandering, by such an experience as Crispin's on the voyage and in Yucatan, and by its results. This dissatisfaction lies behind a good many of Stevens' poems, which deal, if one looks beneath the distracting surface, simply with the opposition between the aridities of middle-class convention and the vivid alertness of the unconventional, as in "Disillusionment at Ten O'clock." Some repeat in smaller compass and with other properties the subject of "The Comedian": as "The Doctor of Geneva." In others he attempts to deal directly with the experience of the sea, but this was a religious experience without the content of traditional religion. In fact, it had no content at all beyond the intuition of a bare reality behind conventional appearance, and hence was an unfertile subject for poetry since it was unproductive of detail. He treated it in one of his best short poems "The Snow Man," but when he had stated it, there was nothing more to be done with it, except to say it over again in another place. This he has repeatedly done, though with a prodigality of invention in phrasing that is astounding.

Most of what is interesting in Stevens issues from this problem. It can be put in various terms. It is the problem of traditional religion and modern life, of imagination and reality, but it can be best put for Stevens in the terms in which it is explicitly put in "The Comedian." The problem is the relationship of a man and his environment, and the reconciliation of these two in poetry and thus in life. The two terms of this relationship are really Wordsworth's two terms: the one, what the eye and ear half create; the other, what they perceive. The reconciliation in Wordsworth is in a religious type of experience:

115

With what strange utterance did the loud dry wind
Blow through my ear! the sky seemed not a sky
Of earth—and with what motion moved the clouds!

Dust as we are, the immortal spirit grows
Like harmony in music; there is a dark
Inscrutable workmanship that reconciles
Discordant elements, makes them cling together
In one society.[7]

The reconciliation in Stevens is sought in poetry, in

those
True reconcilings, dark, pacific words,
And the adroiter harmonies of their fall.

For poetry is the supreme fiction of which religion is a manifes-
tation:

Poetry

Exceeding music must take the place
Of empty heaven and its hymns,

Ourselves in poetry must take their place . . .[8]

What Crispin is seeking is such a reconciliation, a oneness between himself and his environment. He began in the illusion that
he was the intelligence of his soil, but the experience of reality
overwhelmed him, and he came to believe that his soil was his
intelligence. At this extreme he wrote poems in which a person
is described by his surroundings. But he perceived that this too
was sentimental, and so he settled for the ordinary reality of daily
life, married, had four daughters, and prospered. However, he
did not give up poetry entirely; he recorded his adventures in the
poem, and hoped that the reader would take it as he willed: as
a summary

strident in itself
But muted, mused, and perfectly revolved
In those portentous accents, syllables,

116

And sounds of music coming to accord
Upon his law, like their inherent sphere,
Seraphic proclamations of the pure
Delivered with a deluging onwardness.

Such is Stevens' account of the source of his distinctive style and distinctive subjects. But he owed more than he acknowledged to the old and the traditional. He owed "the appointed power" which was "unwielded from disdain."

That he once had the appointed power is clear in his greatest poem, and one of his earliest, "Sunday Morning."[9] The poem is traditional in meter—it is in eight equal stanzas of blank verse— and has as its subject a deep emotional attachment to traditional Christianity and a rejection of Christianity in favor of the clear and felt apprehension of sensory detail in this life, together with an attempt to preserve in the new setting the emotional aspects of the old values.

The poem depicts a woman having late breakfast on a Sunday morning, when of course she should have been at church. She is for the moment at one with her surroundings, which are vivid, sensory, familiar, and peaceful. All this serves to dissipate the traditional awe of Christian feeling, but the old feeling breaks through:

She dreams a little, and she feels the dark
Encroachment of that old catastrophe,
As a calm darkens among water-lights.

Her mood "is like wide water, without sound," and in that mood she passes over the seas to the contemplation of the Resurrection. The remainder of the poem consists of the poet's comment and argument on her situation, on two short utterances she delivers out of her musing, and finally on the revelation that comes to her in a voice.

The poet asserts that Christianity is a religion of the dead and the unreal. In this living world of the sun, in these vivid and sensory surroundings, there is that which can assume the values of heaven:

> Divinity must live within herself:
> Passions of rain, or moods in falling snow;
> Grievings in loneliness, or unsubdued
> Elations when the forest blooms; gusty
> Emotions on wet roads on autumn nights;
> All pleasures and all pains, remembering
> The bough of summer and the winter branch,
> These are the measures destined for her soul.

The truly divine is the human and personal in this world: it consists in the association of feeling with the perception of natural landscape, in human pleasure and pain, in change, as in the change of seasons.

He then argues that the absolute God of religion was originally inhuman, but that the Incarnation by mingling our blood with His, by mingling the relative and human with the Absolute, satisfied man's innate desires for a human and unabsolute Absolute. Certainly, if "the earth" should "Seem all of paradise that we shall know," we would be much more at home in our environment:

> The sky will be much friendlier then than now . .
> Not this dividing and indifferent blue.

At this point the woman speaks in her musing, and says that she could acquiesce in this world, that she could find an earthly paradise, a contentment, in the perception of Nature, in the feel of reality, except that the objects of her perception change and disappear. Nature is an impermanent paradise. The poet, however, answers that no myth of a religious afterworld has been or ever will be as permanent as the stable recurrences of Nature:

> There is not any haunt of prophesy,
> Nor any old chimera of the grave,
> Neither the golden underground, nor isle

118

Melodious, where spirits gat them home,
Nor visionary south, nor cloudy palm
Remote on heaven's hill, that has endured
As April's green endures; or will endure
Like her remembrance of awakened birds,
Or her desire for June and evening, tipped
By the consummation of the swallow's wings.

The woman speaks again, and says:

"But in contentment I still feel
The need of some imperishable bliss."

There remains the desire for the eternal happiness of tradition.
The lines that comment on this present some difficulties to interpretation until it is seen that the poet in his answer proceeds
by developing the woman's position. Yes, he says, we feel that
only in death is there fulfillment of our illusions and our desires.
Even though death be in fact the obliteration of all human
experience, yet it is attractive to us; it has the fatal attractiveness
of the willow in old poetry for the love-lorn maiden. Though
she has lovers who bring her gifts—that is, the earth and its
beauty—she disregards the lovers and, tasting of the gifts, strays
impassioned toward death.

Yet the paradise she would achieve in death is nothing but
an eternal duplicate of this world, and lacking even the principle
of change, leads only to ennui. Therefore, the poet creates a
secular myth, a religion of his irreligion. The central ceremony
is a chant, a poem to the sun,

Not as a god, but as a god might be . . .

It is an undivine fiction that preserves the emotions of the old
religion but attaches them to a poetry in which the sensory objects
of a natural landscape enter into a union in celebration of the
mortality of men:

And whence they came and whither they shall go
The dew upon their feet shall manifest.

119

The biblical phrasing creates a blasphemous religion of mortality.

The poem now concludes with a revelation. Out of the woman's mood a voice cries to her, saying that the place of the Resurrection is merely the place where a man died and not a persisting way of entry into a spiritual world. The poet continues:

> We live in an old chaos of the sun,
> Or old dependency of day and night,
> Or island solitude, unsponsored, free,
> Of that wide water, inescapable.
> Deer walk upon our mountains, and the quail
> Whistle about us their spontaneous cries;
> Sweet berries ripen in the wilderness;
> And, in the isolation of the sky,
> At evening, casual flocks of pigeons make
> Ambiguous undulations as they sink,
> Downward to darkness, on extended wings.

We live, in fact, in a universe suggested by natural science, whose principle is change, an island without religious sponsor, free of the specific Christian experience. It is a sensory world, it has its delights, its disorder, and it is mortal.

The poem is an argument against the traditional Christianity of Stevens' youth, and especially against the doctrine and expectation of immortality, in favor of an earthly and mortal existence that in the felt apprehension of sensory detail can attain a vivid oneness with its surroundings and a religious sense of union comparable to the traditional feeling. The former is undeniably traditional, and much of the deep feeling of the poem is derived from the exposition in sustained and traditional rhetoric of the position which is being denied. In this sense it is parasitic on what it rejects. But the positive argument is almost as traditional in the history of English poetry and in the literary situation of Stevens' youth: it is, with the important difference of a hundred years and the denial of immortality, Wordsworthian in idea, in detail, in feeling, and in rhetoric. Passages comparable to the

120

appositive enumeration of details of natural landscape associated with human feeling, as in

> Passions of rain, and moods in falling snow;
> Grievings in loneliness, or unsubdued elations
> When the forest blooms . . .

are scattered throughout Wordsworth's poetry, especially through the blank verse. I have already quoted a short passage; let me quote another:

> What want we? have we not perpetual streams,
> Warm woods, and sunny hills, and fresh green fields,
> And mountains not less green, and flocks and herds,
> And thickets full of songsters, and the voice
> Of lordly birds, an unexpected sound
> Heard now and then from morn to latest eve,
> Admonishing the man who walks below
> Of solitude and silence in the sky?

The movement of the verse is Stevens', the syntax, and the relation of syntax to the line-ends. The kind of detail is the same. And the idea, if one reads it out of the specific context of Wordsworth's system, is Stevens' idea; for the passage in isolation says, What does man need, what need he desire, more than a live appreciation of the detail of natural landscape, for the world beyond, the birds admonish us—or, Nature tells us—is a world of solitude and silence. This is not precisely what Wordsworth would have endorsed, but certainly what a young man who was drenched in Wordsworth could make of it. And as he read on in the poem—it is "The Recluse"—he would come to the rhetoric of one of his greatest stanzas and the theme of his greatest poem: he would read in Wordsworth:

> Paradise, and groves
> Elysian, Fortunate fields,—like those of old
> Sought on the Atlantic Main—why should they be
> A history only of departed things,

Or a mere fiction of what never was?
For the discerning intellect of Man,
When wedded to this goodly universe
In love and holy passion, shall find these
The simple produce of the common day.[10]

and he would write:

There is not any haunt of prophesy,
Nor any old chimera of the grave . . .

The central concern of Stevens' poetry, the concern that
underlay Crispin's voyage and the poet's meditative argument with
the woman in "Sunday Morning," as well as most of the more or
less curious divergencies of his career, is a concern to be at peace
with his surroundings, with this world, and with himself. He
requires for this an experience of the togetherness of himself and
Nature, an interpenetration of himself and his environment, along
with some intuition of permanence in the experience of absoluteness, though this be illusory and transitory, something to satisfy
the deeply engrained longings of his religious feeling. Now,
there is an experience depicted from time to time in the romantic
tradition—it is common in Wordsworth—and one that has perhaps occured to each of us in his day, a human experience of
absoluteness, when we and our surroundings are not merely related but one, when "joy is its own security." It is a fortuitious
experience; it cannot be willed into being, or contrived at need.
It is a transitory experience; it cannot be stayed in its going or
found when it is gone. Yet though fortuitous and transitory, it
has in its moment of being all the persuasion of permanence; it
seems—and perhaps in its way it is—a fulfillment of the Absolute:

It is and it
Is not and, therefore, is. In the instant of speech,
The breadth of an accelerando moves,
Captives the being, widens—and was there.[11]

122

Stevens attempted to will it into being. He constructed a series of secular myths, like the one in "Sunday Morning," that affirm the traditional religious feeling of the nobility and unity of experience, but the myths remain unconvincing and arbitrary, and conclude in grotesqueries that betray the poet's own lack of belief in his invention, as in "A Primitive Like an Orb," in which he evokes:

A giant, on the horizon, glistening,

And in bright excellence adorned, crested
With every prodigal, familiar fire,
And unfamiliar escapades: whiroos
And scintillent sizzlings such as children like,
Vested in the serious folds of majesty . . .

For, as he asks in an earlier poem:

But if
It is the absolute why must it be
This immemorial grandiose, why not
A cockle-shell, a trivial emblem great
With its final force, a thing invincible
In more than phrase? [12]

He has attempted to contrive it by a doctrine of metaphor and resemblances, which is precisely Wordsworth's doctrine of affinities. He has sought to present in a poem any set of objects and to affirm a resemblance and togetherness between them, but all the reader can see is the objects and the affirmation, as in "Three Academic Pieces," where a pineapple on a table becomes:

1. The hut stands by itself beneath the palms.
2. Out of their bottle the green genii come.
3. A vine has climbed the other side of the wall . . .

These casual exfoliations are
Of the tropic of resemblance . . . [13]

But there is a poem in "Transport to Summer," one of the perfect poems, as far as my judgment goes, in his later work, that achieves and communicates this experience. It is a short poem in couplets entitled "The House Was Quiet and the World Was Calm." There is no fiddle-dee-dee here. The setting is ordinary, not exotic. It is about a man reading alone, late at night. The phrasing is exact and almost unnoticeable. The style is bare, less rich than "Sunday Morning," but with this advantage over that poem, that none of its effect is drawn from forbidden sources, from what is rejected. The meter is a loosened iambic pentameter, but loosened firmly and as a matter of course, almost as if it were speech becoming meter rather than meter violated. It has in fact the stability of a new metrical form attained out of the inveterate violation of the old. It is both modern and traditional:

> The house was quiet and the world was calm.
> The reader became the book; and summer night
>
> Was like the conscious being of the book.
> The house was quiet and the world was calm.
>
> The words were spoken as if there was no book,
> Except that the reader leaned above the page,
>
> Wanted to lean, wanted much most to be
> The scholar to whom his book is true, to whom
>
> The summer night is like the perfection of thought.
> The house was quiet because it had to be.
>
> The quiet was part of the meaning, part of the mind:
> The access of perfection to the page.
>
> And the world was calm. The truth in a calm world,
> In which there is no other meaning, itself
>
> Is calm, itself is summer and night, itself
> Is the reader leaning late and reading there.[14]

124

Notes

I. Poetry, Structure, and Tradition

1 Archibald Macleish, *Collected Poems: 1917-1952* (Boston, 1952), p. 41.
2 *Shorter Oxford English Dictionary* (Oxford, 1933), *s.v.* See also James Craig La Driere, "Poetry and Prose," Joseph T. Shipley, ed., *Dictionary of World Literature* (New York, 1943).
3 Chapter 1. See Gerald Else, *Aristotle's Poetics; The Argument* (Cambridge, Mass., 1957), *ad. loc.*
4 61B.
5 St. Petersburg, April 21, 1914.
6 The theory and point of view here developed closely parallels that of René Wellek in René Wellek and Austin Warren, *Theory of Literature* (New York, 1949), chapter 12.
7 Tr. E. B. Pusey ("Everyman's Library:" London, 1907), pp. 274-5.

II. Classical and Medieval: Statius "On Sleep"

1 *Silvae,* 5.4, ed. Henri Frère, tr. H. H. Izaac (Paris, 1944), p. 205.
2 J. W. Mackail, *Latin Literature* (New York, 1895), pp. 189-90.
3 Robert Yelverton Tyrrell, *Anthology of Latin Poetry* (London, 1901), pp. 302-3; D. A. Slater, *The Silvae of Statius* (Oxford, 1908), pp. 22-3; H. W. Garrod, ed., *Oxford Book of Latin Verse* (Oxford, 1921), pp. 495-500; E. E. Sikes, *Roman Poetry* (London, 1923), pp. 86-8; J. H. Mozley, ed., tr., *Statius* (London and New York, 1928), p. xii; J. Wight Duff, *Literary History of Rome in the Silver Age* (London, 1927), p. 492; Philip Schuyler Allen, *The Romanesque Lyric* (Chapel Hill, 1928), pp. 76-7. In this last the Latin text is printed in an appendix (p. 321) with the Argus passage excised.
4 H. W. Garrod, ed., (Oxford, 1939), pp. 460 and 533.

[5] John W. Cunliffe, ed., *The Complete Works of George Gascoigne* (Cambride, 1907-1910), II, 143; Frank Allen Patterson, ed., *The Student's Milton* (New York, 1931), p. 160.

[6] This is deliberate with Gascoigne: "Certayne notes of Instruction," *Works*, I, 465ff.

[7] Patterson, p. 159.

[8] Whether there is any such playing of accent against quantity in classical Latin is still under dispute.

[9] Fyfe, in fact, reduces the four lines to one—"But my sad eyes their nightly vigil keep"—and expands the second line into two in order to achieve a sonnet. Slater, p. 23.

[10] E. de Selincourt and Helen Darbshire, edd., *Works* (Oxford, 1946), III, 8-9.

[11] *Silvae*, 5.1, 34-5; Ovid, *Metamorphoses*, 14. 708.

[12] Friedrich Vollmer, ed., *Silvae* (Leipzig, 1898), p. 10; *Silvae*, 3.5. 37-42.

III. *Logic and Lyric: Marvell, Dunbar, and Nashe*

[1] Richard von Mises, *Positivism* (Cambridge, Mass., 1951), p. 289.

[2] Harold R. Walley and J. Harold Wilson, *The Anatomy of Literature* (New York, 1934), pp. 143 and 144.

[3] Scholiast cited in Otto Bird, "The Seven Liberal Arts" in Joseph T. Shipley, ed., *Dictionary of World Literature* (New York, 1943), p. 55; J. E. Spingarn, *A History of Literary Criticism in the Renaissance* (2nd ed.: New York, 1908), pp. 24-7; David Hume, *Philosophical Works* (Boston and Edinburgh, 1854), III, 264; von Mises, *loc. cit.*

[4] H. M. Margouliouth, ed., *The Poems and Letters* (Oxford, 1927), II.

[5] T. S. Eliot, *Selected Essays* (new ed., New York, 1950), p. 254; Helen C. White, Ruth C. Wallerstein, and Ricardo Quintana, edd., *Seventeenth Century Verse and Prose* (New York, 1951), I, 454.

[6] John M. Berdan, ed., *The Poems* (New Haven, 1911), pp. 80-1.

[7] Wright Thomas and Stuart Gerry Brown, edd., *Reading Poems* (New York, 1941), p. 702; Douglas Bush, *English Literature in the Earlier Seventeenth Century* (Oxford, 1945), p. 163.

[8] My translation, except for "the brief sum of life forbids our opening

126

a long account with hope," which is Gildersleeve's; see Paul Shorey, ed., Shorey and Gordon J. Lang, *Odes and Epodes* (rev. ed.; Chicago, 1910), *ad loc.*

[9] W. Mackay Mackenzie, ed., *The Poems* (Edinburgh, 1932), pp. 20-3.

[10] Ronald B. McKerrow, ed., *Works* (London, 1904-10), III, 283.

[11] *Contra Gentiles,* 3.27, 29-31, 36, 48, in *Opera Omnia* (Rome, 1882-1948), XIV; Anton C. Pegis, ed., *Basic Writings of Saint Thomas Aquinas* (New York, 1945), II.

[12] James Joyce, *A Portrait of the Aritist as a Young Man* ("Modern Library": New York, 1928), pp. 273-5.

[13] McKerrow, IV, 440.

[14] This essay has been refuted by Frank Towne, "Logic, Lyric, and Drama," *Modern Philology,* LI (1953-4), pp. 265-8.

IV.   *Convention as Structure: The Prologue to the "Canterbury Tales"*

[1] F. N. Robinson, ed., *Works* (Boston, 1933), p. 2; John Livingston Lowes, *Geoffrey Chaucer* (Boston, 1934), p. 198; Robert Dudley French, *A Chaucer Handbook* (2nd ed.; New York, 1947), p. 203.

[2] French, p. 203.

[3] Robinson, pp. 2-3.

[4] William Witherle Lawrence, *Chaucer and the Canterbury Tales* (New York, 1950), p. 38.

[5] Robert Armstrong Pratt and Karl Young in W. F. Bryan and Germaine Dempster, edd., *Sources and Analogues of Chaucer's "Canterbury Tales"* (Chicago, 1941), p. 2.

[6] George Lyman Kittredge, *Chaucer and His Poetry* (Cambridge, Mass., 1915), p. 149: "There is not one chance in a hundred that he had not gone on a Canterbury pilgrimage himself."

[7] Robinson, p. 663.

[8] Robinson, p. 315.

[9] 4. 1245ff. *Works,* ed. G. C. Macaulay (Oxford, 1901), II. 335ff.

[10] Suggested by Émile Legouis, *Geoffrey Chaucer,* tr. L. Lailavoix (London, 1928), pp. 85-6.

[11] Howard R. Patch, "Characters in Medieval Literature," *Modern Language Notes,* XL (1925), pp. 1-14.

[12] Lines 812-6 in the Middle English version; 796-800 in the original, Ernest Langlois, ed., (Paris, 1920), II.

[13] M. E., 160-1, original, 150-1; M. E., 220-1, original, 208-9.

[14] Kittredge, p. 166; Lawrence, p. 30.

V. *Idea as Structure: The Phoenix and Turtle*

[1] George Lyman Kittredge, ed., *The Complete Works* (Boston, 1936),

[2] *Works* (Oxford, 1829), II, xlvi.

[3] *Works,* ed. John Keble, 7th edn. rev. R. W. Church and F. Paget (Oxford, 1888), II, 247-8.

[4] *ST: Summa Theologica* in St. Thomas Aquinas, *Opera Omnia* ("Leonine edition": Rome, 1882-1948). Some details of the following interpretation have been anticipated by other scholars, particularly by the Indian scholar, Ranjee. See William Shakespeare, *The Poems,* ed. Hyder Edward Rollins ("The New Variorum": Philadelphia, 1938), pp. 323-31 and 559-83.

[5] Alexander B. Grosart, ed., *Robert Chester's "Love Martyr"* (London, 1878), top pagination 169.

[6] John Gerard, *The Autobiography of an Elizabethan,* tr. Philip Caraman (London, 1951), p. 48: "I must not forget to mention a certain lady and her husband (they were gentlefolk) who made a vow of chastity . . . I kept in touch with them for many years afterward and I can say that during all that time they remained faithful to their vow." See also p. 86 on Mrs. Line: ". . . she made a vow of chastity, a virtue she practiced in her married life." Father Gerard was a noted Jesuit; the events described occurred in the 1590's.

The only testimony relating to the circumstances of this poem, if it does relate to this poem, is the remark made in passing by Fr. Henry More, S.J. (1660) about Ann, Lady Stourton: "a daughter of Edward, Earl of Derby, and sister to the Stanley whose epitaph Shakespeare wrote." (Rollins, p. 578) There were five sisters (John Seacome, *The History of the House of Stanley* [Preston, 1793], pp. 130-1) but none of them seems to fit the apparent specifications of the poem. Sir John Salusbury's wife, of course, was a natural daughter of the fourth Earl of Derby, and hence a niece of Lady Stourton's, as was Dorothy Halsall, her sister, with whom Sir John seems to have been in love. (Carleton Brown, ed., *Poems by Sir John Salusbury and Robert Chester* [E.E.T.S., e.s. cxiii: London, 1914], pp. xxx-viiiff). I add, for the fun of it, that Salusbury's motto, "posse et nolle nobile" (Brown, p. xxix) is the theme of Shakespeare's Sonnet 94.

[7] Grosart, top pagination, 177 and 181-6.

[8] The last line of the *Epode* appears in *England's Parnassus* (1600).

[9] A. J. Denomy, "An Inquiry into the Origins of Courtly Love," *Medieval Studies,* Pontifical Institute of Medieval Studies, Toronto, VI (1944), 175-260, especially p. 209.

VI. *Plots and Errors: "Hamlet" and "King Lear"*

[1] A. C. Bradley, *Shakespearean Tragedy* (London, 1912), p. 89; Allardyce Nicoll, *Studies in Shakespeare* (London, 1927), p. 43.

[2] E. M. Forster, *Aspects of the Novel* (New York, 1927), p. 144: "The plot, then, is the novel in its logical intellectual aspect . . ."

[3] Henry James, *The Ambassadors* (New York, 1909), II, 200-1 (Bk. X, ch. 3).

[4] Mark Twain, *The Adventures of Huckleberry Finn,* introductory Notice; Sherwood Anderson in Robert E. Spiller, et al., ed. *Literary History of the United States* (New York, 1948), II, 1230-1; Forster, p. 152; Elizabeth Bowen, *Collected Impressions* (London, 1950), p. 249; Edwin Muir, *The Structure of the Novel* (London, 1928), pp. 38, 39, 40, 43, and 47-8.

[5] Ben Jonson, *Masque of Blackness*, line 6.

[6] *Discoveries,* 2747-9: "For the episodes and digressions in a fable are the same that household stuff and other furniture are in a house."

[7] *Lectures and Notes on Shakespeare* (London, 1897), p. 472.

[8] T. W. Baldwin, *Shakespeare's Five-Act Structure* (Urbana, 1947); Marvin Theodore Herrick, *Comic Theory in the Sixteenth Century* (Urbana, 1950); Madeleine Doran, *Endeavors of Art* (Madison, 1954).

[9] Kittredge, *ad loc.*

[10] Iodocus Willichius, ed. (Cologne, 1567), on *Andria,* 1.1: "Quod autem actus fabularum partimur in scenas, aliamque primam, aliam

secundam, et sic deinceps dicimus, quam perite et intelligenter id fiat, quaerendum puto. Equidem libere ut dicam, grammaticorum hanc, non poetarum, esse partitionem arbitror." *Orationes, Epistolae, et Poemata* (Leipzig, 1698), p. 696: "omnino autem illam inutilem et supervacaneam, et a stultis literatoribus excogitatam actuum in scenas divisionem, quaeso te, ut tollas. Baldwin, p. 277, cites these passages and the Jonson.

11 Quintilian, 3.5.5

12 Allan H. Gilbert, *Literary Criticism: Plato to Dryden* (New York, 1940), p. 511.

13 Baldwin, chapter 2; text, ed. Paul Wessner (Leipzig, 1902), 2 vols.

14 5.4.255-6.

15 *Discoveries,* 2625.

16 Geraldi Cinthio in Gilbert, p. 254.

17 Gilbert, pp. 528-9.

VII. *Tradition and Modernity: Wallace Stevens*

1 *Collected Poems* (New York, 1954), p. 239.

2 "Bantams in Pine-Woods," p. 75.

3 "Academic Discourse at Havana," p. 142.

4 "Le Monocle de Mon Oncle," p. 14.

5 "The Comedian as the Letter C," IV, pp. 37, 39, 37.

6 *The Necessary Angel* (New York, 1951), p. 26.

7 *Prelude,* 1.337-44.

8 "Academic Discourse at Havana," IV, p. 144; "The Man with the Blue Guitar," V, p. 167.

9 pp. 66-70.

10 Lines 126-33 and 800-8.

11 "A Primitive Like an Orb," II, p. 440.

12 "Life on a Battleship," *Opus Posthumus,* ed. Samuel French Morse (New York, 1957), p. 79.

13 *The Necessary Angel,* p. 86.

14 pp. 358-9.

WOE OR WONDER

The Emotional Effect
of Shakespearean Tragedy

TO THE MEMORY OF W. D. BRIGGS

Introduction:
Ripeness is All

I am concerned in these essays with understanding precisely what Shakespeare meant. It is true that "when we read Shakespeare's plays," as one scholar says, "we are always meeting our own experiences and are constantly surprised by some phrase which expresses what we thought to be our own secret or our own discovery."[1] But the danger is that the meaning we find may really be our own secret, our own discovery, . rather than Shakespeare's, and the more precious and beguiling for being our own. The danger I have in mind can be illustrated by our attitude toward one of the most famous of Shakespearean phrases, "Ripeness is all." It is a favorite quotation of Mr. Eliot's. "It seems to me," he says in discussing the question of truth and belief in poetry, "to have profound emotional meaning, with, at least, no literal fallacy."[2] He does not specify what this meaning is, but I take it that it is something not strictly denotative though emotionally compelling.

The phrase, indeed, has seemed to many to represent a profound intuition into reality and to sum up the essence of Shakespearean, or even of human, tragedy. It speaks quite nearly to us. What it means to each will perhaps depend on his own experience and his own way of relating the texture of experience to the insights of literature. Yet all would agree that "Ripeness is all" gathers into a phrase something of the ultimate value of this life; it reassures us that maturity of experience is a final good, and that there is a fulness of feeling, an inner and emotional completion in life that is attainable and that will resolve our tragedies. Such at least seems to be the interpretation of a recent critic. "After repeated disaster," he says of Gloucester in *King Lear:*

he can assent, "And that's true too," to Edgar's "Ripeness is all."
For man may ripen into fulness of being, which means, among
other things, that one part of him does not rule all the rest and
that one moment's mood does not close off all the perspectives
available to him.[3]

In this way we discover in Shakespeare's phrase the secret morality of our own times. It is a meaning I can enter into quite
as deeply as anyone, but it is not what Shakespeare meant.

Shakespeare meant something much more traditional. The
phrase occurs in *King Lear*. In an earlier scene Edgar had pre-
vented Gloucester from committing suicide, that act which
consummates the sin of despair, and Gloucester had accepted
the situation in the true spirit of Christian resignation:

> henceforth I'll bear
> Affliction till it do cry out itself
> 'Enough, enough,' and die.
>
> 4. 6. 75-7

But now Gloucester seems to relapse for a moment, saying:

> No further, sir; a man may rot even here.

And Edgar stiffens his resolution with these words:

> Men must endure
> Their going hence even as their coming hither:
> Ripeness is all.
>
> 5. 2. 9-11

The context is the desire for death. The conclusion is that
as we were passive to the hour of our birth so we must be passive
to the hour of our death. So far, surely, the speech is an affirmation of the spirit of resignation, and it would be reasonable
to suppose that the summary clause at the end, "Ripeness is
all," is but the final restatement of this attitude. It was certainly an available attitude. The experience of Christian
resignation was dense with the history of the Western spirit,
and that history was alive and present in Shakespeare's time;
it spoke daily from the pulpit and in the private consolations of

intimate friends. The theme, furthermore, was a favorite with Shakespeare. It had been fully explored in the Duke's great speech in *Measure for Measure*:

> Be absolute for death. Either death or life
> Will thereby be the sweeter. Reason thus with life:
> If I do lose thee I do lose a thing
> That none but fools would keep. A breath thou art,
> Servile to all the skyey influences
> That do this habitation where thou keep'st
> Hourly afflict. Merely thou art death's fool;
> For him thou labour'st by thy flight to shun,
> And yet runn'st toward him still. . .
> Yet in this life
> Lie hid moe thousand deaths; yet death we fear
> That makes these odds all even.
> 3. 1. 5-13, 39-41

But the finest expression, other than in the passage from *Lear*, is Hamlet's speech to Horatio as he goes to the catastrophe:

> . . . we defy augury; there's a special providence in the fall of
> a sparrow. If it be now, 'tis not to come; if it be not to come,
> it will be now; if it be not now, yet it will come: the readiness
> is all. 5. 2. 230-3

This is as much as to say that we must endure our going hence, be it when it may, since the hour of our death is in the care of Providence: *the readiness is all.*

It has been said that this is Stoic, and certainly *augury* hints toward Antiquity. But he who speaks of a special providence in the fall of a sparrow could trust an audience in the age of Elizabeth to think of Christian theology and the New Testament:

> And fear not them which kill the body, but are not able to kill
> the soul: but rather fear him which is able to destroy both body
> and soul in hell. Are not two sparrows sold for a farthing? *and
> one of them shall not fall on the ground without your Father.*
> But the very hairs of your head are all numbered. Fear ye not
> therefore, ye are of more value than many sparrows.

137

Watch therefore: for ye know not what hour your Lord doth come. But know this, that if the goodman of the house had known in what watch the thief would come, he would have watched, and would not have suffered his house to be broken up. *Therefore be ye also ready*: for in such hour as ye think not the Son of man cometh.

It was not only Seneca and his sons who could urge men to meet death with equanimity. Bishop Latimer, the Protestant martyr, in a sermon preached before King Edward VI speaks the thought and almost the words of Hamlet:

Unusquisque enim certum tempus habet praedefinitum a Domino: "For every man hath a certain time appointed him of God, and God hideth that same time from us." For some die in young age, some in old age, according as it pleaseth him. He hath not manifested to us the time because he would have us at all times ready; else if I knew the time, I would presume upon it, and so should be worse. But he would have us ready at all times, and therefore he hideth the time of our death from us. . . . But of that we may be sure, there shall not fall one hair from our head without his will; and we shall not die before the time that God hath appointed unto us: which is a comfortable thing, specially in time of sickness or wars. . . . There be some which say, when their friends are slain in battle, "Oh, if he had tarried at home, he should not have lost his life." These sayings are naught: for God hath appointed every man his time. To go to war in presumptuousness, without an ordinary calling, such going to war I allow not: but when thou art called, go in the name of the Lord; and be well assured in thy heart that thou canst not shorten thy life with well-doing.[4]

The similarity of the phrase in *Hamlet* to the one in *Lear* is so close that the first may be taken as the model and prototype of the other. But in *Lear* the phrase has been transmuted, and with it the idea and attitude. The deliberate and developed rhetoric of *Measure for Measure* has served its purpose to explore the area of experience, and has been put aside. The

138

riddling logicality of Hamlet's speech has been simplified to
the bare utterance of:

> Men must endure
> Their going hence even as their coming hither

and the concept of the arbitrariness of birth has been introduced to reinforce the arbitrariness of death. Finally, Hamlet's
precise and traditional statement, "the readiness is all," has
been transformed into a metaphor.

What does the metaphor mean? There is no need for
conjecture; it had already by the time of *Lear* become trite
with use, and with use in contexts closely related to this. In
Thomas Wilson's *Art of Rhetoric* (1560) we read:

> Among fruit we see some apples are soon ripe and fall from the
> tree in the midst of summer; other be still green and tarry till
> winter, and hereupon are commonly called winter fruit: even so
> it is with man, some die young, some die old, and some die in
> their middle age.[5]

Shakespeare has Richard in *Richard II* comment on the death
of John of Gaunt:

> The ripest fruit first falls, and so doth he:
> His time is spent . . .
>
> 2. 1. 153-4

That is, as fruit falls in the order of ripeness, so a man dies when
his time is spent, at his due moment in the cosmic process. Again,
Touchstone's dry summary of life and time in *As You Like It*:

> And so, from hour to hour, we ripe and ripe,
> And then, from hour to hour, we rot and rot . . .
>
> 2. 7. 26-7

does not mean that we ripen to maturity and then decline, but
that we ripen toward death, and then quite simply and with
no metaphors rot.

But death is not incidental to Shakespearean tragedy; it
is rather the defining characteristic. Just as a Shakespearean

comedy is a play that has a clown or two and ends in marriages, so a tragedy involves characters of high estate and concludes with violent deaths. The principle of its being is death, and when this is achieved the play is ended. In this sense, then, "Ripeness is all" is the structural principle of Shakespearean tragedy. Thus in *Richard III* the Cassandra-like chorus, the old Queen Margaret, enters alone as the play draws rapidly on to the final catastrophe and says:

> So now prosperity begins to mellow
> And drop into the rotten mouth of death
>
> 4. 4. 1-2

And in *Macbeth,* Malcolm says toward the close:

> Macbeth
> Is ripe for shaking, and the pow'rs above
> Put on their instruments.
>
> 4. 3. 237-9

In this passage the powers above, who are the agents of Providence, are associated with the ripened time. Providence is destiny, and in tragedy destiny is death.

By "Ripeness is all," then, Shakespeare means that the fruit will fall in its time, and man dies when God is ready. The phrase gathers into the simplest of sentences, the most final of linguistic patterns, a whole history of attempted formulations, and by the rhetorical device of a traditional metaphor transposes a state into a process. Furthermore, the metaphor shifts our point of view from a man's attitude toward death, from the "readiness" of Hamlet and the "Men must endure" of the first part of Edgar's speech, to the absoluteness of the external process of Providence on which the attitude depends.

But this is not what the phrase means to the uninstructed modern reader, and this poses a problem. The modern meaning is one that is dear to us and one that is rich and important in itself. It would be natural to ask, Need we give it up? I see no reason why we should give up the meaning: maturity of experience is certainly a good, and the phrase in a modern context is well enough fitted to convey this meaning. But it is our phrase now, and not Shakespeare's, and we should accept the responsibility for it. The difference in meaning is unmistakable: ours looks toward life and his toward death; ours finds its locus in modern psychology and his in Christian theology. If we are secure in our own feelings we will accept our own meanings as ours, and if we have any respect for the great we will penetrate and embrace Shakespeare's meaning as his. For our purpose in the study of literature, and particularly in the historical interpretation of texts, is not in the ordinary sense to further the understanding of ourselves. It is rather to enable us to see how we could think and feel otherwise than as we do. It is to erect a larger context of experience within which we may define and understand our own by attending to the disparity between it and the experience of others.

In fact, the problem that is here raised with respect to literature is really the problem of any human relationship: Shall we understand another on his terms or on ours? It is the problem of affection and truth, of appreciation and scholarship. Shakespeare has always been an object of affection and an object of study. Now, it is common experience that affection begins in misunderstanding. We see our own meanings in what we love and we misconstrue for our own purposes. But life will not leave us there, and not only because of external pressures. What concerns us is naturally an object of study. We sit across the room and trace the lineaments of experience on the face of concern, and we find it is not what we thought it was. We come to see that what Shakespeare is saying is not what we thought he was saying, and we come finally to appreciate it for what it is. Where before we had constructed the fact from our feeling, we now construct our feeling from the fact. The end of affection and concern is accuracy and truth, with an alteration but no dimunition of feeling.

II

Aught of Woe or Wonder

Whatever emotion and whatever tragedy may be, it has always been said that tragedy, and especially the tragic catastrophe, evokes strong and specific emotions. The doctrine is common to Antiquity and the present day as well as to Shakespeare and the Renaissance. "In undertaking any piece of literature," Erasmus remarks in a little Renaissance treatise on how to teach, "it is advisable to show what kind of work it is, the nature of its subject-matter, and what especially is to be looked for in that kind of work. . . . In tragedy one looks especially for the emotional effects, which are quite strong, and then for the means by which these effects are excited."[1] The nature of the effects, however, alters from period to period as the nature of tragedy alters and as the quality and structure of the emotional life varies from society to society, for there is a history of the emotions as well as a history of ideas. The effects we are concerned with here are those of Shakespearean tragedy and those specifically intended by the author and supported by his tradition. The question is, What emotional effects did Shakespeare intend to be evoked by the catastrophe of his greater tragedies?

I

We are told explicitly at the end of *Hamlet* what the emotional effect of the tragic catastrophe is: it is one of fear, sorrow, and wonder. The point is made in two passages, the first of which reads:

142

I follow thee.
I am dead, Horatio. Wretched queen, adieu!
You that look pale and tremble at this chance,
That are but mutes or audience to this act,
Had I but time (as this fell sergeant, Death,
Is strict in his arrest) O, I could tell you—
But let it be. Horatio, I am dead;
Thou liv'st; report me and my cause aright
To the unsatisfied.

5. 2. 343-51

The scene is familiar to every reader: the King and Queen
are dead, Laertes has uttered his last words. And now Hamlet,
in a fashion conventional to the Elizabethan drama, addresses
his remarks rapidly to one character after another—to the dying
Laertes, to Horatio, to the Queen; and finally he turns to the
other actors on the stage, to the "mutes" who serve as "audience to this act." These "look pale and tremble": it is their
function to express the proper emotional attitude and so to convey that attitude directly to the larger audience who witness
the play, for emotional effects are directly transferrable; indeed,
they are much more communicable than ideas.

The way in which this process was understood in Shakespeare's time is explained by his contemporary, Thomas Dekker,
in the prologue to one of his plays:

That man give me whose breast filled by the Muses
With rapture into a second them infuses;
Can give the actor sorrow, rage, joy, passion,
Whilst he again by self-same agitation
Commands the hearers, sometimes drawing out tears,
Then smiles, and fills them both with hopes and fears.[2]

The dramatist derives emotions from his sources of inspiration,
infuses them into the actor, who in turn communicates them to
the audience. The scheme of thought here is Platonic. It is that
which Socrates explains to the professional reciter of Homer in
Plato's dialogue *Ion* under the figure of a magnetic chain of

143

attraction (533C), and doubtless is borrowed from that model. The Muse inspires Homer as a magnet moves an iron ring, the reciter Ion is moved by Homer as another ring by the magnetized one, and the audience finally is moved by Ion, so that three rings hang like a chain from the magnet. Thus feeling runs directly from the sources of poetry to the audience through the medium of poet and actor, and the emotions which in this case Ion excites in his hearers—fear, sorrow, and wonder (535B-C)[3]—are curiously enough those which Shakespeare in *Hamlet* ascribes to the tragic catastrophe. They are also, of course, the emotional effects which Aristotle ascribes to Greek tragedy—pity and fear, certainly, and as we shall see, wonder, too.[4]

The particular emotion denominated in the first passage from *Hamlet* is the conventional tragic effect of fear or terror, for to "look pale and tremble" are the very marks and signs of this. Richard in *Richard III* queries Buckingham on his qualifications for the role of tragic villain:

> Come, cousin, can'st thou quake and change thy color . . .
> As if thou wert distraught and mad with terror?

And Buckingham reassures him:

> Tut. I can counterfeit the deep tragedian . . .
>
> 3. 5. 1, 4-5

The emotion of fear is evoked by "this chance," in men who are "mutes or audience to this act." What is the precise meaning of "this act" and "this chance," since it is with respect to these that the effect is predicated? *Act* in such contexts signifies the particular course of events under consideration. So the First Gentleman comments on the narration of those extraordinary events that untangle the knot of the *Winter's Tale*: "The dignity of this act was worth the audience of kings and princes, for by such was it acted" (5. 2. 86-8). And Prospero in the *Tempest*, referring to the whole business of his deposition and exile, says to Alonso: "Thy brother was a furtherer in this act"

144

(5. 1. 73). But the closest parallel to the present passage is in the final speech in *Othello* where Lodovico, the representative of the Venetian state, closes the play thus:

> Myself will straight aboard, and to the state
> This heavy act with heavy heart relate.

This heavy act—that is, "The tragic loading of this bed," the deaths of Desdemona and Othello. There is here an exact correspondence between the quality of the events and the quality of the emotion they evoke, between the heaviness of act and the heaviness of heart. Similarly the emotion of fear or terror would naturally be provoked by such fearful and terrible events as the deaths of the King, Queen, and Laertes, and the imminent death of Hamlet himself.

"This chance" has a meaning similar to "this act." It is, furthermore, a notion and a term intimately associated with the central Elizabethan conception of tragedy, and especially of the tragic catastrophe. It concentrates in a word the two main aspects of that event, aspects that had long been fused in the Latin equivalent, *casus*. For that word may signify, as it does in the late medieval collections of tragic stories, the fall and death of a great figure which constitutes the catastrophe; and it may also signify the external cause of such a fall, the operation of that agency which to man seems Chance or Fortune, but which from a true and theological point of view is to be regarded as the unfolding of Divine Providence. Indeed, nothing really happens by Chance or Fortune with respect to an absolute God, but only with respect to secondary causes: *nihil est a casu vel fortuna respectu Dei, sed respectu ceterarum causarum.*[5] Hence the display on the stage of the operation of Chance, which is but the inscrutable ways of Divine Providence, strikes the witnesses with fear and terror when the case is notable, for it illuminates the disparity between the relative world of man and the absoluteness of the Eternal Cause.

The bare word, of course, though shot through with the

larger meanings of that historic term, does not carry with it such a full and explicit theory as has just been sketched. Yet its use here does imply the prior existence of such a context. What the bare word means can be ascertained by glancing through a Shakespeare concordance: the meaning ranges from the relatively colorless significance of "ordinary happening or event," through the denomination of such events as make up a narrative (*Cymb* 5. 5. 391), to the strictly philosophical significance of "Chance or Fortune." But the phrase, "this chance," has also a special and restricted meaning. It means the fall and death of notable persons and has in it an element of suddenness and surprise, of the apparently fortuitous.

For example, in the *Tragedy of Locrine* (about 1591), a bad but representative play, the chorus promises us:

> the sequel shall declare
> What tragic chances fall out in this war.
> 2 Prol., 16-7[6]

And fall they do, one after another. So also King Henry in *3 Henry VI* speaks of the dead slain in battle:

> How will the country for these woful chances
> Misthink the king, and not be satisfied!
> 2. 5. 107-8

But the best example is in *Macbeth*, where Macbeth speaks of the murder of Duncan after its accomplishment:

> Had I but died an hour before this chance,
> I had liv'd a blessed time.
> 2. 3. 96-7

That is, "My life had ended in the state of grace *(I had liv'd a blessed time)* if I had died before resolving to murder my King *(an hour before this chance),*" for the fall from the state of grace was coincident with the moral decision. "This chance," then, is the murder of Duncan, a notable fall. In the passage

146

from *Hamlet* it is the tragic catastrophe. And the immediate emotional effect of this on the audience is said to be fear.

But fear is not the only effect ascribed to the catastrophe. In another passage the effects are designated as those of sorrow and astonishment, or woe and wonder. After the death of Hamlet, the young Fortinbras enters in the majesty of state, and as he enters asks:

> Where is this sight?

Horatio answers him:

> What is it you would see?
> If aught of woe or wonder, cease your search.
>
> 5. 2. 373-4

The tableau of destruction remains on the stage—

> O proud Death,
> What feast is toward in thine eternal cell
> That thou so many princes at a shot
> So bloodily hast struck?
>
> 5. 2. 375-8

And Horatio, who was privy to it all, defines this sight as one of woe and wonder, *doloris et admirationis*. It is interesting to note that in the First Quarto, the mangled stage version of *Hamlet,* the passage reads:

> enter Fortinbrasse with his traine.
> FORT.   Where is this bloody sight?
> HOR.   If aught of woe or wonder you'ld behold
> Then looke upon this tragicke spectacle.

In both texts the spectacle is characterized by its proper effects. One of these is *woe* or sorrow, which is the ground of pity, as it was to the Watch who discovered the bodies of Romeo and Juliet:

> We see the ground on which these woes do lie,
> But the true ground of all these piteous woes
> We cannot without circumstance descry.
>
> 5. 3. 179-81

147

Hence pity is evoked by the woes of the catastrophe of *Romeo*, the tragic deaths, by what the chorus-character, Friar Laurence, had already called in the same scene "this lamentable chance" (146). Nevertheless, woe is not precisely pity. It is the more general term, of which pity is a species. It is the English equivalent of that *dolor sive tristitia* which in the medieval tradition of literary criticism is noted, rather than pity *(misericordia sive commiseratio)*, as the subject and effect of tragedy,[7] and which in the medieval tradition of psychological analysis, which is substantially the Renaissance tradition, is treated at length along with fear as one of the basic and most powerful passions of the soul. The others are joy and hope (Thomas, *ST*, 1-2. 25.4).[8] Pity, then, denotes precisely the relationship of the spectator to the catastrophe; but the nature of the catastrophe itself is woeful.

The relationship of the terms is that expounded by Edgar in *Lear*. To Gloucester's question:

> Now, good sir, what are you?

he answers:

> A most poor man, made tame to fortune's blows,
> Who, by the art of known and feeling sorrows,
> Am pregnant to good pity.
>
> 4. 6. 224-7

If we may apply this passage to the general notion of tragedy, we may say that Edgar is the ideal spectator. He has attained the moral effect of that excitation of feeling; he has been "made tame" by participating in "fortune's blows," which are the material of tragedy; he has penetrated into that experience consciously and has realized its significance in feeling, and so has attained to the habit of, the capacity for exercising, the virtue of pity.

The catastrophe is sorrowful and naturally begets pity. It is also sudden, surprising, on a large scale, and involves great persons; hence it evokes wonder. This is an emotion less discussed in connection with tragedy than either fear or sorrow, and one that the literary person today does not easily think of as an emotion, but it is a commonplace in the Renaissance especially in connection with the deaths of notable persons and with the effects of drama and fiction. Dekker, for instance, with reference to the death of Queen Elizabeth, speaks of "the sorrow and amazement that like an earthquake began to shake the distempered body of this island (by reason of our late sovereign's departure)." And Sidney characterizes tragedy as "stirring the affects of admiration and commiseration."[9] *Admiration*, of course, is simply the Latin term for "wonder," as *commiseration* is for "pity." The emotion itself is that state of overpowering surprise, the shocked limit of feeling, which represents either the extreme of joy or, as in this case, the extreme of fear. Indeed, in the medieval tradition of psychological analysis it is defined as a species of fear (*ST*, 1-2. 41. 4), and thus the relation of wonder to fear is similar to that of pity to sorrow.

II

Fear, sorrow, and wonder are the explicit effects of the tragic catastrophe of *Hamlet*, or so at least it is here argued. But even if one grants that the effects are named in the particular passages cited, they are not spoken by the author in his own person. They are spoken by characters in a play. The remarks are in character, no doubt, and have some bearing on the delineation of character, but they can hardly be taken as expressing the author's intention with regard to the play as a whole, for drama by its very nature denies the author not only the right but even the possibility of speaking in his own person. Whatever a character thinks, says, or does must be taken only as an expression of character, and as an action in the sense that character and action are but aspects of each other. Hence Hamlet's remarks and Horatio's are elements in the

149

effect of the play, functionally related to all other elements, but not to be taken as explicit comments which furnish a guiding principle of order for the whole and consequently represent the author's intention.

But the assumptions that lie behind this point of view do not apply to Elizabethan drama though they do apply to a good many modern works. The principal assumption is that the work as a whole is an indissoluble unit that exists only in its total effect. This is one aspect of the doctrine of organic form. The assumption operates in this way among others: whatever is said in a play is construed in the light of the critic's total impression of the work, or more often of the character who speaks since the delineation of character is usually taken to be the primary end of fiction. Hence a speech is first read as contributing to the whole, either of the play or of the character, and then reinterpreted so as to conform to the whole which the critic has constructed. Whatever is discordant with this must be reconciled, often by the invocation of "irony," a device as fertile as Stoic allegory for disposing of the difficulties which the original text puts in the way of an interpretation.

Now, if every speech of an effective character is dramatic, in the modern sense, then it never means what it says but is only an expression of what the critic thinks the character's character is. What this leads to in practice can be made clear by an example. A modern critic, and a scholar quite learned in Renaissance thought, sees in Iago's rejoinder to Roderigo's confession of moral helplessness (*Othello*, 1. 3. 319ff.) "a grand perversion of the theory that good is the end and purpose of reason."[10] Roderigo has confessed with a shameless determinism his love for Desdemona, even though she is Othello's wife:

> What should I do? I confess it is my shame to be so fond, but it is not in my virtue to amend it.

And Iago replies:

150

Virtue, a fig! 'Tis in ourselves that we are thus or thus. Our bodies are our gardens, to the which our wills are gardeners; so that if we will plant nettles or sow lettuce, set hyssop and weed up thyme, supply it with one gender of herbs or distract it with many—either to have it sterile with idleness or manured with industry—why, the power and corrigible authority of this lies in our wills.

The critic notes, "This passage states the ethics, the infidelity, of selfishness."

Perhaps he is misled by *Virtue, a fig!* (the punctuation is mine), overlooking the fact that in the context *(it is not in my virtue to amend it)* virtue has quite obviously the common Elizabethan meaning of "power," and that Iago is consequently by no means making light of that virtue which is the opposite of vice. For what does Iago say? He picks up Roderigo's assertion that it is not in his power not to be a sinning fool, to go kill himself for love, and maintains that we do have the power to make ourselves one thing or the other, good or evil, to control or not to control our bodies, our lower natures, and that this power is our will. This, so far as I can see, is a notorious commonplace of the Christian tradition, as well as of the Aristototelian. It is plain and hoary orthodoxy, and there is no perversion in it. Of course, a theologian might object that Iago's position is too Pelagian, that it makes no provision for the Grace of God, but the statement is brief and is not theological in context: in fact, you will hardly restrain a man from killing himself for love by suggesting that the Grace of God may prevent his accomplishing his purpose.

The second objection that could be made against the orthodoxy of this passage is that it is, perhaps, too voluntaristic, that nothing is said of reason. But this objection fails if we quote the whole passage, for Iago continues:

If the balance of our lives had not one scale of reason to poise another of sensuality, the blood and baseness of our natures would conduct us to most prepost'rous conclusions. But we

151

have reason to cool our raging motions, our carnal stings, our unbitted lusts; whereof I take this that you call love to be a sect or scion.

That is, Iago identifies the power and corrigible authority which lies in our wills with reason. Hence, it is evident that it is the medieval and Christian concept of the reasonable will which he opposes to the deterministic sensuality of Roderigo. Finally, no one, I trust, will maintain that Iago slanders in this instance true Love by designating Roderigo's infection as lust, which it is.

Yet on this latter passage the critic remarks: "Iago understands the warfare between reason and sensuality, but his ethics are totally inverted; reason works in him not good, as it should according to natural law, but evil, which he has chosen for his good." This, as a remark on Iago's character and actions in general, is aptly and accurately put. But the remark purports to be on this particular passage, and as such it is precisely wrong.

The passage is one of the finest statements, especially in its rhythm, of the traditional and orthodox view of the relation of the reasonable will to the sensitive soul; it has, then, its own absolute value as "thought," as the accomplished saying of something very much worth saying. It has also its function in the plot and its relation to Iago's character, but this function and relationship is rather "mechanical" (in fact, hierarchical) than "organic" (that is, monistic). Yet the passage serves the larger purposes of the plot without losing and altering its own quality as such. In the plot, it is an argument to persuade Roderigo from suicide, and is such an argument as a divine might use. But Iago's purpose in persuasion is not to save Roderigo's soul but to save his person and his purse for the benefit of Iago's own designs. The evil lies in the end, the intention; the means and the accidental effects are in themselves good, nor do they lose that quality in being used for an evil end. It is good to prevent a man from killing himself. The argument employed is orthodox and true, and no less true for the circumstances. The devil quotes Scripture to his purpose, but you need not for this reason take Scripture as an expression of the devil's character.

A Shakespearean speech, then, takes its point in part from itself, especially if it goes beyond the bare gist of what is needed for the plot, and in part from its context, from who says it and under what circumstances. But the relation of context and speech is one that depends on relevant considerations, and relevance is construed in terms of what is appropriate. It is beside the point, then, in considering the last scene of *Hamlet,* that Hamlet occupies a privileged position among Shakespeare's heroes, that he is said to be of all those the most lovingly and sympathetically presented, so much so that many feel in this instance the author has been partial to his character. It is beside the point, even, that earlier in the play Hamlet has shown a critical interest in the discussion of drama. His remarks to the players are called forth by that situation and are appropriate to it, though they are also interesting in themselves and go quite beyond what is needed for the action.

It is somewhat in point that Hamlet is the hero, and especially that he is at the moment he speaks the sole surviving member of the royal family, and hence for that moment the head of the state; he has the right to speak authoritatively. Besides, he is dying, and one's last words are commonly supposed to be truthful. But the real point is that his remarks are addressed to the standers-by as to an audience. They are a comment on the reactions of an audience, and must be taken as expressing how an audience would and should react. His remarks simply put into words what the other actors on the stage are to express in gesture, and if the actual audience does not feel the like, the play has been a failure.

The character of Horatio, however, and the circumstances under which he speaks are, in this respect, a little more complicated. In the first place, he speaks at the request of Fortinbras. And what is the significance of Fortinbras? He is the principle of renewed order in the state. He is the indispensable character for concluding a Shakespearean play; for each play, with the notable exception of *Troilus and Cressida*, begins with disorder in the state and concludes only on the restoration of order. As the representative of order he is in virtue of his office conceived of as reason: for authority is order, and order is reason. This is common doctrine. He speaks the truth and the truth is spoken to him. Consequently, his presence is almost a necessary condition for Horatio's remarks.

But what is the position of Horatio himself? Horatio, as has often been noted, is a kind of chorus. He is a special character outside of the plot, except in so far as he is the confidant of and spokesman for Hamlet. But he is not the kind of chorus that is swayed now to this side and now to that as the tides of sympathy and fortune shift, as is the Greek chorus, or the chorus in Jonson's *Cataline*. Horatio is the well-tempered man. He is the man of whom Hamlet has said:

> Since my dear soul was mistress of her choice
> And could of men distinguish, her election
> Hath seal'd thee for herself. For thou hast been
> As one, in suff'ring all, that suffers nothing;
> A man that Fortune's buffets and rewards
> Hath ta'en with equal thanks; and blest are those
> Whose blood and judgement are so well commingled
> That they are not a pipe for Fortune's finger
> To sound what stop she please. Give me that man
> That is not passion's slave, and I will wear him
> In my heart's core, ay, in my heart of hearts,
> As I do thee.
>
> 3. 2. 68-79

154

This speech has its own function in the scene—it is the play scene— and it serves particularly as a contrast with the later bitter ragging of Rosencrantz and Guildenstern: "You would play upon me; you would seem to know my stops; you would pluck out the heart of my mystery . . . ," and so on (3. 2. 380ff.). It has its own function as a thought worthy of being expressed and not inappropriate to the circumstances. But it is also the speech that establishes in fairly full and explicit terms the relevance of Horatio to the play.

One of the key terms in the passage is *election*. This is a technical term in the medieval tradition for the act of moral choice (*ST*, 1-2, 13, translating Aristotle's *proairesis*) with respect to choosing the means to an end. The end is happiness, or some aspect of it, and true friendship with a just man is the means—

> Horatio, thou art e'en as just a man
> As e'er my conversation cop'd withal.
> 3. 2. 59-60

Thus election chooses Horatio. But moral choice is a function of reason, of the soul, and is exercised as soon as one attains the "age of reason," but not before (*ST*, 1. 100. 2, and 1-2. 13. 2. *contra*). Finally, the metaphor of sealing derives from the common Aristotelian and scholastic figure of imposing a seal on wax, which represents the relationship of form and matter: the choice of means gives determinate form to the end desired (*ST*, 1-2. 13. 1. c., especially *ad fin.*). The meaning is illustrated in the following passage:

> NESTOR.   . . . It is suppos'd
> He that meets Hector issues from our choice;
> And choice, being mutual act of all our souls,
> Makes merit her election . . .
> *Troilus*, 1. 3. 346-9

Choice is an act of the soul; the particular act of choosing this or this as means is *election*. Sometimes the choice is erroneous,

155

the will is carried away by the sensitive appetite (*ST*, 1-2 .77):

> HECTOR. But value dwells not in particular will:
> It holds his estimate and dignity
> As well wherein 'tis precious of itself
> As in the prizer. 'Tis mad idolatry
> To make the service greater than the god;
> And the will dotes that is attributive
> To what infectiously itself affects
> Without some image of th'affected merit.
> TROILUS. I take to-day a wife, and my election
> Is led on in the conduct of my will,
> My will enkindled by mine eyes and ears,
> Two traded pilots 'twixt the dangerous shores,
> Of will and judgement. How may I avoid,
> Although my will distaste what it elected,
> The wife I chose? . ..
>
> *Troilus*, 2. 2. 53-67

Similarly in *Cymbeline*:

> SECOND LORD. If it be a sin to make a true election
> She is damn'd.
>
> 1. 2. 29-30

To return, Hamlet says that Horatio is the man whom Hamlet, when he comes to the age of reason, selected by a reasonable choice as the fit co-respondent of his dear soul, which is in its essence reason. For Horatio is one who is open to all experience but who suffers by it no inner alteration of his reasonable form. He is impassive to all passions. He is indifferent to the external operations of fortune, for he is a man of perfected self-mastery, sealed by grace, in whom the irrational and the rational are in due relation, the one subordinated to the other; and thus the inner unalterable core of reasonable order is not subject to the irrational alterations produced by the impingement of external circumstances. Hence Horatio should be regarded as the ideal commentator, like the similar characters in Jonson's plays, Cordatus, Crites, and Horace: he is reason expressing reasonable judgment on the action.

156

The point perhaps calls for some elaboration. The ideal spokesman in Elizabethan literature is always spokesman by virtue of his reasonableness. He is never intended to be biographically identifiable with the author, though of course it would be impossible for authors so individual as Shakespeare and Jonson not to infuse some of their own qualities into a character. But the Elizabethan author had no intention of expressing his own personality, either in a character or in his work as a whole. In fact, he did not know that he had such a thing as a personality, for the concept of personality can hardly be said to have been formed. It was the reasonable soul that was the central psychological concept of the Renaissance, and a man was praiseworthy, as Horatio was, in so far as the reasonable soul spoke in him and was hearkened to. It is true that a man was considered to have certain individualising properties derived from his sex, his time of life, and his position in society, but these were comprised in the concept of decorum. They were the differentiations of reasonableness in accordance with circumstance. Whatever traits he might have beyond these, as for instance, melancholy or foppery, were the result of a disturbance of reasonable balance and a deviation from the ideal norm, and they were vicious in so far as they deviated. All this is familiar to the student of the Renaissance, but the conclusion is that the character who is presented as conforming to the ideal norm is presented as a standard by which deviations from the norm may be charted, and when he speaks he speaks in the light of reason, and what he says represents the author's explicit intentions. For the author himself is reason.

IV

The question of under what circumstances Horatio speaks has now been answered in part. He speaks in reply to Fortinbras' request, and Fortinbras is the principle of reason and order in the state, who expounds and exacts the truth; and he himself is the reasonable commentator.

But the situation is more complicated than this. The situation at the end of *Hamlet* is the kind of final one which is customary in Shakespeare's plays. The loose ends, or most of them, are now tied up; the course of action is recapitulated and in part explained; and the representative of the state invites the principal remaining characters to "go hence, to have more talk of these sad things" (*Romeo*, 5. 3. 307), "where we may leisurely / Each one demand and answer to his part" (*Winter's Tale*. 5. 3. 152-3). But in *Hamlet* this basic situation is given a curious expansion and development.

We have already seen how Hamlet treats the cast on the stage as spectators of the catastrophe, and have quoted the passage in which he turns to Horatio, and, as it were, deputizes him. He lays on Horatio the charge "to tell my story," a charge which Horatio accepts when he proposes later to "speak to th' yet unknowing world / How these things came about." Indeed Fortinbras accepts the proposal: "Let us haste to hear it," he says, "And call the noblest to the audience" (5. 2. 360, 390, 397-8).

The lines are so familiar that the reader may not notice what is happening. It is implied in a series of ambiguities, as was implied more openly in Hamlet's speech, that the minor characters who remain on the stage are to be regarded as an audience. Such a notion is involved in Fortinbras' pun, to "call the noblest to the audience," for they shall attend the audience of the new king, and they shall be an audience to whom the events will be related. In like fashion, Horatio asks, before he begins his resumé of the plot, that orders be given that the bodies of the main characters in the catastrophe "High on a stage be placed to the view"; these bodies, then, which are to be placed on a ceremonial stage become by virtue of an obvious pun the characters who will act on a theatrical stage. For the difference between Hamlet's relation to his quasi-audience and Horatio's is this: the other characters are treated by Hamlet as spectators of the events which just took place on the stage; they are treated by Horatio as spectators or auditors of the events that he is about to recount or present. Horatio, who has been deputized by Hamlet to tell his story, is treated in the end almost as if he were the author of the play of *Hamlet*. The events which we have just seen on the stage are treated according to the usual dramatic convention as if they had just now really happened. They are reality, and the play about this reality will only begin when the play we have seen is over.

Thus Horatio, who is about to give an account of these events, is the imitator and expounder of the reality we have seen. It is in keeping with this curious sleight-of-hand that, in preparation for the play which will follow the final bare stage, Horatio presents the argument of the events in a kind of prologue:

> . . . give order that these bodies
> High on a stage be placed to the view;
> And let me speak to th' yet unknowing world
> How these things came about. So shall you hear
> Of carnal, bloody, and unnatural acts;
> Of accidental judgements, casual slaughters;
> Of deaths put on by cunning and forc'd cause,
> And, in this upshot, purposes mistook
> Fall'n on th' inventors' heads. All this can I
> Truly deliver.
>
> 5. 2. 388-97

The passage is in effect a summary of the preceding action. It is in form an argument of the relation which is supposed to follow, and it has the stylistic qualities of the conventional argument. But what is more—it is the truth: "All this can I truly deliver," for I am the repository of Hamlet's trust, I am the reasonable man and hence the ideal spokesman, I am the intention of the author.

Consequently, Horatio's *Hamlet* is also Shakespeare's *Hamlet*. Each is constituted by the plot, by what happens. Each

159

is concerned with "carnal, bloody, and unnatural acts," and these are, respectively, the adultery, murder, and incest which precede and lay the foundation for the play. The accidental judgment which leads to the casual slaughter is Hamlet's mistaking Polonius for the King, a judgment based upon misconstrued signs and hence not a true or substantial judgment. This is clear to anyone who is familiar with the scholastic discussion of manslaughter, or casual homicide. To employ the Latin terminology which Shakespeare uses in its anglicized form, this judgment *per accidens* leads to a slaughter which is *praeter intentionem,* and so casual, not causal *(ST,* 2-2. 64. 8).

Perhaps the idea here deserves a short digression. It appears again in an extraordinary passage in the *Winter's Tale.* Florizel says, in reply to the question, "Have you thought on a place whereto you'll go?" after marrying Perdita:

> Not any yet;
> But as th'unthought-on accident is guilty
> To what we wildly do, so we profess
> Ourselves to be the slaves of chance and flies
> Of every wind that blows.

4. 4. 548-52

The philosophy, no doubt, is too great for the occasion, but there is no reason to assume that it is not pertinent. Nevertheless, this is surely an odd passage, and the oddness lies in the comparison, in the *as* clause. For, to profess oneself the slave of chance and fly of every wind that blows is a common notion and fairly easy to understand: it is an indulgence often granted to young lovers by those whom their actions are not liable to hurt. But the notion is qualified by the preceding clause: we are the slaves of chance, Florizel says, in the sense in which the unthought-on accident is guilty to what we wildly do. What does this mean?

It depends on the distinction in casuistry which is drawn in Horatio's phrase above, that between causal and casual actions.

160

The distinction is especially clear in the discussions of actions which arise from drunkenness, or any similar state of "wildly doing." For example, if a man gets drunk and in that state "unintentionally" kills another, he is not directly guilty of homicide spiritually, whatever he may be legally, for the result is beyond his intention. But he does not on this account get off spiritually easily. He is guilty of such a degree of irrational drunkenness as rendered the homicide possible, or even probable. The substance of his sin, then, lay in the choice by which he came into the condition of "wildly doing." The example is St. Thomas'. Hooker in the *Laws of Ecclesiastical Polity* deals with an analogous case:

> Finally, that which we do being evil, is notwithstanding by so much more pardonable, by how much the exigence of so doing or the difficulty of doing otherwise is greater; unless this necessity or difficulty have originally arisen from ourselves. It is no excuse therefore unto him, who being drunk committeth incest, and allegeth that his wits were not his own; inasmuch as himself might have chosen whether his wits should by that mean have been taken from him. 1. 9. 1[11]

In brief, then, the initial choice is intentional; the precise consequences may be accidental and the result of chance. Such is the scheme of thought that lies behind the *as* clause. The initial choice of going off with Perdita is within Florizel's power, and he will make it, for he has embraced the condition of "wildly doing":

FLORIZEL. From my succession wipe me, father! I
    Am heir to my affection.
CAMILLO. Be advis'd.
FLORIZEL. I am, and by my fancy. If my reason
    Will thereto be obedient, I have reason;
    If not, my sense, better pleas'd with madness,
    Do bid it welcome.
CAMILLO. This is desperate, sir.

4. 4. 491-6

He is heir to his emotions; he is advised by imagination to which his reason must subscribe. Hence what follows, as particularly the place whereto they'll go, will be accidental and the result of chance. It will be, like the death of Polonius, casual.

But to return to Horatio's speech in *Hamlet*—the "deaths put on by cunning and forced cause" are, of course, the deaths of Rosencrantz and Guildenstern, and "this upshot" in which the intrigue with dramatic justice recoils on the intriguers is the final scene of the play.

There is obviously a point for point correspondence between the items of Horatio's list and the main events of the central plot of *Hamlet*. However, the items themselves are not particularized as in the traditional argument, but generalized.[12] No names are mentioned, no particular circumstances alluded to. And the generalization is pointed by the consistent use of the generalized plural: *acts, judgements, slaughters, deaths, purposes, inventors*; for, though some of these items may be considered to be proper plurals, it is significant that all are pluralized. The items listed are such classes of action as generally form the subject-matter of tragedy. They do not precisely correspond to, but they are of the same nature as, the items in the Donatan tradition, or in, for example, Scaliger's list of the subject-matters of tragedy: "The matters of tragedy are great and terrible, as commands of kings, slaughters, despairs, suicides, exiles, bereavements, parricides, incests, conflagrations, battles, the putting out of eyes, weeping, wailing, bewailing, funerals, eulogies, and dirges." Nor are such lists simply to be found in critical treatises: they are the common property of the times. Mr. Harding in his theological controversy with Bishop Jewel seizes the occasion of Jewel's mention of Sophocles to insert a summary description of tragedy. "A tragedy," he says, "setteth forth the overthrows of kingdoms, murder of noble personages, and other great troubles, and endeth in woful lamentations." And Jewel retorts with a full list of the terrible tragic events associated with the villainous Popes of Rome.[13]

In brief, Horatio promises his audience a tragedy. "So shall you hear," he says—and then follows a generalized list of items which every member of the audience recognized at once as equivalent to the single word—"tragedy." The implication is that *Hamlet* is a tragedy because it presents such tragic actions. Furthermore, the effects of tragedy which Shakespeare mentions in this scene—pity, fear, astonishment—arise from the nature of the tragic actions themselves, for these actions are, as Scaliger says, great and terrible, and they evoke a corresponding response. They are terrible in that they are great, and pitiable and wonderful for the same reason. Such an equation between the greatness of the persons and the action and the greatness of the tragic response is explicitly formulated in the final comment of Octavius, the representative of the state at the conclusion of *Antony and Cleopatra:*

> High events as these
> Strike those that make them; and their story is
> No less in pity than his glory which
> Brought them to be lamented.
>
> 5. 2. 363-6.

A tragedy, then, is defined by the kind of actions it presents, and the effect of tragedy is the direct result of the presentation of such actions, though the validity of the effect may depend upon other considerations. The effect, moreover, is one of fear, sorrow, and wonder. This is no doubt a relatively crude aesthetic, but it is substantially Aristotle's, and it is Shakespeare's. It is also true.

III

The Donatan Tradition

Fear, sorrow, and wonder are the emotions explicitly associated with tragedy, not only in *Hamlet*, but generally in the tradition of literary criticism of Shakespeare's day. The tradition is well-known. It derives from a few time-worn texts which were repeated with the singlemindedness with which one recites the penny catechism.[1]

I

The basic text for the theory of tragedy comes from a schoolbook of the late classical period, Donatus on Terence:

> There are many differences between tragedy and comedy, but the principal difference is that in comedies the characters are of moderate estate, the difficulties that arise are slight, and the outcome of it all is joyful; but the marks of tragedy are precisely the opposite; the characters are great, the actions fearful in the extreme, and the outcome is sad and involves deaths. Again, in comedy all is disturbed at the beginning and tranquil at the close; in tragedy the order of progression is exactly reversed. The moral of tragedy is that life should be rejected; of comedy, that it should be embraced. And, finally, in comedy the story is always made-up; in tragedy, the story is commonly true and based on history.[2]

Tragedy and comedy are precise contraries; from this center the particular marks of distinction are evolved and disposed. Such a way of looking at things was quite congenial to the medieval mind, whose basic discipline was the logic of Aristotle and the principles of identity, contradiction, and the law of the excluded middle, and whose view of men was conditioned by the doctrine of Heaven and Hell, good and evil, grace and

164

sin, and of the irreparable differences between them. There went along with this the clarity of definition and discrimination which this habit of mind encouraged. If the clarity broke down in practice, if in the hurly-burly of the stage comedy intruded on tragedy, this could only be ascribed, so long as the habit of mind persisted, to the imperfect nature of man which it was the duty of thought and intention to remedy. Hence tragicomedy, for example, did not pose a practical problem since it was actually in existence, nor a problem of authority since it had the warrant of Plautus, but a logical problem, and almost an insuperable one, for the two elements were defined by their opposition.

The distinctions which Donatus establishes between the two forms are firmly held throughout the tradition. They are distinctions of 1) character, 2) order of progression in the plot, 3) source and kind of plot, 4) moral purpose, 5) kind of incident and the accompanying emotional effect, 6) kind of conclusion and the accompanying emotional effect, together with three additional principles stated in other texts than Donatus — 7) the nature of the subject matter, 8) the principle which accounts for the turn in the fortune of the characters, and 9) the nature of the style. Several of these imply each other, and a few corollary distinctions enter in the later tradition, but on the whole these principles, the first six of which are clearly stated in Donatus, sufficiently characterize the tradition and amply account for the nature of tragedy on the Elizabethan stage. Indeed, if these distinctions are taken seriously and regarded as principles of order by which the dramatist writes as he does rather than as rules external to the work, it will be seen that Elizabethan tragedy, including Hamlet, is in large part given merely by the acceptance of these principles. It follows that the historian of Elizabethan drama might more plausibly begin with the traditional definition than with the earliest examples of medieval drama. The latter are historical forerunners which only in small part account for the developed product; the definition is almost the Archetype itself, in which the seminal ideas, the principles of order, explicitly dwell.

The first distinction is that the tragic characters must be great, and this means of high rank. It is the modern feeling that this is an artificial stipulation, explicable only in light of the erroneous social ideas of our ancestors. But *The Death of a Salesman* is not a tragedy in the old sense, and so one might conjecture there is something else involved: there is involved a radical difference in the nature of the tragic effect. For the field of tragedy will be the state, since men of high rank are rulers of the state. Tragedy will then involve not private life and private feeling—this is the province of comedy —, but public life and public feeling. But public feeling is different in kind from private.[3] A public calamity moves us in a different way than does a private one. The murder of John Doe is one thing; the assassination of Trotsky or of Admiral Darlan is another. Hence the tragic emotions in the older tradition will be predominantly communal and public, and we will find that a similar qualification is implied in the other principles of order which Donatus distinguishes.

The second distinction is that the direction of the action in tragedy is from order to disorder; in comedy the converse. How deeply this scheme had entered into Shakespeare's thought can be conjectured from the passage in *Lear* in which it forms the structural framework of the expression. Edgar soliloquizes on the heath:

> To be worst,
> The lowest and most dejected thing of fortune,
> Stands still in esperance, lives not in fear.
> The lamentable change is from the best;
> The worst returns to laughter.

4. 1. 2-6

The change appropriate to tragedy *(the lamentable change)* is from the best; the change from the worst is comedy. Yet Shakespearean tragedy does not exhibit this progression in its

166

simple form. The greater part of a Shakespearean tragedy does, it is true, consist of a progression toward deeper and deeper disorder, but a) the beginning is not tranquil since there is already some disorder (as in the opening scenes of *Romeo*, *Hamlet*, and *Othello*), and b) the end always involves (with the curious exception of *Troilus* whose literary form is still a matter of dispute) the restoration of order and tranquility. That is, the principle is clearly operative, but under certain limitations.

We can see, however, why the limitations are introduced. a) Since the play deals with disorder, it is simple craftsmanship to begin with at least the first motions of disorder, and if a traditional precept be needed, Horace is at hand with the admonition to begin in the middle of things, which Shakespeare himself invokes in the prologue to *Troilus*. b) As for the conclusion, the concept of order was of such importance to Shakespeare and his contemporaries, and politically of such importance, that we may assume that he neither cared to end a play in disorder (except for *Troilus*), nor perhaps would he have felt safe in so doing. But beyond this, order at the end of such harrowing experiences as constitute tragedy implies an intention to communicate to the spectators a commensurate order in feeling—by a tranquil close to dismiss them in calm of mind, all passion spent. But this calm of mind is correlative with order in the state: the aesthetic feeling is in part political in nature.[4]

The third distinction is that the plot of tragedy is commonly historical and true, not feigned. We can understand, then, the fusion of the historical chronicle play and tragedy in Elizabethan drama, for it has its critical justification in this tenet. But if tragedy is historical, it is not merely realistic as distinguished from being fanciful; it has rather the compelling absoluteness of accomplished fact. Hence its effect will be accompanied by the recognition that things could not be otherwise, since this is how in fact they were. It follows from this,

167

as from the principles of high rank in personages and of concluding order in the state, that the emotional effects of tragedy will be of a kind consonant with these requirements. They will be more impersonal than personal. The experiences which the spectator will associate with these effects, the traces and memories which will give them substance, will be drawn not from the guarded and private world of his sensibility, but from the more communal world of his public self. The content of the effects will thus be different in kind from that which the uninstructed modern reader will experience, and a comparable difference in kind is implied in the next principle.

This, the fourth, is the moral purpose of tragedy. Donatus tells us that the lesson expressed in tragedy is the rejection of life *(fugienda vita)*. Thus, in a Christian and political context tragedy will be regarded as a warning against pride and against trusting in worldly prosperity. Sidney, for example, maintains that tragedy "with stirring the affects of admiration and commiseration teacheth the uncertainty of this world and upon how weak foundations gilden roofs are builded";[5] and Jonson closes *Sejanus* with these massive reflections:

> Let this example move th' insolent man
> Not to grow proud and careless of the gods.
> It is an odious wisdom to blaspheme,
> Much more to slighten or deny their powers;
> For whom the morning saw so great and high,
> Thus low and little fore the even doth lie.

But if one takes into account the subsequent principles in Donatus' definition, the fifth, that the incidents of tragedy involve great fears, and the sixth, that the catastrophe involves deaths and is sorrowful *(exitus funesti)*, it will be clear that resignation to death in the Christian sense is the natural moral to such tragedy. It is, in fact, the moral of *Hamlet*, expressed by the hero as he goes to the catastrophe, disturbed by forebodings of the tragic issue:

we defy augury; there's a special providence in the fall of a
sparrow. If it be now, 'tis not to come; if it be not to come, it
will be now; if it be not now, yet it will come: the readiness
is all.

5. 2. 230-3

Such acquiescence, if we should take the Donatan moral seriously, would constitute the catharsis of this kind of tragedy,
the effect of the tragic effect. It would be one of logic and
theology, whose instrument is teaching, and whose end is
Christian resignation.

But what must be the nature of the emotional effects themselves if they are to conduce to such an end? They must be
impersonal to a marked degree. For resignation is the subsumption, and almost the loss, of the individual under the general.
One's own death cannot be a matter of frightened concern,
since it is not peculiar but common, since it is inevitable and
given. So Caesar:

> Of all the wonders that I yet have heard,
> It seems to me most strange that men should fear,
> Seeing that death, a necessary end,
> Will come when it will come.
>
> *Julius Caesar*, 2. 2. 34-7

And Gertrude to Hamlet:

> Thou know'st 'tis common. All that lives must die,
> Passing through nature to eternity.
>
> 1. 2. 72-3

Thus the emotional disturbance of tragic incident is resolved
in resignation.

The process is traditional in Christianity. Thomas Aquinas,
for example (*ST*, 1-2. 42. 2. ad 3) tells us that death and
other lapses of Nature have Universal Nature, or Eternal Law,
as cause; but the nature of a particular being fights against
such lapses as much as it can, and from this striving springs
sorrow and anguish when death is seen as present, fear and

169

terror when it looms in the future. These are the tragic
emotions, and aroused by the tragic fact of death. Resignation in this tradition is nothing other than the acquiescence of
Particular in Universal Nature. It is nothing other than an
effective belief in logic, so that to perceive the subsumption of
instance under rule is to be satisfied. If all men are mortal, then
Hamlet, being a man, is also mortal.

But emotional effects that are ordered toward acquiescence,
disturbances that are intended to subside, are different in kind
from those that are exploitable and are intended to be enjoyed.
The latter are sentimental and private; the former are in potency
to the impersonal order of their envisaged end.

II

A tragedy is a succession of fearful incidents, enacted by
persons of high rank, that progresses from initial calm into
ever-deepening disaster, and concludes sadly in deaths. Fear
and sorrow are its appropriate emotions, fear of the catastrophe
and sorrow at its accomplishment. They are appropriate because they are the natural emotions with which men regard
death in prospect and in fulfilment. They are, furthermore,
emotions of a public and impersonal order.

The similarity of this definition to that of Aristotle's
Poetics is obvious, and in all likelihood the tradition derives
partly from Aristotle himself, if not from the Poetics (which
seems to have been little known in Antiquity and to have been
recovered in the West only in the Thirteenth Century), then
from his lost dialogue On Poets and from his student Theophrastus and the Peripatetic School. From such sources the
tradition descended to the Alexandrian and Roman scholars,
and from them to the school texts of late Antiquity.[6] But the
history is not important in this connection. What is important is that these notions entered into the texture of medieval
thought, and came to the Renaissance as commonplaces. Hence,

I shall present now a few additional texts in which may be distinguished certain further and corollary principles of order, together with a text from the late Middle Ages and one from Shakespeare's day in which can be seen the consistency of the tradition and the liveliness of reapprehension with which it was entertained two thousand years after Aristotle.

Of equal importance with that of Donatus is the definition of Diomedes, a grammarian of the Fourth Century A.D.:

> Tragedy involves the full cycle of fortune turning to adversity in characters of the heroic age—this is Theophrastus' definition. . . . Comedy—we render the Greek definition—involves a full cycle in the fortune of private citizens, but never the danger of death. . . . The fortunes involved in comedy are those of little streets and unimportant households, not as in tragedy of princes and men of state. . . . The distinctions between comedy and tragedy are these: the characters of tragedy are semi-divine, leaders of the state, kings; those of comedy are unimportant and private persons. The subjects of tragedy are woes, exiles, deaths; of comedy, love affairs and seductions. Finally, the movement of events in tragedy is almost always from happy circumstances to bitter deaths, accompanied at the end with the perception that the fortunes of the house involved have gone to ruin. Hence comedy and tragedy are by definition distinct: the one a full cycle of harmless incident, the other a reversal of great fortunes. Sorrow, then, is characteristic of tragedy.
>
> *Ars Grammatica*, 3[7]

To this may be added two passages from Isidore of Seville's encyclopedia, the *Britannica* of ten centuries. The first is from the section "On Poets":

> The tragic writers have attained considerable fame, principally for the plots of their plays, which are fashioned in the image of truth. . . . The comic writers deal with the lives of private citizens; the tragic, however, with affairs of state and the histories

of kings. Similarly, the plots of tragedies deal with woful material; of comedies, with happy.

Etymologiae, 8. 7. 5-6

The second passage is from the section "On Shows":

> Tragedians are those who recite to an audience a lamentable poem about historical events and the crimes of wicked princes.
>
> 18. 45

As early as the tenth century this is contracted into the curt phrase: *tragoedia luctuosum carmen.* Tragedy is a lamentable tale, a woful story. To these texts may be added the influential sentence from Boethius' *Consolation of Philosophy: quid tragoediarum clamor aliud deflet nisi indiscreto ictu fortunam felicia regna vertentem?* which Chaucer translates:

> What other thyng bywalen the cryinges of tragedyes but oonly the dedes of Fortune that with unwar strook overturneth the realmes of great nobleye? *(Glose. Tragedye is to seyn a dite of a prosperite for a tyme, that endeth in wrecchidness.)*
>
> 2. Prose 2

together with Ovid's remark, "Tragedy is weightier in style than any other genre" *(Tristia,* 2. 381).

From these texts we may distinguish some additional principles of order. The seventh defines the range of subject matter: woes, exiles, slaughter, the crimes and villainies of princes, the ruin of a noble house, the downfall of kingdoms. The eighth defines the organization of the plot, which describes a period, a full circle, so that the tragic character may say at the end as Edmund says in *Lear:*

> The wheel is come full circle; I am here.
>
> 5. 3. 174

The principle of alteration, the power that turns the circle of prosperity, is Fortune, whose indiscriminate blow overturns prosperous kingdoms. The importance of this principle is well-known and generally conceded. It accounts for the dominant

172

conception of tragedy in the late Middle Ages and the Renaissance, that tragedy is the fall from prosperity of a character of high estate.

A classic example is Marlowe's *Edward II,* where in the final scene the Queen says to Mortimer:

> Now, Mortimer, begins our tragedy.
>
> 2591

And the nature of the tragedy is defined a few lines later by Mortimer himself:

> Base Fortune, now I see that in thy wheel
> There is a point to which when men aspire
> They tumble headlong down. That point I touched,
> And, seeing there was no place to mount up higher,
> Why should I grieve at my declining fall?
> Farewell, fair Queen, weep not for Mortimer
> That scorns the world and, as a traveller,
> Goes to discover countries yet unknown.
>
> 2627-34

The fall in this case is followed by Mortimer's death, and in general the tragic fall is consummated by death, so that the principle of Fortune and the principle of death are identified. Nevertheless, it is probably significant to ascertain upon which of the two emphasis is laid: here the emphasis is clearly on the fall; in Shakespeare it is clearly on death. Furthermore, the fall is generally sudden and absolute: note Chaucer's mistranslation as "unwar strook," or unforeseen, of *indiscreto ictu,* which means "a random stroke." This introduces the element of surprise, which will in part account for the addition of the effect of wonder, and which will obviously serve to transfer the effect of fear from the incidents that precede the catastrophe to the catastrophe itself.

The ninth is the principle of style: tragedy requires the weighty or high style, a requirement which is implied by the principle of decorum—

But to present a kingly troop withal,
Give me a stately-written tragedy,
Tragoedia cothurnata, fitting kings,
Containing matter, and not common things.
                              Spanish Tragedy. 4. 154-7

For, only the high style in its aspect of gravity is fitted to
deal with affairs of state, and only the high style in its aspect
of forceful utterance, of passion and vividness, is fitted to deal
with crimes and villanies, and to call forth the terror, the woe,
and especially the wonder which it is the peculiar function of
high rhetoric to produce.

These texts, with others which need not be cited here,
were copied again and again throughout the Middle Ages,
repeatedly glossed, and indeed became so trite and commonplace that they can scarcely be said to have a history, only a
continued and recurrent existence. One example will suffice
to illustrate the continuation. It is a passage from Lydgate's
Troy Book (about 1420) in which he develops a remark by
Guido delle Colonne to the effect that tragedies and comedies
were said to have been first acted at Troy:

And first also, I rede, that in Troye	
Wer song and rad lusty fresche comedies,	
And other dites, that called be tragedies.	
And to declare, schortly in sentence	845
Of bothe two the final difference:	
A comedie hath in his gynning,	
At prime face, a maner compleyning,	
And afterward endeth in gladnes;	
And it the dedis only doth express	850
Of swiche as ben in pouert plounged lowe;	
But tragidie, who so list to knowe,	
It begynneth in prosperite,	
And endeth euer in aduersity;	
And it also doth the conquest trete	855
Of riche kynges and of lordys grete,	
Of mighty men and olde conquerou[ri]s,	

Whiche by fraude of Fortunys schowris
Ben ouercast and whelmed from her glorie
    Of a Theatyre stondynge in the princypale
    paleys of Troye, declarenge the falle of
    Pryncys and others.
And whilon thus was halwed the memorie   860
Of tragedies, as bokis make minde,
Whan thei wer rad or songyn, as I fynde,
In the theatre ther was a smal auter
Amyddes set, that was half circuler,
Whiche in-to the Est of custom was directe;   865
Up-on the whiche a pulpet was erecte,
And ther-in stod an aw[n]cien poete,
For to reherese by rhetorikes swete
The noble dedis, that wer historial,
Of kynges, princes for a memorial,   870
And of thes olde, worthi Emperours,
The grete emprises eke of conquerours,
And how thei gat in Martis high honour
The laurer grene for fyn of her labour,
The palm of knyghthod disservid by [old] date,   875
Or Parchas mad hem passyn in-to fate.
And after that, with chere and face pale,
With stile enclyned gan to turne his tale,
And for to synge, after al her loos,
Ful mortally the stroke of Antropos,   880
And telle also, for al her worthihede,
The sodeyn brekyng of her lives threde:
How pitiously thei made her mortal ende
Thorugh fals Fortune, that al the world will schende,
And how the fyn of al her worthines   885
Endid in sorwe and in highe tristesse,
By compassyng of fraude or fals tresoun,
By sodeyn mordre or vengaunce of poysoun,
Or conspirynge of fretyng fals envye,
How unwarly that thei dide dye;   890
And how her renoun and her highe fame
Was of hatrede sodeynly made lame;

And how her honour drowe un-to decline;
And the meschef of her unhappy fyne;
And how Fortune was to hem unswete—   895
Al this was tolde and rad of the poete,
And whil that he in the pulpet stood,
With dedly face al devoide of blood,
Singinge his dites, with muses al to-rent,
Amydde the theatre schrowdid in a tent,   900
Ther cam out men gastful of her cheris,
Disfigurid her facis with viseris,
Pleying by signes in the peples sight,
That the poete songon hath on hight;
So that ther was no maner discordaunce   905
Atwen his dites and her contenaunce:
For lik as he aloft[e] dide expresse
Wordes of Ioye or of heuynes,
Meving and cher, bynethe of hem pleying,
From point to point was alwey answering—   910
Now trist, now glad, now hevy, and [now] light,
And face chaunged with a sodeyn sight,
So craftily thei koude hem transfigure,
Conformyng hem to the chaunt[e]plure,
Now to synge and sodeinly to wepe,   915
So wel thei koude her observaunces kepe . . . [8]

Here are all the elements of the tradition, though jumbled together and in no particular order. The concept of tragedy is essentially determined, as it is in Donatus and Diomedes, by contrast with the concept of comedy (845-6). Tragedy begins happily and ends in adversity (852 ff.); the external principle of the reversal is Fortune (858-9; 884; 895); the characters are rich kings and great lords (856); tragedy is rhetorical (868), that is, in high style — "stile enclyned" (878) —, and in verse (844); the subject-matter is historical (869); the narrator clearly displays fear (877) and this is associated with the rhetorical manner and with the subject of death (878 ff.); in fact, the terror which the narrator displays "with dedly face al devoide of blood" as he tears the cat ("the muses al torente") in bombastic high style is mirrored in the pantomime of the dumb-show, and, in general, there is an exact correspondence between the fear, sorrow, emotional excitation ("meving"), and the joy of the text and of the illustrative action, together with a considerable range in the emotions called forth (897-916). Furthermore, the catastrophe is piteous (883) and sorrowful (886); it is sudden (882), and is brought about by violence and deceit — fraud, false treason, sudden murder, the vengeance of poison, or the conspiracy of biting envy (887-9); in fact, the tragic catastrophe is precisely sudden and violent death (880 ff.).

But here are also most of the elements of Elizabethan tragedy, and some which, though corollaries to the principles enunciated in the earlier tradition, are not explicit there. For example: if Marlowe's *Tamburlaine* is a tragical discourse and its presentation a "tragic glass," as it is called on the title-page and in the prologue to the original edition, this is because the play is in high style and as Lydgate here says:

doth the conquest trete
Of riche kynges and of lordys grete,
Of mighty men and olde conquerou[ri]s.

The introduction of the notion of the "conspiringe of fretyng fals envye" as engineering the tragic catastrophe will help account — to choose one example among many — for the curious circumstance that the debate between Comedy and Tragedy in the Induction to the popular Elizabethan play of *Mucedorus* is conducted by Comedy and by Envy, who speaks for tragedy. It accounts also for many an Elizabethan play, particularly for the motivation of *Othello* and of Jonson's *Sejanus*. The concern for the honor and reputation of the protagonist after his tragic death is peculiarly relevant to the last scene of *Hamlet*. The "vengaunce of poysoun" is *Hamlet* again. Finally, the confusion of high style with bombast — "the muses al to-rente" — is markedly Elizabethan; the first we hear of Shakespeare in London is that — as Greene querulously complains — he thinks he can bombast out a blank verse with the best of them, even as Hamlet later thinks he can swing it as well as Laertes — "Nay, an thou'lt mouth, / I'll rant as well as thou" (5. 1. 306-7). In brief, if the words of the narrator were distributed among the actors of the dumb-show and the Globe were erected in Troy, Lydgate's play could be the *Spanish Tragedy* or *Hamlet*.

The persistence of a critical awareness of these principles may be illustrated from a single text, the Prologue to *Henry VIII*, usually said to be by Shakespeare and Fletcher. Who wrote the prologue is unknown, but it does not matter:

> I come no more to make you laugh. Things now
> That bear a weighty and a serious brow,
> Sad, high, and working, full of state and woe,
> Such noble scenes as draw the eye to flow,
> We now present. Those that can pity, here   5
> May (if they think it well) let fall a tear:
> The subject will deserve it. Such as give
> Their money out of hope they may believe,
> May here find truth too. Those that come to see
> Only a show or two and so agree   10
> The play may pass — if they be still and willing,
> I'll undertake may see away their schilling
> Richly in two short hours. Only they
> That come to hear a merry bawdy play,
> A noise of targets, or to see a fellow   15
> In a long motley coat guarded with yellow,
> Will be deceiv'd. For, gentle hearers, know,
> To rank our chosen truth with such a show
> As fool and fight is, beside forfeiting
> Our own brains and the opinion that we bring   20

To make that only true we now intend,
Will leave us never an understanding friend.
Therefore, for goodness sake, as you are known
The first and happiest hearers of the town,
Be sad, as we would make ye. Think ye see   25
The very persons of our noble story
As they were living. Think you see them great,
And follow'd with the general throng, and sweat
Of thousand friends. Then, in a moment, see
How soon this mightiness meets misery.   30
And if you can be merry then, I'll say
A man may weep upon his wedding day.

The basis for discussion is again the sharp distinction of comedy
from tragedy, which is expressed not only in the opening lines
(1-2), but also is introduced with a certain truculence into
the middle where the historical nature of tragedy is affirmed
(13-22, but especially 17-21), and lies behind the turn of
thought in the final lines: for it would be as proper to weep
at the weddings which are the external signs that a comedy has
been concluded:

> Our wooing doth not end like an old play:
> Jack hath not Gill. These ladies' courtesy
> Might well have made our sport a comedy.
> *Love's Labor's Lost,* 5. 2. 883-5

as to be merry at the deaths which conclude a tragedy. For
tragedy is woful. Its subjects are grave and of serious aspect
(2); they are sad, lofty, and have a strong emotional effect
("working," 3); they are noble scenes which evoke tears and
pity (3-7), being full of affairs of state and at the same time
of woe, with the implication that the former qualifies the latter.
Furthermore, the height of the persons and the richness of the
emotional effect are, it is almost implied, proportional
to each other; this is a notion which we shall find made explicit
at the conclusion of *Antony and Cleopatra:*

179

High events as these
Strike those that make them; and their story is
No less in pity than his glory which
Brought them to be lamented.

5. 2. 363-6

In the final part of the Prologue the spectators are abjured to achieve the full emotional effect intended; they are to be as sad as the authors and actors wish them to be (23-5). They can attain this end (the process is clearly described) by vividly realizing the events on the stage as if they were real, or, indeed, by imputing to them the reality which in fact they have because of the warrant of their historical truth (23-7); in this way the spectators are to achieve the emotional end of historical tragedy, woe or pity — "for sorrow is characteristic of tragedy," as Diomedes says. This effect culminates in the tragic catastrophe, the sudden and violent ("in a moment see," 29) fall from mightiness to misery (27-30).

III

So much for the tradition. But what does Shakespeare himself mean by tragedy? What does the term denote in his works, and with what notions is it associated in context? It denotes primarily violent death, and the notions with which it is associated are the principles of the Donatan tradition. I give now a number of representative passages from Shakespeare's works in which the term *tragedy* or one of its derivatives appears.

A. Talbot in *1 Henry VI*:

Speak, Salisbury; at least, if thou canst speak.
How far'st thou, mirror of all martial men?
One of thy eyes and thy cheek's side struck off?
Accursed tower! Accursed fatal hand
That hath contriv'd this woful tragedy!

1. 4. 73-7

180

Tragedy is death in battle, the sudden and violent death of a notable person. It is woful. It is brought about by circumstances *(Accursed tower!)* and by a responsible agent *(Accursed fatal hand)*.

B. Gloucester in 2 *Henry VI:*

> I know their complot is to have my life;
> And if my death might make this island happy
> And prove the period of their tyranny,
> I would expend it with all willingness.
> But mine is made the prologue to their play;
> For thousands more, that yet suspect no peril,
> Will not conclude their plotted tragedy.
> 3. 1. 147-53

Tragedy is the consequence of political intrigue; it involves the destiny of the state; and it concludes with unexpected deaths. But the point of the prophecy in this instance is that here not even holocausts, or tragedy on tragedy, will conclude the plot.

C. Warwick and Queen Margaret over the dead body of Gloucester in 2 *Henry VI*—The Queen speaks:

> Then you belike suspect these noblemen
> As guilty of Duke Humphrey's timeless death?

And Warwick:

> Who finds the heifer dead, and bleeding fresh,
> And sees fast-by a butcher with an axe,
> But will suspect 'twas he that made the slaughter?
> Who finds the partridge in the puttock's nest
> But may imagine how the bird was dead,
> Although the kite soar with unbloodied beak?
> Even so suspicious is this tragedy.
> 3. 2. 186-94

Tragedy is "timeless death"; that is, untimely, violent, as in *Titus Andronicus* (E, below).

D. Henry VI to Richard in the Tower, 3 *Henry VI:*

181

Ah, kill me with thy weapon, not with words!
My breast can better brook thy dagger's point
Than can my ears that tragic history.

5. 6. 26-8

The tragic history is an account of the death of the young
Prince Edward.

E. *Titus Andronicus*, 2. 3. 265: "timeless tragedy" means
murder, untimely death.

F. *Titus Andronicus*, 4. 1. 45-60: tragedy is rape and
murder.

G. *Richard III*. "Enter Queen with her hair about her
ears, Rivers and Dorset after her."

QUEEN. Ah, who shall hinder me to wail and weep,
To chide my fortune, and torment myself?
I'll join with black despair against my soul
And to myself become an enemy.
DUCHESS OF YORK. What means this scene of rude impatience?
QUEEN. To make an act of tragic violence.
Edward, my lord, thy son, our king, is dead!

2. 2. 34-40

The nature of the act of tragic violence is defined in the preceding speech as sin (*And to myself become an enemy*), and
specifically as the sin of despair. The characteristic act of
despair is suicide. The act of tragic violence, then, is suicide.

H. Hastings in *Richard III*:

But I shall laugh at this a twelvemonth hence,
That they which brought me in my master's hate,
I live to look upon their tragedy.
Well, Catesby, ere a fortnight make me older,
I'll send some packing that yet think not on't.

3. 2. 57-61

Tragedy is violent unexpected death.

I. *Richard III*. "Enter old Queen Margaret":

182

> So now prosperity begins to mellow
> And drop into the rotten mouth of death.
> Here in these confines slyly have I lurk'd
> To watch the waning of mine enemies.
> A dire induction am I witness to,
> And will to France, hoping the consequence
> Will prove as bitter, black, and tragical.
>
> 4. 4. 1-7

The preliminaries are dire — that is, the tragic atmosphere is one of fear —, and promise by the law of aesthetic congruity that the consequence will be bitter and black — that is, tragical. The principle of order that connects preliminaries and consequence is the waning of prosperity: the wheel of Fortune.

J. *Midsummer's Night's Dream:*

> THESEUS. '. . . very tragical mirth.'
> Merry and tragical? tedious and brief?
> That is hot ice and wondrous strange snow . . . .
> PHILOSTRATE. And tragical, my noble lord, it is;
> For Pyramus therein doth kill himself . . . .
> THESEUS. . . . Marry, if he that writ it had played
> Pyramus and hang'd himself in Thisby's garter,
> it would have been a fine tragedy . . .
>
> 5.1. 57-9; 66-7; 365-7

Tragedy and comedy are precise contraries. The distinguishing mark of tragedy is violent death, suicide.

K. The Archbishop of Canterbury in *Henry V*, 1. 2. 105-6, speaks of "Edward the Black Prince," whose warlike spirit "on the French ground play'd a tragedy" by slaughtering the French army.

L. *Othello*, 5. 2. 363: the representative of the state speaks of the dead bodies of Desdemona and Othello as "the tragic loading of this bed."

M. *The Phoenix and Turtle*, 52: "the tragic scene" is the death of the phoenix and the dove.

N. Lucrece in the *Rape of Lucrece:*

"O comfort-killing Night, image of hell!
Dim register and notary of shame!
Black stage for tragedies and murthers fell!
Vast sin-concealing chaos! nurse of blame!
Blind muffled bawd! dark harbour for defame!
Grim cave of death! whisp'ring conspirator
With close-tongu'd treason and the ravisher!"
764-70

This passage constitutes a congeries of the fundamental notions and attitudes associated with the concept of tragedy; its objective content is murder, death, whispering conspiracy, close-tongued treason, rape; it deals in sin — night, its symbol, is the image of Hell, where grace dies *(comfort-killing)* and chaos spreads, for chaos is the issue of sin as order is of grace; tragedy is preoccupied with fame (cf. *Hamlet*, 5.2.355-60); its atmosphere is dim, vast (that is, "disordered"), black, blind (that is, "irrational"), dark, grim.

O. The lover in *A Lover's Complaint* is portrayed as a master of insincere rhetoric and capable of expressing all the external signs of the appropriate emotions:

To blush at speeches rank, to weep at woes,
Or to turn white and sound at tragic shows . . .
307-8

The effect of tragedy is fear or terror.

In brief, the tragic atmosphere and the anticipation of the tragic catastrophe is fearful; the catastrophe woful. The process by which the catastrophe comes about involves intrigue, hypocrisy, political conspiracy and treason, acts of sin, and is conducted by responsible agents. These are the connotations of *tragedy*. The denotation is violent, unexpected death — murder, death in battle, suicide. To these is added rape.

This denotation of *tragedy*, however, is not merely Shakespearean; it is generally Elizabethan, as indeed is well known. Death in *Soliman and Perseda*, speaking as a chorus at the be-

184

ginning of the play, says: "And what are tragedies but acts of death?" (1. 1. 7). And, again, at the conclusion:

> Packe *Loue* and *Fortune*, play in comedies,
> For powerfull Death best fitteth Tragedies.[9]

In the Induction to *A Warning for Fair Women*, which was produced by Shakespeare's company, the characters are Tragedy, History, and Comedy. Tragedy is called "a common executioner," "murther's Beadle," "The common hangman unto Tyranny," and a little later it is remarked:

> Then we shall have a tragedy indeed;
> Pure purple buskin, blood and murther right.
>   Induction, 6, 19, 20, 61-2[10]

Finally, Fletcher in the preface to the *Faithful Shepherdess* distinguishes tragi-comedy from tragedy "in respect it wants deaths, which is enough to make it no tragedy. . . ." Hence death is the essential mark — note the technical language of "in respect"—, the defining characteristic.

The tragic fact is death. Even the most natural death has in it a radical violence, for it is a transition from this life to something by definition quite otherwise; and, however much it may be expected, it is in its moment of incidence sudden, for it comes as a thief in the night, you know not the day nor the hour. Hence the characteristics of suddenness and violence which are attached to death in tragedy may be viewed as only artistic heightenings of the essential character of death: the unnaturalness of the tragic event is only pointed and emphasized by the unnatural precipitancy of its accomplishment. If Elizabethan dramas often end in almost indiscriminate butchery, the intention, even if mistaken, is only to make them the more tragic.

That tragedy is death is a conception which will account for a puzzling feature in the history of Elizabethan drama: namely, that we have a number of interesting plays, particularly those traditionally associated with Shakespeare's name, *Arden of Feversham, A Warning for Fair Women,* and the *Yorkshire Tragedy,* in which recent and actual murders are dramatized. These were regarded as tragedies; indeed one of them has the extensive Induction which was quoted from above, in which Tragedy after an argument with History and Comedy introduces the play. Nevertheless, in these plays the usual notion that tragedy involves a notable reversal of prosperity and the fall of a person from high estate to low is little attended to, though not unnoticed, and at the same time the corollary notion that the chief characters should be of princely, or at least of noble, rank is deliberately violated. These are domestic tragedies. The characters involved are usually of what we would call the middle class — they are normally gentlemen. The situation is sordid, not splendid.

It is obvious that such a play, if the principle of decorum is to be observed, must forego the high style appropriate to traditional tragedy. It must forego at the same time the splendor and universality of great events; it must temper its effect to the meanness of its theme. The advantage which such tragedy claims for itself in exchange for the advantages of traditional tragedy is that of unadorned truth — truth in the literal historical sense, and unadorned in the sense of unrhetorical, or lacking the high style. So Tragedy in *A Warning for Fair Women* introduces the sordid story of murder with these remarks:

> My scene is London, native and your own.
> I sigh to think my subject too well-known.
> I am not feigned.

l. 86-8

I am not feigned. Again, the author of *Arden of Feversham,* invoking the age-old commonplace of simple truth as opposed to artful feigning, a commonplace that derives from the early Christian defense of the unliterary character of the New

186

Testament and from the older classical commonplace of nature and art, concludes the play with these words:

> Gentlemen, we hope you'll pardon this naked Tragedy,
> Wherein no filed points are foisted in
> To make it gracious to the ear or eye;
> For simple truth is gracious enough,
> And needs no other points of glosing stuff.
>
> Epilogue, 14-18[11]

A *naked tragedy* is unrhetorical, lacking in ornament, a tragedy in other than high style. Perhaps one should remark that the play does have a good deal of Kydian ornament in it, but this is beside the point, being only another lamentable example of the gap between profession and practice.

To conclude: if violent death is the distinguishing mark of tragedy, and this seems to be Shakespeare's understanding of the term, it follows 1) that domestic tragedy is a legitimate species since it has the defining characteristic and the associated property of historical truth; 2) that high tragedy will by logical implication involve the fall of princes since the violent death of a high character is such a fall, but that this theme is not logically primitive, but derived; 3) that the tragic attitude will be the attitude toward death; 4) that the tragic effects will be those appropriate to violent death: fear, sorrow, and perhaps wonder at the suddenness and violence; and 5) that the effect of tragedy is consequently not infinitely subtle but quite obvious. On this account the tragedy of *Hamlet* is the holocaust which concludes it, and the tragedy of Hamlet himself is his death.

IV

Wonder

But is wonder a traditional effect of tragedy? Does it appear in the tradition so closely associated with tragic woe that Horatio's *aught of woe or wonder* could be taken as a designation of the tragic effect? Certainly it is not explicit, if present at all, in Donatus or Diomedes. Yet about twenty years before the publication of *Hamlet* Sir Philip Sidney had defined tragedy in the passage already quoted as "stirring the affects of admiration and commiseration."[1] The literal meaning of *admiration* in the Renaissance — it is the meaning of the Latin word *admiratio*—is "wonder." Hence Horatio's phrase is simply a translation from Latin to Germanic diction of Sidney's, with the substitution of the more general and more traditional notion of sorrow for the more special and more Aristotelian notion of pity. Of course, we need not picture Shakespeare as filching his phrase from Sidney, though this is not at all improbable. The question is rather, How did wonder, or admiration, come to be recognized as an effect proper to tragedy, and on what authority was it raised to an equal status with sorrow and fear? On what precedent did Sidney and Shakespeare speak? For surely neither intended to say anything novel on this subject.

I

The precedent is as old as Aristotle's *Poetics*.[2] It is true that in the famous definition of tragedy (1449b24-8) Aristotle speaks only of "incidents arousing pity and fear, wherewith to accomplish its catharsis of such emotions." There is, however, another emotion explicitly associated elsewhere in the *Poetics* with tragic incident and with the tragic catastrophe, and this is wonder or astonishment *(ekplexis, to thaumaston)*.

188

Three principal texts bear on this point. The first occurs toward the end of the *Poetics,* in the comparison of tragedy and epic:

> The marvellous is certainly required in tragedy. Epic, however, offers more opening for the improbable, the chief factor in the marvellous, because in it the agents are not visibly before us. The scene of the pursuit of Hector would be ridiculous on the stage—the Greeks halting instead of pursuing him, and Achilles shaking his head to stop them; but in the poem the absurdity is overlooked. The marvellous, however, is a cause of pleasure, as is shown by the fact that we all tell a story with additions, in the belief we are doing our hearers a pleasure.
>
> 1460a11-17[3]

The marvellous is certainly required in tragedy. Furthermore, from the example which Aristotle gives of telling a story with additions it is clear that the marvellous derives its value from the point of view of its effect on the audience: wonder, for like begets like.

The point is supported by a later passage, the second principal text, in which Aristotle is discussing the sort of criticisms one may make of the poet's art:

> As to the criticisms relating to the poet's art itself. Any impossibilities there may be in his descriptions of things are faults. But from another point of view they are justifiable, if they serve the end of poetry itself—if (to assume what we have said of that end) they make the effect of either that very portion of the work or some other portion more astounding. The Pursuit of Hector is an instance in point.
>
> 1460b23ff.

That is, impossibilities can be defended on the grounds that they make some portion of the work more astounding. The astounding has therefore a kind of absolute value. As such, it is not merely permissible, but necessary. In fact, the implication of this passage, which occurs in the extended comparison

189

of tragedy and epic, is that epic surpasses tragedy in this respect: you can get away with more of the marvellous in a narration than on the stage, for what seems marvellous when told may seem ridiculous when seen. What is presented on the stage and before our eyes cannot "fly from all humanity." Thus, the element of wonder, which rests upon the improbable, cannot bulk so large or be handled so indiscreetly as in straight narrative, but it cannot be dispensed with. So Aristotle arrives at his canon for the stage: "a likely impossibility is always preferable to an unconvincing possibility" (1460a26-27).

Furthermore, Aristotle posits here that wonder is an end —if it be not the end—of poetry, of which tragedy is a species. Now the end in the Aristotelian scheme is that toward which all things conspire and to which they are subordinated. It will be worth our while, then, to reconcile if possible this passage in which wonder is spoken of as the end of poetry with those others in which is implied that a specific kind of pleasure (involving pity and fear) is the end of tragedy (1448b18; 53a36; 53b11 and 12; 62a16; and 62b13). This passage will furnish the general solution; the third principal text, which will be noticed later, will furnish the specific solution applicable to tragedy.

The relationship of wonder and pleasure is that wonder is pleasurable (1460a17). It is pleasurable in itself. It is pleasurable also in that it is the occasion and motive for learning, as is clear from the famous passage in the *Metaphysics*:

> For it is owing to their wonder that men both now begin and at first began to philosophize. . . . And a man who is puzzled and wonders thinks himself ignorant (whence even the lover of myth is in a sense a lover of Wisdom, for the myth is composed of wonders) . . .
>
> 1. 2. 982b11-19

Furthermore myth, which furnished the material for Greek tragedy, is described as composed of wonders, and the lover of myth is a lover of Wisdom in that he, too, seeks to know.

Wonder is the occasion and motive for learning; learning is pleasurable: by this chain are wonder and pleasure connected. This is explained in the *Rhetoric*:

Again, since learning and wondering are pleasant, it follows that such things as acts of imitation must be pleasant—for instance, painting, sculpture, poetry—and every product of skilful imitation; this latter, even if the object imitated is not itself pleasant; for it is not the object itself which here gives delight; the spectator draws inferences ('That is a so-and-so') and thus learns something fresh. Dramatic turns of fortune and hairbreadth escapes from perils are pleasant, because we feel all such things are wonderful.

1. 11. 1371b4-12

Wonder and pleasure are the principal effects of art, and consequently of tragedy and the tragic catastrophe; they are its end. The two are correlative, for the one is the motive for inference, the other its natural accompaniment. Furthermore, what we now call aesthetic experience is for Aristotle substantially the experience of inferring. This is clear from the passage just cited, and is reinforced by the well-known passage early in the *Poetics* in which Aristotle analyzes the general origin of poetry. He points out that men, and especially the young, are natural copy-cats and prone to make-believe. This is how they learn. Secondly, he says, "it is natural for all to delight in works of imitation":

The truth of this second point is shown by experience: though the objects themselves may be painful to see, we delight to view the most realistic representations of them in art, the forms for example of the lowest animals and of dead bodies. The explanation is to be found in a further fact: to be learning something is the greatest of pleasures not only to the philosopher but also the rest of mankind, however small their capacity for it; the reason of the delight in seeing the picture is that one is at the same time learning—gathering the meaning of things, e.g. that the man there is so-and-so; for if one has not seen the thing

191

before, one's pleasure will not be in the picture as an imitation
of it, but will be due to the execution or colouring or some
similar cause.

4. 1448b4-19

Wonder, then, is associated with pleasure as the end of poetry,
and it is also posited as required in tragedy. But is it specifically
associated, as it is in *Hamlet,* with the proper tragic effects of
pity and fear? It is, as one would expect, since Aristotle tells
us that through pity and fear tragedy attains its proper pleasure
(1453b10-11), and pleasure involves wonder. The text, which
is the third of the principal texts, reads:

> Tragedy, however, is an imitation not only of a complete action,
> but also of incidents arousing pity and fear. Such incidents have
> the very greatest effect on the mind when they occur unex-
> pectedly and at the same time in consequence of one another;
> there is more of the marvellous in them then than if they hap-
> pened of themselves or by mere chance. Even matters of chance
> seem most marvellous if there is an appearance of design as it
> were in them; as for instance the statue of Mitys at Argos killed
> the author of Mitys's death by falling down on him when a
> looker-on at a public spectacle; for incidents like that we think
> to be not without a meaning. A Plot, therefore, of this sort is
> necessarily finer than others.

9. 1452a1-11

It is implied again that wonder has an absolute value in itself.
Furthermore, the degree of surprise, the amount of the marvellous, in the plot of a tragedy is the measure of the pity and
fear it provokes, so that in the strict mathematical sense
wonder is a function of pity and fear: $PF = W$.

Two further passages may be cited in this connection. In
discussing the kinds of incidents which will produce the tragic
pleasure of pity and fear, Aristotle remarks that

> A better situation [than the one previously discussed] is for the
> deed to be done in ignorance, and the relationship [of the parties

involved] discovered afterwards, since there is nothing odious in it, and the Discovery will serve to astound us.

14. 1454a2-4

And later, in analyzing the kinds of Discovery, he remarks:

> The best of all Discoveries, however, is that arising from the incidents themselves, when the great surprise comes about through a probable incident, like that in the *Oedipus* of Sophocles . . .

16. 1455a16-18

In brief, let wonders happen, but make them—at least at the moment of their happening—plausible and convincing. This can best be accomplished by making the tragic incident unexpected, and yet, as soon as it has happened, obviously logical and supported by the situation and the preceding action. The incident is not what we expected, but what, as soon as we see it, we realize that we should have expected. Something of this sort is involved when we understand a person: he acts spontaneously at a crisis in a way we would never have predicted, yet the moment the thing has happened we know that we knew that was the sort of person he was. The point will be clear if we contrast this with our attitude toward the critical actions of those whom we do not understand: their actions simply puzzle us, and the measure of our bewilderment is the measure of our lack of understanding.

There is no need to think all this original with Aristotle: both rhetoric and poetic—the latter in Antiquity is only partially distinguishable from the former—had already a long history by this time. Much of the evidence, it is true, has been lost, and much must be reconstructed by divining earlier features in later texts.[4] But it is clear from the remarks of the rhapsode Ion in Plato's dialogue that fear, pity, and wonder were the commonly recognized effects of the recitation of epic, and particularly of the striking passages: for the whole point of the dialogue, which is simple-mindedly ironic, is that what Ion says should represent common opinion:

193

ION. . . . When I speak of anything piteous, my eyes are filled with tears; when I mention anything fearful or terrible, my hair stands on end with fear and my heart throbs . . .

SOC. And do you not know that you produce the same effects on many of the spectators?

ION. I know it right well, for when I look down from the platform I see them weeping and showing signs of terror and astonishment at my words.

Ion. 535B-C[5]

Nevertheless, most of the subsequent history of the concept of wonder can be derived from the Aristotelian texts. Wonder is, first of all, the natural effect of a marvellous story, and hence of those myths which furnished the plots of ancient tragedy and epic, as well as of those extraordinary events which in later Hellenistic times, as earlier in Herodotus, are narrated in certain types of history and in the marvellous tale. Apuleius, for instance, in the first sentence of the *Metamorphoses* claims that his purpose is to evoke wonder: "I have told these stories," he says, "in this style that you may wonder *(ut mireris)*."

Wonder is, in the second place, the result of a surprising and unexpected turn in events, and is thus intimately involved in the tragic catastrophe and in its proper effect. Furthermore, since in tragedy the turn is toward the worse, the effect of surprise will be inwoven with sorrow or pity as well as astonishment, and the astonishment will take that form which is akin to fear. From this line of thought, though not necessarily from Aristotle, is derived the following passage from a little scrapbook of short treatises by the famous rhetorician Hermogenes of Tarsus, which goes under the title of *How to Speak Effectively:*

> Phillipics, dialogue, comedy, tragedy, and the Socratic symposia weave the whole by a kind of double method. . . . The web and woof of tragedy are woe and wonder, as is to be seen both in the tragedies of tragic writers and in those of Homer whom Plato called the father of tragedy and the choregus.[6]

Thirdly, wonder is an end of poetry. This concept is generalized in the Neo-Platonist Plotinus, to whom wonder is an effect of beauty:

> This is the effect that Beauty must ever induce, wonderment and a pleasant astonishment, longing and love and a dread that is pleasurable.
>
> *Enneades*, 1. 6. 4[7]

However, the more restricted view, which we found in Aristotle, that wonder is along with pleasure the end of poetry is a commonplace in later Antiquity; it is chiefly associated with the name of Eratosthenes, the poet-scholar, friend and disciple of Callimachus. We gain our knowledge of his position principally from the criticisms which Strabo levels against it in the *Geography*. "Eratosthenes," he says, "is wrong in his contention that the aim of every poet is to entertain, not to instruct" (1. 1. 10).[8] The argument is long and somewhat tedious. In brief, Strabo holds that the poet either pleases or instructs,—pleases when what he says is false, instructs when what he says is true (1. 2. 3, and 7-9). On this basis the ends of the various branches of composition are distinguished:

> Now the aim of history is truth, . . . the aim of rhetorical composition is vividness, as when Homer introduces men fighting; the aim of myth is to please and excite amazement.
>
> 1. 2. 17

The purpose of myth—that is, of a story—is pleasure and wonder.

Eratosthenes' distinction, as preserved by Strabo, appears also in the historian Polybius. He is criticizing one of his predecessors, Phylarchus, of whom he says:

> Leaving aside the ignoble and womanish character of such a treatment of his subject, let us consider how far it is proper or serviceable to history. A historical author should not try to thrill his readers by such exaggerated pictures, nor should he, like a tragic poet, try to imagine the probable utterances of his

195

characters or reckon up all the consequences probably incidental to the occurrences with which he deals, but simply record what really happened and what really was said, however commonplace. For the end of tragedy is not the same as that of history but quite the opposite. The tragic poet should amaze and charm his audience for the moment by the verisimilitude of the words he puts into his characters' mouths, but it is the task of the historian to instruct and convince for all time serious students by the truth of the facts and the speeches he narrates, since in the one case it is the probable that takes precedence, even if it be untrue, the purpose being to create illusion in spectators, in the other it is the truth, the purpose being to confer benefit on learners.

2. 56[9]

The passage is intellectually more respectable, of course, than that from Strabo. For Polybius, though he does not exclude— as no one should since literature is a part of life—general ethical judgments ("Leaving aside the ignoble and womanish character of such a treatment of his subject"), is nevertheless capable of discussing literature on its own terms and with reference to its own proper ends ("let us consider how far it is proper and servicable to history"). The end of tragedy is to astonish and please—but not without qualifications, for he points out in the passage that follows this quotation that unless we know the causes of a catastrophe and the course of events which led up to it, it is impossible to feel due indignation or pity. In brief, the effect must be adequately motivated.

Plutarch in his essay on *How a Young Man Should Study Poetry* repeats the commonplace:

But when poetic art is divorced from the truth, then chiefly it employs variety and diversity. For it is the sudden changes that give to its stories the elements of the emotional, the surprising, and the unexpected, and these are attended by very great astonishment and enjoyment; but sameness is unemotional and prosaic.

7.25[10]

In an earlier passage he applies Eratosthenes' formulation of the end of poetry to a play of Aeschylus:

> But it is patent to everybody that this is a mythical fabrication which has been created to please or astound the hearer.
>
> 7.17

The following passage from the ancient Life of Aeschylus obviously springs from the same context of critical notions: Aeschylus "has few devices for drawing tears" and "uses the spectacle and plot more to strike by the marvellous than to effect artistic illusion."[11]

II

The marvellous is pleasurable. Thus wonder is an end of poetry, or it is with pleasure the end of poetry. Hence it would obviously be involved in the effect of any particular kind. It is, however, associated with the specific, rather than with the generic, effect of tragedy even in Aristotle, since the specific effects of pity and fear are most truly effective when they also involve wonder. Indeed, the marvellous is required in tragedy. Consequently, it becomes traditional to distinguish the purpose of fiction, especially of epic and tragedy, from that of history and of rhetoric on these grounds: fiction aims at wonder and pleasure; history at truth and instruction; rhetoric at vividness and persuasion. But, of course, these lines of distinction were not fixed and unalterable in Antiquity, since the subjects of the distinctions were not simple. Poetry and rhetoric had a great deal in common; fiction commonly involved history, and history fiction. Furthermore, from the time of Aristotle poetry was often identified with fiction, and the mythical was a characteristic property. Thus, the end of poetry was often said to be pleasure and instruction, as in Horace and Strabo, and its methods were usually rhetorical.

However, wonder is not only an effect of a story or of a

subject matter, it is also an effect of language and of style. It is precisely the effect of characteristically poetic, or tragic, style, as opposed to the plain straightforward style proper to prose and to dialectic. For the fundamental distinction which prevails in Antiquity and informs the traditional theory of the three (or four) styles is the distinction in diction between the unornamented language native to prose and the unusual, figurative, ornamented language of poetry, and especially of tragedy. The distinction remained current even though poetry appropriated the language of prose, as in the later tragedians, and prose in the rhetorical tradition of Gorgias appropriated the language of poetry (Aristotle, *Rhet.* 3. 1. 1404a20-34; Strabo, 1. 2. 6). The point is made clear by Aristotle in the *Rhetoric.* The effect of poetic diction is wonder.

> People do not feel toward strangers as they do towards their own countrymen, and the same thing is true of their feeling for language. It is therefore well to give everyday speech an unfamiliar air: wonder is a characteristic of things off the beaten track, and the wonderful is pleasant. In verse such effects are common, and there they are fitting; the persons and things there spoken of are comparatively remote from ordinary life. In prose passages they are far less often fitting because the subject-matter is less exalted.

3. 2. 1404b8-15[12]

The later theory on the subject derives partly from such passages as this, probably by way of Theophrastus' work on style, and partly no doubt from Sophistic theory as developed by Gorgias among others. (Diodorus, 12. 53; Gorgias, *Helena,* 9.) It seems to have been based, at least originally, upon a distinction between style which employs plain language and to the point, whose aim is merely truth, and whose concern is simply with content *(rem tene, verba secuntur),* and a style cultivated as such. The former uses proper expressions only; the latter intermingles figurative. Its aim is to move, to convince, to please; its concern is with the effect on the audience. The former is the style of dialectic and, in general, of philosophy; and the latter is the style of poetry and of rhetoric. So Theophrastus in a passage preserved in one of the later commentaries on Aristotle's logic:

> Language is divided into two types, according to the philosopher Theophrastus, the one having reference to the hearers, the other to the matter concerning which the speaker aims to convince his audience. To the division with reference to the hearers belong poetry and rhetoric. Therefore its function is to choose the more stately words, and not those which are common or vulgar, and to interweave them with each other harmoniously, to the end that, by means of them and the effects which result from the employment of them, such as vividness, sweetness and other qualities of style, together with studied expansion and contraction, all employed at the suitable moment, the listener shall be charmed and astonished and, with respect to intellectual persuasion, overmastered. The division looking to the matter will be the especial concern of the philosopher, refuting the false and setting forth the true.[13]

The effect of astonishment or wonder is the natural correlative of unusual diction, as it is of the unusual event. The proper word satisfies by its exactness; the unusual pleases or displeases by its startling effect. Upon this basis, which though obvious is not unimportant, together with the doctrine of the appropriateness of style to subject, rests the whole later theory of the kinds and characters of style in all its elaboration. Hence, the theorists will ascribe to any style which is noticeable as such the quality of wonder. That style which is elaborated for the purpose of charm or pleasure—the *genus floridum*—will evoke the kind of pleasant wonder that the marvellous story does, and will be appropriate to such subjects: for instance, the Milesian style of Apuleius, for the effect of wonder is ascribed in the passage cited above not only to the subject matter but also to the style. The high style, the forceful, the grand—the style of Demosthenes and of Aeschylus—will evoke that wonder which is akin to fear, and will be especially appropriate to tragedy. Yet wonder may be on a lesser scale than this: it corresponds to the displacement, large or small, that initiates internal movement: with respect to the intellect, inference, the processes of logic, and learning; with respect to the irrational part of the soul, feeling and emotion. Hence style can evoke emotion in the audience, and at the same time by the law of decorum the degree of unusual diction should be proportionate to the height and intensity of the feeling inherent in the subject-matter. Again, to wonder at style is to regard it highly, to approve of it, to admire in the modern sense, but this attitude, though not unaccompanied by feeling, nevertheless implies no specific shade of emotional coloring.

This much may serve to introduce the following citations in which is exhibited the continuity in antiquity of the Peripatetic and Sophistic tradition that wonder is an effect of style, and especially of the high style appropriate to tragedy. The treatise on style by Demetrius (probably first century A. D.) is clearly in this tradition. He cites a line of Homer in which a figurative shift in construction elevates the style, and contrasts this with the ordinary way of saying the same thing. "But everything ordinary is trivial," he says, "and so fails to attain wonder" (59-60). Again, to take a longer quotation:

The sayings of Demades, too, possess power, although their expression sounds peculiar and unusual. Their power arises partly from their significance and partly from their allegorical form and lastly from their exaggerated character.

This is an example: "Alexander is not dead, Athenians. If he were, the whole world would smell the corpse." The use of the word "smell" for "perceive" involves both allegory and exaggeration. The fact that the world perceived it signifies Alexander's strength, and at the same time the sentence has an effect of astonishment which is due to a combination of three causes.

200

Everything that astonishes is powerful, because it creates fear.
282-3[14]

The rhetorical concept of wonder is the subject of the famous treatise on elevated style *(On the Sublime)*, which has been ascribed to Longinus. The subject is announced in the opening chapter. The author premises that the eminence and renown of great writers, both in prose and in verse, is derived from distinction in language (1. 3). The effect of such distinction he conceives of in the traditional way—the doctrine is precisely that of the passage cited above from Theophrastus — as astonishment, which overpowers the hearer and puts him in a state of transport. This effect is differentiated from that of persuasion, and incidentally of pleasure, on the grounds that this is irresistible while persuasion for the most part involves voluntary assent, and secondly that this is a matter of detail and that of the work as a whole (1. 4).

In this way the differences which Eratosthenes, Polybius, and Strabo, among others, had established between the various kinds of literary works are here applied in the context of rhetorical theory to single out the special effect of certain details in a work. The analysis gets sometimes a little complicated. Thus, in discussing the kind of image in which out of an inspired passion the writer thinks he sees what he is describing and makes his hearer see it—a well-known rhetorical device in Antiquity — Longinus distinguishes between the purpose of such images in oratory and in the poets. In poetry the end is astonishment; in prose vividness; though both alike seek to stir up excitement (15. 36). But the poetic image tends to be fabulous, exaggerated, and to go beyond what is believable, whereas the virtue of imagery in prose is always its reality and truth (15. 40). Nevertheless, imagery in prose can exceed persuasion and attain astonishment, combining vigor and passion with argument and fact so that the hearer is not merely persuaded but actually enslaved, for the stronger effect of wonder will absorb the weaker of persuasion (15. 41).[15]

201

The notion also appears, as we might expect, in the Latin authors. Cicero, for example, in the teacher-pupil dialogue on the *Classification of Oratory* associates wonder with ornate or figurative diction, and hence with the charming style *(genus suave)*. He points out that style will be charming if something unusual, original, or novel is said — he is thinking of phrasing —, "for anything wonderful pleases" (22). Again, a charming account is one that has causes of wonder, suspense, and emotional outcomes, along with interpolated emotional passages, dialogues, sorrow, anger, fear, joy, and desire (32). Cicero is here speaking of those expositions of events which form part of a speech, but the description could easily apply to a play, and particularly to such as the *Winter's Tale* or to many of Beaumont and Fletcher. In another passage he says that in developing a subject in the decorative style we should take up those aspects that produce suspense, wonder, and delight (58). Finally, he points out in an extended passage that in epideictic speeches, whose chief purpose is to please and entertain an audience, the speaker should make use of striking phrases, which have a great deal of charm; that is, he should use coined words, archaisms, and metaphors, and in constructing the phrase one should echo another by similarity of rhythm and ending, thus giving doublets and a verbal rhythm, not sounding like verse yet satisfying the ear with an appropriate harmony. But the ornament should not be merely verbal; there should also be in the matter a good deal of what is wonderful and unexpected, things foreshadowed by portents, prodigies, and oracles, and what seems to the man to whom this happens to be the result of divine intervention or of fate. For the feeling of suspense in the audience, and wonder, and the unexpected outcome always give a certain pleasure in the hearing (72-3).[16] What is described here is represented in Elizabethan times by Lyly's *Euphues,* and all its progeny in the Elizabethan drama. Wonder is an effect both of style and of subject.

202

The doctrine of Antiquity on wonder is summed up and transmitted to posterity by Quintilian:

> . . . those words are the most to be commended which express our thoughts best, and produce the impression which we desire on the minds of the judges. Such words undoubtedly must make a speech both worthy of admiration and productive of pleasure; but not of that kind of *admiration* with which we wonder at monsters; or of that kind of *pleasure* which is attended with unnatural gratification, but such as is compatible with true merit and worth.
>
> 8. *Pr.* 32-3

> It was the sublimity, magnificence, splendour, and dignity of his [Cicero's] eloquence, that drew forth that thunder of approbation. No such extraordinary commendation would have attended on the speaker, if his speech had been of an everyday character, and similar to ordinary speeches. I even believe that his audience were insensible of what they were doing, and that they gave their applause neither voluntarily nor with an exercise of judgment, but that, being carried away by enthusiasm, and unconscious of the place in which they stood, they burst forth instinctively into such transports of delight.

> But this grace of style may contribute in no small degree to the success of a cause; for those who listen with pleasure are both more attentive and more ready to believe; they are very frequently captivated with pleasure, and sometimes hurried away in admiration. Thus the glitter of a sword strikes something of terror into the eyes, and thunder storms themselves would not alarm us so much as they do if it were their force only, and not also their flame, that was dreaded. Cicero, accordingly, in one of his letters to Brutus, makes with good reason the following remark: *That eloquence which excites no wonder, I account as nothing.* Aristotle, also, thinks that to excite wonder should be one of our greatest objects.
>
> 8. 3. 2-6[17]

203

III

So much for Antiquity. It will be sufficient now to establish the continuity of the tradition in the Middle Ages, and later in the Renaissance. The effect of wonder will be a familiar notion to any Christian since it is frequently noted in the New Testament as the effect of the words and works of Christ:

> And the disciples were astonished at his words. . .
>
> Mt. 13. 54
>
> And straightway the damsel arose and walked, for she was of the age of twelve years. And they were astonished with a great astonishment.
>
> Mk. 5.42

Wonder, of course, is the natural effect of miracles, real or apparent. St. Augustine makes the point in the text which furnishes the standard definition for medieval theology: "I call a miracle anything great and difficult or unusual that happens beyond the expectation or ability of the man who wonders at it" *(De Utilitate Credendi,* 16. 34).[18] And St. Thomas, in turn, integrates the Augustinian definition with the Aristotelian. In the *Summa* he takes up the question, "Whether everything that God does outside of the natural order is miraculous?" He cites an authoritative text from St. Augustine: "When God does anything contrary to the course and custom of nature as we know it, we call it a miracle." For the term is indeed derived from the word for wonder, and wonder arises whenever an effect is manifest and its cause hidden, as Aristotle says in the *Metaphysics.* Consequently, what is wonderful to one man may not be wonderful to another, but a miracle is fully wonderful since it has a cause absolutely hidden from all, namely, God (*ST* 1. 105.7).

The marvellous event, and so the marvellous story, provokes wonder. The explicit recognition of this effect is common throughout the literature of the Middle Ages, and has behind

204

it a tradition derived from Christian dogma. Thus the German *Niebelungenlied* of the twelfth century begins by promising us that now we will hear a wonder told, and so likewise in countless romances.

But with the recovery of the Aristotelian writings in the twelfth and thirteenth centuries, the concept of wonder as the end of poetry again enters firmly into the tradition under the authority of Aristotle and in association with most of the other elements in the tradition which were distinguished in the preceding sections of this essay. One of the most interesting texts is to be found in the works of St. Albert the Great, the teacher of Thomas Aquinas. It occurs in Albert's *Commentary on the Metaphysics of Aristotle;* I shall cite it at length:

> Ch. 6: *In which it is shown that philosophy is a speculative, not a practical, science.*
>
> That philosophy is speculative, not practical, is clear from the motive that first moved men to philosophize. For everyone who has philosophized, now or in the past, has been motivated only by wonder. Now, wonder is defined as a constriction and suspension of the heart caused by amazement at the sensible appearance of something so portentous, great, and unusual, that the heart suffers a systole. Hence wonder is something like fear in its effect on the heart. This effect of wonder, then, this constriction and systole of the heart, springs from an unfulfilled but felt desire to know the cause of that which appears portentous and unusual: so it was in the beginning when men, up to that time unskilled, began to philosophize—they marvelled at certain difficulties, which were, as a matter of fact, fairly easy to solve. The Pythagoreans, for example, were concerned with the theory of number, with even and odd numbers, with complete, increasing, and diminished number. Then men advanced bit by bit in learning and, becoming more proficient, raised graver questions whose causes were not easy to see: such as the changes of the moon with respect to mansions, accessions, and eclipses, or questions about the sun and the stars. . . . In like fashion they advanced in Physics, and began to wonder

205

about generation in general, asking whether the universe was created or given.

Now the man who is puzzled and wonders apparently does not know. Hence wonder is the movement of the man who does not know on his way to finding out, to get at the bottom of that at which he wonders and to determine its cause. A token in proof is that the famous Philomithes according to this way of looking at the matter is a Philosopher, for he constructed his stories out of wonderful events. I hold that Philomithes was a poet who loved to fashion stories: for *mithes*, with the first syllable long, is the word for stories, and *Philomithes*, then, means a lover of stories, if you make the penultimate syllable long. Thus Aristotle shows in that branch of logic which is called poetic that the poet fashions his story for the purpose of exciting wonder, and that the further effect of wonder is to excite inquiry. Such is the origin of philosophy, as Plato shows with respect to the stories of Phaeton and Deucalion. The single purpose of these stories is to excite one to wonder at the causes of the two deluges of fire and of water (which issued from the circut of wandering stars), so that through wonder the cause would be looked for, and the truth discovered.

Hence poetry offers a method of philosophizing, just as do the other sciences of logic. But the other sciences or branches of logic offer a method of proving a proposition by reasoning, that is, by conclusive or probable argument; poetry, however, offers no method of proof but rather a method of wonder by which we are incited to inquiry. Therefore, though poetry is a subdivision of grammar with respect to prosody, with respect to its purpose it is one of the branches of logic.

To get back to the point: we define the man who wonders as one who is in suspense as to the cause, the knowledge of which would make him know instead of wonder. . . .

In I Met., Tr. 2,ch. 6[19]

The poet Philomithes, of course, is a character that grew from a misreading of the Greek text in the passage in which Aristotle states that "the lover of myth *(philomuthos)* is in a sense a lover of Wisdom, for the myth is composed of wonders" *(Metaphysics,* 1. 2. 982b18-9). But he is a charming character, and he makes the point. The end of poetry is wonder, and the end of wonder is to excite inquiry; thus poetry is a branch of logic with respect to its purpose, and distinguished from other branches in that they offer methods of proof but poetry offers a method of motivation. Its physiological effect is similar to that of fear.

St. Thomas holds substantially the same position, and cites Aristotle in the *Poetics* to the same effect. He is discussing the causes of pleasure, and comes finally to the question, Does wonder cause pleasure? He first takes up the objections:

> Apparently it doesn't 1) since wonder is a property of ignorance, and ignorance is not pleasurable, but rather knowledge. 2) Furthermore, wonder is the beginning of wisdom, being as it were a way of looking for the truth, as is said in the *Metaphysics,* 1, 2. But it is more pleasurable to contemplate what is already known than to inquire into the unknown, as Aristotle says in the *Ethics* X, 7. (1177a23ff.), since the latter offers difficulties and impediments, but the former does not, and pleasure arises from unimpeded operation. Therefore wonder is not a cause of pleasure, but rather a hinderance. 3) Furthermore, everyone delights in what he is used to; hence the operation of habits acquired through daily use is pleasurable. But what one is used to is not wonderful, as Augustine says (at the beginning of *In Joan.,* tr. 24). Therefore wonder is precisely not a cause of pleasure.

> But to the contrary is the text of Aristotle (Rhet. 1. 11. 1371a31): *wonder is a cause of pleasure.*

> My position is that to attain anything one feels a want of is pleasurable; and the measure of anyone's desire for something he loves is the measure of his pleasure in attaining it. Indeed, in the very augmentation of desire there is an augmentation of pleasure,

in that there arises a hope of what is loved, and desire itself is pleasurable in its aspect of hope. But wonder is a kind of desire for knowledge. The situation arises when one sees an effect and does not know its cause, or when the cause of the particular effect is one that exceeds his power of understanding. Hence wonder is a cause of pleasure in so far as there is annexed the hope of attaining understanding of that which one wants to know.

For this reason, everything wonderful is pleasurable: for example, anything that is infrequent, as well as any representation of things, even of those that are not in themselves pleasant. For the soul delights in comparing one thing with another, since this is a proper and connatural activity of reason, as Aristotle says in his *Poetics* (4. 1448b13ff.). And for this reason even to be released from great danger is quite pleasurable, as is said in the *Rhetoric* (1.11.1371b10ff.).

As to the first objection, wonder is not pleasurable in so far as it involves ignorance, but in so far as it involves learning the cause, and learning something new: namely, that such-and-such is such-and-such, though we had not thought it was.

As to the second objection, there are two kinds of pleasure: acquiescence in the Good, and awareness of such acquiescence. With respect to the former, since it is a more complete experience to contemplate known truth than to inquire into the unknown, the contemplation of things known is in itself more pleasurable than inquiry into things unknown; nevertheless, it sometimes happens that, with respect to our awareness of experience, inquiry is more pleasurable in that it has more drive and springs from a greater desire. For desire is especially aroused by the awareness of ignorance, and consequently a man takes the greatest pleasure in those things which he discovers for himself or learns from the ground up.

As to the third objection, doing what we are used to is pleasurable in so far as it is in a way natural to us. Still, on the other hand, what is unusual can be pleasurable, either with respect to the process of learning, since our desire for knowledge is proportional to the marvellousness of the subject, or with re-

spect to the actual doing, since the mind is strongly impelled by desire to that which is felt intensely because of its novelty. But an activity, the more full it is, the greater the pleasure it causes.
$$1\text{-}2.\ 32.\ 8^{20}$$

Wonder is also a species of fear, as the Damascene teaches. To the objection that wonder and amazement *(admiratio et stupor)* are not species of fear, since fear refers only to evil, and wonder and amazement refer to the unusual, whether good or evil; and again, to the further objection that philosophers are moved by wonder to inquire into the truth, whereas fear does not move one to investigate but rather to run from the scene of investigation; Thomas answers that the authority of the Damascene and of Gregory of Nyassa is sufficient to establish the point. He then solves the objections by dividing the six traditional species of fear into three whose source is internal and three whose source is external — wonder *(admiratio)*, which arises when one contemplates some great evil whose issue he cannot see; amazement *(stupor)*, which arises when one contemplates some unaccustomed evil, for it will seem to be great because it is unaccustomed; shocked surprise *(agonia)*, which arises from the unforeseen. Hence to the former objection Thomas answers that only that wonder and amazement which arises from the contemplation of evil is a species of fear; to the latter objection he answers that a man who wonders does fear at the moment to give a judgment, fearing that he will fail, but that he looks into the matter in the future; the amazed man, however, fears both now and in the future; hence wonder is the beginning of philosophizing, but amazement an impediment to it *(ST, 1-2. 41. 4)*.

IV

Whatever appears in the scholastic philosophers and at the same time in Aristotle, as well as in Cicero and Quintillian, is likely to appear anywhere in Renaissance literature. It will be commonplace. Thus the rhetorical tradition is gathered up, assimilated, and integrated into a consistent structure in Pontanus' dialogue on poetry (*Actius,* about 1500). There the end of poetry is said to be "to speak well and appropriately so as to attain wonder," and this is later corrected by one of the speakers into the form, "to speak exceptionally well," so as to distinguish the poet from the orator who also must speak well and appropriately. The wonder referred to is conceived under two aspects: it is admiration, in the modern sense, for the eloquence of the poet himself, who from this source derives his fame and glory; at the same time, it is the emotion of wonder in the audience. The poet moves wonder not only by sublime words, but also by his subject matter, and since truth alone cannot guarantee this he shades truth with fiction and myth. Nor is wonder only the effect of the grave and serious; it is also the effect of the pleasant and delightful. And in speaking so sweetly, sublimely, and marvellously, the poet teaches others to speak well, so that every literary form derives from poetry.[21]

The same line of thought is developed in Fracastoro's dialogue *Navagero* (published 1555), in which the emphasis, however, is laid on the final remark, and poetry is distinguished from all other forms in that it is the master-art of eloquence. For, though poetry excites wonder, this is not its exclusive characteristic since wonder is also the effect of oratory and history: "Who can read Cicero himself without wonder?"[22]

The idea is common throughout the Renaissance. Minturno, who is in the same line of tradition as Pontanus and Fracastoro, begins his dialogue on the poet, *De Poeta* (1559), with the statement that "no one can be called a poet who does not excel in the power of arousing wonder." Minturno, however, goes beyond the rhetorical tradition, making a good deal of Aristotle's *Poetics* which had lately been translated, paraphrased, and expounded by a good many of his fellow-countrymen. Thus he introduces the notions of wonder and pleasure in connection with tragedy:

The poet does not deal with what does not please, nor does he move the emotions without delight. Rather, excited by the force of language and the weight of his ideas he rouses, attracts, and moves the audience intensely to the point of wonder—either through fear or pity, or both.[23]

In fact, the idea of wonder is so commonplace in the Renaissance it would be surprising not to find it in Sidney or in Shakespeare. Hence, to establish the availability of the idea, I will only add to these citations and that from Sidney's *Defense* the following passages from Spenser.

A. Wonder is the effect of theological discourse, being, of course, the highest subject-matter and hence affording by its very nature the highest eloquence; as such, however, it is an effect of subject, not of style:

> And that her sacred Booke, with blood ywritt,
> That none could reade, except she did them teach,
> She unto him disclosed every whitt,
> And heavenly documents thereout did preach,
> That weaker witt of man could never reach,
> Of God, of grace, of justice, of free will,
> That wonder was to heare her goodly speach:
> For she was hable with her wordes to kill
> And rayse againe to life the hart that she did thrill.
>
> *Faerie Queene*, 1. 10. 19

Compare Milton's *Paradise Lost:* At Raphael's speech Adam,

> with his consorted Eve,
> The story heard attentive, and was filled
> With admiration and deep muse, to hear
> Of things so high and strange . . .
>
> 7. 50-3

B. The palmer finds good Guyon, "slumbering fast, in senseles dreame":

> Whom when the palmer saw, abasht he was
> Through fear and wonder, that he nought could say . . .
>
> *F. Q.*, 2. 8. 7. 1-2

211

Fear and wonder is the effect of apparent unexpected death.

C. Ruth (that is, pity or woe) and wonder is the effect on the bystanders at a mortal combat:

> With that they both together fiercely met,
> As if that each ment other to devoure;
> And with their axes both so sorely bet,
> That neither plate nor mayle, whereas their power
> They felt, could once sustaine the hideous stowre,
> But rived were like rotton wood a sunder,
> Whilest through their rifts the ruddie bloud did showre,
> And fire did flash, like lightning after thunder,
> That fild the lookers on attonce with ruth and wonder.
>
> F. Q., 4. 3. 15

Attonce means "both."

D. The following marvellous events quite properly provoke great wonder of a kind akin to fear, as do the prodigies of Nature:

> Then forth he brought his snowy Florimele,
> Whom Trompart had in keeping there beside,
> Covered from peoples gazement with a vele.
> Whom when discovered they had throughly eide,
> With great amazement they were stupefide;
> And said, that surely Florimell it was,
> Or if it were not Florimell so tride,
> That Florimell her selfe she then did pas.
> So feeble skill of perfect things the vulgar has.

> Which when as Marinell beheld likewise,
> He was therewith exceedingly dismayd;
> Ne wist he what to thinke, or to devise,
> But, like as one whom feends had made affrayd,
> He long astonisht stood, ne ought he sayd,
> Ne ought he did, but with fast fixed eies
> He gazed still upon that snowy mayd;
> Whom ever as he did the more avize,
> The more to be true Florimell he did surmize.

As when two sunnes appeare in the azure skye,
Mounted in Phoebus charet fierie bright,
Both darting forth faire beames to each mans eye,
And both adorn'd with lampes of flaming light,
All that behold so strange prodigious sight,
Not knowing Natures worke, nor what to weene,
Are rapt with wonder and with rare affright:
So stood Sir Marinell, when he had seene
The semblant of this false by his faire beauties queene.

F. Q., 5. 3. 17-19

Then Artegall steps forth and says this " 'is not (I wager) Florimell at all' . . . For proof whereof he bad them Florimell forth
call."

Then did he set her by that snowy one,
Like the true saint beside the image set,
Of both their beauties to make paragone,
And triall, whether should the honor get.
Streight way so soone as both together met,
Th' enchanted damzell vanisht into nought:
Her snowy substance melted as with heat,
Ne of that goodly hew remayned ought,
But th' emptie girdle, which about her waste was wrought.

As when the daughter of Thaumantes faire
Hath in a watry cloud displayed wide
Her goodly bow, which paints the liquid ayre;
That all men wonder at her colours pride;
All suddenly, ere one can looke aside,
The glorious picture vanisheth away,
Ne any token doth thereof abide:
So did this ladies goodly forme decay,
And into nothing goe, ere one could it bewray.

Which when as all that present were beheld,
They stricken were with great astonishment,
And their faint harts with senselesse horrour queld,
To see the thing, that seem'd so excellent,

213

So stolen from their fancies wonderment:
That what of it became none understood.
And Braggadochio selfe with dreriment
So daunted was, in his despeyring mood,
That like a lifelesse corse immoveable he stood.

F. Q., 5. 3. 24-6

E. "Calidore sees young Tristram slay / A proud discourteous knight":

Which when he saw, his hart was inly child
With great amazement, and his thought with wonder fild.

F. Q., 6. 2. *Argum.* and 4. 8-9

F. In *The Ruines of Time*:

Before mine eyes strange sights presented were,
Like tragicke pageants seeming to appeare.

489-90

Then follows a series of visions in which a gold image, a stately tower, a pleasant paradise, a giant, a gold bridge over the sea, and two white bears successively fall to ruin:

Much was I troubled in my heavie spright,
At sight of these sad spectacles forepast,
That all my senses were bereaved quight,
And I in minde remained sore agast,
Distraught twixt feare and pitie; when at last
I heard a voyce, which loudly to me called,
That with the suddein shrill I was appalled.

'Behold,' said it, 'and by ensample see,
That all is vanitie and griefe of minde,
No other comfort in this world can be,
But hope of heaven, and heart to God inclinde;
For all the rest must needs be left behinde.'

575-86

The effect of these tragic pageants is wonder ("That all my

214

senses were bereaved quight") which suspends and mediates between fear and pity. The ultimate effect is to teach the rejection of this life.

v

Certainly the aesthetic effect of wonder was a notion easily available to Shakespeare. But if Horatio's *aught of woe or wonder* is to be taken as aesthetically significant, it must be shown not only that Shakespeare could have been but also that he was aware of the tradition. Does Shakespeare use the notion of wonder, and the synonymous *amazement, astonishment,* and *to be struck senseless,* in any other contexts than this one in Hamlet? He does. In fact, he uses almost the full range of meanings which are to be found in the tradition.

Wonder is the effect of such an incident, conventional to tragedy, as the appearance of the Ghost in *Hamlet* and the recognition of his likeness to the dead King:

> BERNARDO. Looks it not like the King? Mark it, Horatio.
> HORATIO. Most like. It harrows me with fear and wonder.
>
> 1. 1. 43-4

The appearance is regarded by Horatio (1. 1. 113-25) as of the same nature as those signs and portents, those foreshadowings of tragic consequences, which preceded the death of Caesar. Indeed, such "precurse of fierce events," such "harbingers preceding still the fates / And prologue to the omen coming on" have precisely the same effect upon Casca in the play of *Julius Caesar:*

> CASCA. It is the part of men to fear and tremble
> When the most mighty gods by tokens send
> Such dreadful heralds to astonish us.

To which Cassius replies;

> . . . You look pale, and gaze
> And put on fear, and cast yourself in wonder,
> To see the strange impatience of the heavens. . . .
>
> 1. 3. 54-6 and 59-61

215

Wonder, then, is an emotion which is a kind of fear and is produced by striking and supernatural events. But, truly, one doesn't have to see the ghost in order to experience the effect: the Ghost in the closet scene is invisible to Hamlet's mother, yet the effect on her of Hamlet's apparently wild actions, his holding discourse with the incorporeal air, and the communicated effect of his manifest fear and wonder—

> Forth at your eyes your spirits wildly peep;
> And, as the sleeping soldiers in th' alarm,
> Your bedded hairs, like life in excrements,
> Start up and stand an end. —

are characterized by the Ghost himself as an effect of amazement:

> But look, amazement on thy mother sits.
> 3. 4. 119-22, 112

Wonder is also an effect of the plot as a whole, and not merely of incident. Theseus and Hippolyta in *Midsummer Night's Dream* discuss the events of the same play, the plot of the criss-crossing lovers, from the point of view of literary criticism (the passage contains the famous remarks on "the poet's eye in a fine frenzy rolling"):

> HIPPOLYTA. 'Tis strange, my Theseus, that these lovers speak of.
> THESEUS. More strange than true. . . .
> HIPPOLYTA. But all the story of the night told over,
> And all their minds transfigur'd so together,
> More witnesseth than fancy's images
> And grows to something of great constancy;
> But howsoever, strange and admirable.
> 5. 1. 1-2 and 23-27

The plot, whether true or not, is certainly strange and wonderful *(admirable)*.

Wonder, however, is especially the effect of the denouement of those plays which the literary historian calls romances, especially if they conclude with a marvellous and surprising turn of events. Thus, in the *Winter's Tale* the "discovery" that Perdita is the King's daughter is described by the First Gentlemen as "a little amazedness." He goes on:

> . . . but the changes I perceived in the King and Camillo were very notes of admiration. They seem'd almost, with staring on one another, to tear the cases of their eyes. There was speech in their dumbness, language in their very gesture. They look'd as they had heard of a world ransom'd, or one destroyed. A notable passion of wonder appeared in them; but the wisest beholder that knew no more but seeing, could not say if th' importance were joy or sorrow; but in the extremity of the one it must needs be.

> 5. 2. 5-6, 9-21

He, however, had been commanded out of the chamber, and did not have the full story; hence, so far as he was concerned, it was "a little amazedness," provoked mainly by the wonder of the King and Camillo. The Second Gentleman, who now enters, is better informed and tells us:

> Such a deal of wonder is broken out within this hour that balladmakers cannot be able to express it.

> 5. 2. 25-7

Wonder, then, is the effect of the surprising and the marvellous; it is an extremity of feeling, and hence may be either joy or sorrow, fear or rapture. It is, if not the actual effect of such plots as the *Winter's Tale*, at least the effect aimed at. Thus Paulina, the mistress of ceremonies in the following scene, remarks as she discloses Hermione standing like a statue:

> I like your silence; it the more shows off
> Your wonder.

> 5. 3. 21-2

And the disclosure certainly has such an effect on Perdita; witness the King's speech:

217

O royal piece,
There's magic in thy majesty, which has. . .
From thy admiring daughter took the spirits,
Standing like stone with thee!

$$5. 3. 38-9, 41-2$$

But there is more wonder still! Paulina warns her audience that
they remain at their own risk:

Quit presently the chapel, or resolve you
For more amazement.

$$5. 3. 86-7$$

And when the King commands, "No foot shall stir," she speaks
to the statue:

'Tis time; descend; be stone no more; approach;
Strike all that look upon with marvel.

$$5. 3. 98-100$$

So, if the reader finds the events of the play improbable, that
is the point. They are intended to be improbable. The effect
aimed at is pleasurable wonder.

In comparable circumstances, at the denouement of the
serious plot of *Much Ado,* when Hero appears alive, the Friar
says:

All this amazement can I qualify . . .
Meantime let wonder seem familiar. . .

$$5. 4. 67 \text{ and } 70$$

Wonder, then, is associated not only with extreme fear but also
with extreme joy, and is marked by silence and immobility. It
is the shocked limit of feeling. Hence, Descartes a few years
later chose wonder as the first, and indeed the principal, passion
of the soul (*Les Passions du Ame,* 2. 53; 69-78).

It is easy to understand that the marvellous is intended to
be wonderful, whether in fact the reader finds it so or not.
But tragedy should not so fly from all probability. In what way,
then, does Shakespearean tragedy in general, and the tragic

218

catastrophe in particular, admit of the effect of wonder? I have already shown how certain conventional tragic incidents and certain conventional appurtenances of tragic atmosphere involve fear and wonder. But a tragedy is not merely a spectacle and a plot, it is also something written and spoken; it is in large measure a series of declamations. This is obviously true of Elizabethan tragedy and of Shakespearean.

In fact, the revolution in the English theatre of the 1580's out of which came the great plays of the succeeding decades consisted largely in the introduction of an adequate rhetoric. Nashe, for example, characterizes the pre-Shakespearean *Hamlet* and related plays as "handfuls of tragical speeches." Again, it is Greene's dying complaint against the companies of actors that he has been "of them forsaken," "those puppets . . . that spake from our mouths, those antics garnished in our colors" — that is, in our colors of rhetoric. It is his complaint against Shakespeare himself that he "supposes he is as well able to bombast out a blank verse as the best of" Greene's companions.[24] Marlowe's *Tamburlaine, Parts I* and *II* are, according to his printer, "tragical discourses"; and Marlowe himself enunciated in the prologue to *Tamburlaine I*, in those lines which constitute the charter of the greater Elizabethan tragedies, the rhetorical principle of high style in tragedy and its concomitant effect of wonder or astonishment:

> From jigging veins of rhyming mother wits
> And such conceits as clownage keeps in pay,
> We'll lead you to the stately tent of war
> Where you shall hear the Scythian Tamburlaine
> Threatening the world with high astounding terms
> And scourging kingdoms with his conquering sword.
> View but his picture in this tragic glass,
> And then applaud his fortunes as you please.

Though these lines have often been quoted, they are

worth noticing again, for they are packed with critical doctrine. They are a manifesto. The first two lines constitute an explicit rejection of the old theatrical tradition of the fourteener with its rhyme and its marked regularity of metre *(jigging veins)*; of the uneducated, unartful writer *(mother wits)*; and of the tradition of the irresponsible clown. In its stead is proposed the modulated and rhymeless line, and the wholly serious play. This play involves a high subject, *war*, and by implication and the enjoinment of decorum a *stately* style, a high and royal style. The effect will be largely one of language and of rhetoric, for there *you shall hear*, and you shall hear what is grand, or even grandiose, a *threatening the world*, expressed in *high astounding terms*.

Let us dwell on this phrase. A *term* is not any word, but a word belonging to a special vocabulary; so we speak of logical terms, and philosophical terms, and in the field of rhetoric there is, for example, that specialized literary diction which the Scots called "aureate terms." And Chaucer says in the *Canterbury Tales*:

> Youre termes, youre colours, and youre figures —
> Keep hem in stoor til so be that ye endite
> Heigh style, as whan that men to kinges write.
> *Clerk's Prologue*, 16-8

Tamburlaine will speak, then, in a choice and sifted language, the diction of *high* style, whose effect is here defined as that of wonder or astonishment, the *astounding*. This effect is supported by the kind of action involved, *scourging kingdoms with his conquering sword*.

The manifesto concludes with the proposition that the work of literature should merely present the object and leave the question of judgment to the spectator. This last, it seems to me, is Marlowe's one distinctive contribution to literary theory (I do not say that it is correct), and *Tamburlaine* is perhaps the only play of the period — perhaps the only play of Marlowe's — that clearly adheres to the doctrine. Yet it is only an extreme statement of a general trend in Elizabethan drama, the trend towards emancipating the story from the exemplum. However, it is the other ideas which are of concern here, and these ideas are the common critical property of the time. They enunciate the principle of high style, high characters, and high matters, to which Shakespeare gave allegiance, though a less thorough-going allegiance. The significance of this passage is that they are here expressed for the first time in Elizabethan drama, that they are expressed memorably, that the play to which these ideas are prologue is, if we leave aside Kyd and *The Spanish Tragedy*, the first notable application of the ideas, and, finally, that the play itself was a great success and had great influence on the course of Elizabethan drama.

The reader today is fairly unmoved by grand speeches, but the testimony of our fathers as to the overwhelming effect of the grand style is explicit and pretty unanimous. It should cause no surprise, then, to find that Shakespeare ascribes the quality of wonder to eloquence. He echoes *Tamburlaine* at the beginning of *I Henry the Sixth* (if the passage be indeed his); there the Dauphin, deeply impressed by Joan of Arc's long speech, exclaims seriously:

> Thou hast astonish'd me with thy high terms.
> 1. 2. 93

Again, in *Henry the Fifth* the Archbishop of Canterbury in delineating the ideal character of the King ascribes the same quality to the eloquence of theology and to the sweet style.

> Hear him but reason in divinity,
> And, all-admiring, with an inward wish
> You would desire the King were made a prelate. . .
> Turn him to any cause of policy,
> The Gordian knot of it he will unloose,
> Familiar as his garter; that, when he speaks,

221

> The air a charter'd libertine, is still,
> And the mute wonder lurketh in men's ears
> To steal his sweet and honey'd sentences. . .
>
> 1. 1. 38-40, 45-50

But the point is clear enough in *Hamlet* itself, and in connection with "tragical speeches." In the graveyard scene, after Laertes' outburst of rhetoric, Hamlet discloses himself and answers rant with rant:

> Nay, an thou'lt mouth,
> I'll rant as well as thou. . . .

> What is he whose grief
> Bears such an emphasis? whose phrase of sorrow
> Conjures the wand'ring stars, and makes them stand
> Like wonder-wounded hearers?
>
> 5. 1. 306-7, 277-80

The terms *emphasis* and *phrase* make quite clear that Hamlet refers to Laertes' style, which is at least intended to wound (that is, "to strike") the hearers with wonder.

Wonder in Shakespeare is the effect of tragic incident and tragic style, as well as of the marvellous turn in events. But this does not exhaust the complexity of the notion of wonder; one more strand at least remains to be unravelled. For the notion derives not only from the tradition of literary criticism, as the proper effect of marvellous events, and the tradition of rhetoric, as the proper effect of marvellous eloquence, but it derives also from the tradition of philosophy, in which wonder is the primary cause of learning.

Wonder, in this sense, is that which strikes our attention and provokes intensity of interest and intensity of curiosity. Hence it is obviously relevant to drama and fiction, for a story that does not interest us may as well not exist, as Mine Host will instruct us, who commented on the Monk's famous, but deadly, tragedies:

222

Sire Monk, namoore of this, so God you blesse! . . .
Nor certeinly, as that thise clerkes seyn,
Where as a man may have noon audience,
Noght helpeth it to tellen his sentence.

VII. 3978, 3990-2

It is especially relevant to the conclusions of Shakespearean plays, which are as persistently occupied with the explanation of "How these things came about" (*Hamlet*, 5. 2. 391) as are the conclusions of the modern detective story. For wonder, as the motive for acquiring knowledge, demands explanation and is satisfied by it. Now, to satisfy by explanation, though it may seem a misguided impulse to the modern reader who lives by the current maxim of "Never explain," was not unimportant to the Elizabethan: it is the chief concern of the dying Hamlet. He charges Horatio:

> report me and my cause aright
> To the unsatisfied. . . .
> O good Horatio, what a wounded name
> (Things standing thus unknown) shall live behind me!
> If thou didst ever hold me in thy heart,
> Absent thee from felicity awhile,
> And in this harsh world draw thy breath in pain,
> To tell my story.

5. 2. 350-1,355-60

For this reason, to satisfy the unsatisfied as to Hamlet's motives and actions, Horatio soon summarizes the events of the play, but not for this reason only. The unexplained gives scope to the irrational: hence

> let this same be presently perform'd
> Even while men's minds are wild, lest more mischance
> On plots and errors happen.

5. 2. 404-6

There is, then, in the resolution of wonder a kind of *catharsis*, a further effect of the effect of the catastrophe, and one appropriate to Shakespearean drama. To understand is to acquiesce. The movement of the drama is from this point of view an increasing intensity of interest which culminates in the striking events of the climax. These astonish the spectator so that he stands for the moment stone-still, but at the same time they demand explanation, and with the explanation his emotion subsides and order prevails, as on the stage at the close of the play order prevails in the state.

Certainly the philosophical notion of wonder enters into the explanation of the catastrophe. In the passage already cited from *Much Ado*, the Friar hastens to remark on the marvel of the catastrophe:

> All this amazement can I qualify,
> When, after that the holy rites are ended,
> I'll tell you largely of fair Hero's death.
>
> 5. 4. 67-9

First wonder, then explanation. So also in *As You Like It* Hymen, who enters to conclude the comedy, speaks thus:

> Peace ho! I bar confusion.
> 'Tis I must make conclusion
>   Of these most strange events . . .
> Whiles a wedlock hymn we sing,
> Feed yourselves with questioning,
> That reason wonder may diminish
> How thus we met, and these things finish.
>
> 5. 4. 131-3 and 143-6

And the general scheme is very well explained by Quince, as prologue to the "tragical mirth" that concludes *Midsummer Night's Dream*:

> Gentles, perchance you wonder at this show;
> But wonder on, till truth make all things plain.
>
> 5. 1. 128-9

224

To sum up: the primary effect of tragedy is sorrow or woe, of which pity is a species. The tragic atmosphere and the incidents leading to the catastrophe are fearful. This is the Donatan tradition in which the tragic fact is violent, unexpected death, and corresponds to the medieval tradition of psychology in which the anticipation of death is fearful and its accomplishment woful. But since the catastrophe is unexpected, it will startle the audience, and so the emotion of fear which has accompanied the course of tragic incident will become attached in special measure to the catastrophe. But this will be that fear which results from external events: wonder, astonishment, or shocked surprise. Hence woe and wonder are the effects of the tragic spectacle. Horatio's phrase, then, as is Sidney's, is only a distillation of the tradition, and *woe* is even a more proper term than pity, *wonder* than fear.

In the preceding section, I have cited texts in which Shakespeare explicitly names wonder as an effect of tragic incident, of tragic style, and as the principal effect of the catastrophe of those non-tragical plays which involve marvellous events, being the natural correlative of marvels and the motive for understanding them. But is wonder named in any other work of Shakespeare as an effect of the tragic catastrophe, or does it appear only in the one passage from *Hamlet?* Again, is it customary to name explicitly the intended effect at the end of other Elizabethan plays?

It will be expected that woe or pity will be the most commonly named, and in fact there are more texts than anyone wishes to look through. To cite one example, the anonymous *Tragedy of Locrine* is drenched with mournful complaints. These occur after each of the successive tragic catastrophes which constitute the play (1. 1. 227 ff.; 3. 1. 1 ff.; and especially 43 ff.; 3. 6. 1 ff.; 5. 1. 1 ff. and especially 16 ff.), but most notably at the end. Here in Estrild's lament over the death of Locrine, the concept of lamentation and pity is explicitly associated with the concept of tragedy as involving both the fall and death of the great, and the lesson of the instability of this world — for here as in glass we plainly see that all our life is but as a tragedy, a confused chaos of mishaps:

> Break, heart, with sobs and generous suspires!
> Stream forth, you tears, from forth my watery eyes!
> Help me to mourn for warlike Locrine's death!
> Pour down your tears, you watery regions,
> For mighty Locrine is bereft of life!
> O fickle Fortune! O unstable world!
> What else are all things that this globe contains
> But a confused chaos of mishaps?
> Wherein as in a glass we plainly see
> That all our life is but as a tragedy,
> Since mighty kings are subject to mishap . . .
>
> 5. 4. 111-21[25]

But the effect of wonder is common enough. In Greene's *Orlando Furioso* the Emperor of Africa, who is the representative of the state, replies after hearing an account of the action from Orlando:

> I stand amazed, deep overdrenched with joy,
> To hear and see this unexpected end:
> So will I rest content.
>
> 5. 2. 1425-7[26]

This is the kind of wonder we have already met at the end of the *Winter's Tale*. Of like kind is the effect of the discovery in Marston's *Malcontent* that Malevole is Altofont, the former and legitimate Duke of Genoa:

> MALEVOLE. Banish amazement; come, we four must stand
> Full shock of fortune. Be not so wonder stricken. . . .
> PIETRO. . . . Give leave to recollect
> My thoughts dispersed in wild astonishment.
>
> 4. 5

This is the principal catastrophe of the play, though there follows in the fifth act, amid masquing and comedy, a second reversal — the fall of Mendoza. Of a similar nature is the discovery of Andrugio at the end of Marston's *Antonio and Mellida:*

> We are amazed, our royal spirits numbed
> In stiff astonished wonder at thy prowess . . .

And, a little later, when Antonio rises from the coffin:

> Stand not amazed, great states! . . .
> Most wished spectators of my tragedy. . . .

There is a different, but not too dissimilar, kind in the 1610 *Mucedorus,* the version played before King James. Here Comedy and Envy in the Epilogue suddenly kneel before the majesty of James:

> ENVY. My power has lost her might; Envy's date's expired.
> Yon splendent majesty hath felled my sting,
> And I amazed am. *Fall down and quake.*
>
> 65-7[28]

But for wonder as the immediate effect of the catastrophe of a tragic, rather than of a comic or heroic, catastrophe, Shakespeare himself gives precedent. The catastrophe of Shakespeare's poem the *Rape of Lucrece* is Lucrece's suicide — at which:

> Stone-still, astonish'd with this deadly deed,
> Stood Collatine and all his lordly crew. . .
>
> 1730-1

This is the wonder that is a species of fear; but, as the shock subsides, woe and pity rise:

> About the mourning and congealed face
> Of that black blood a wat'ry rigoll goes,
> Which seems to weep upon the tainted place;
> And ever since, as pitying Lucrece' woes,
> Corrupted blood some watery token shows, . . .
>
> 1744-48

The poem ends finally with Brutus' speech, which again provokes wonder:

> This said, he struck his hand upon his breast
> And kiss'd the fatal knife to end his vow;
> And to his protestation urg'd the rest,
> Who, wond'ring at him, did his words allow.
>
> 1842-5

Quite parallel to this is the conclusion of Jonson's *Sejanus*.
Here signs and prodigies precede the fall of Sejanus:

> But now a fiery meteor in the form
> Of a great ball was seen to roll along
> The troubled air, where yet it hangs unperfect,
> The amazing wonder of the multitude!
>
> 5. 4. 48-51

The fall itself provokes wonder:

> MACRO. Wherefore, fathers,
> Sit you amazed and silent . . .
>
> 5. 10. 246-7

But the final effect is a curious kind of terror, emotionally
rather subtle, for, though terror is not directly named, no one
can miss it: the more our pity is solicited in the subsequent
speeches for the attendant circumstances of Sejanus' fall, the
more our terror rises. The pity which these accounts summon
is really a kind of aghast terror at the mob and at the political
corruption which still persists and is not resolved with Sejanus'
fall. The pity we feel is certainly not pity for Sejanus himself,
who had disclaimed any such softness:

> When I do fear again, let me be struck
> With forked fire, and unpitied die . . .
>
> 5. 6. 75-6

to whom it had been denied by Macro:

> And no man take compassion of thy state . . .
>
> 5. 10. 242

228

and whose fall is described thus by Lepidus:

> And this man fall! Fall? Ay, without a look
> That durst appear his friend, or lend so much
> Of vain relief to his changed state as pity!
>
> 5. 10. 283-5

Finally Arruntius at the very end of the play sums it all up:

> Forbear, you things
> That stand upon the pinnacles of state
> To boast your slippery height: when you do fall
> You pash yourselves to pieces, ne'er to rise;
> And he who lends you pity is not wise.
>
> 5. 10. 458-62[29]

The immediate effect of the fall is wonder, but its final effect is a terror begotten by the detailing of the occasions for pity. But the pity is simply for the human state and the innocent bystanders; there can be no real pity for the fall of a thorough villain. And here is disclosed how fear or terror enters properly into the catastrophe of an Elizabethan play. We feel pity for the death of the good and for death itself, but the violent end of the wicked begets fear. Thus Shakespeare's Queen Margaret anticipates the fall of Richard III:

> But at hand, at hand
> Ensues his piteous and unpitied end.
>
> 4. 4. 73-4

and Richmond later comes from the field of battle:

> God and your arms be prais'd, victorious friends!
> The day is ours; the bloody dog is dead.
>
> 5. 5. 1-2

Contrast this with Bolingbroke's comment on Richard II, who was weak but not villainous:

> Lords, I protest my soul is full of woe
> That blood should sprinkle me to make me grow.

229

Come, mourn with me for what I do lament. . .
                            5. 6. 45-7

In like fashion the death of Macbeth is not mourned — he is
spoken of as "this dead butcher and his fiendlike queen" (5. 8.
69) — though that of Siward's son is:

> Your cause of sorrow
> Must not be measur'd by his worth, for then
> It hath no end.
>   5. 8. 44-6

   Sorrow and pity are reserved for the deaths of the good,
or for the human fact itself — even Richard III's end will
be piteous, though unpitied. Hence, at the end of *Lear*, Albany,
the representative of the state, says after the deaths of Lear and
Cordelia:

> Bear them from hence. Our present business
> Is general woe.
>   5. 3. 318-19

But on the earlier reported deaths of Goneril and Regan, one
of whom was his wife, he only says:

> This judgement of the heavens, that makes us tremble,
> Touches us not with pity.
>   5. 3. 231-2

Fear, then, is the effect of the violent death of the wicked as
distinguished from that of the good, whose fall evokes sorrow
and pity.

   The striking effect of pity and sorrow is explicitly named
at the end of two later Shakespearean tragedies. Octavian, the
representative of the state, sums up *Antony and Cleopatra:*

> High events as these
> Strike those that make them; and their story is
> No less in pity than his glory which
> Brought them to be lamented.
>   5. 2. 363-6

230

The verb *strike* here denotes the effect of wonder — at least, this is its ordinary meaning. Aufidius utters similar sentiments at the end of *Coriolanus:*

> My rage is gone,
> And I am struck with sorrow. Take him up.

Again, to be struck is the effect of wonder. Consequently, these three plays at least — *Hamlet, Anthony and Cleopatra, Coriolanus* — together with the *Rape of Lucrece,* are intended explicitly to evoke the emotional effect of woe and wonder.

From the later tradition I will quote only the following close parallel: The Cardinal in Middleton's *Women Beware Women* characterizes the catastrophe thus:

> The greatest sorrow and astonishment
> That ever struck the general peace of Florence
> Dwells in this hour.
>
> 5. 1. 240-2[30]

V

Reason Panders Will

The emotional effect of the catastrophe, of course, is not equivalent to the experience of the work. It is a final element in that experience, enters into it, and in part determines it. But there is more to the experience of art than the emotional effect even of the whole, and certainly more than the effect of the conclusion. There is, among other things, the experience of the language of the work. (There is, especially in the Renaissance, the intellectual experience of persistent sententious thought. And there is in the typical play the central intellectual experience of plotting, counter-plotting, and mistakes: the events of *Hamlet* are characterized by Horatio at the end of the play as "mischance" that "on plots and errors happen" (5. 2. 405-6). This is an experience of the same sort as that of a game of chess, and is like chess intense in its kind, for though it is intellectual it is not without emotion: otherwise it would not be experience. Nevertheless, the other aspects of a work are related to the effect of the conclusion, and not only as elements in the larger experience of the whole. They are related in this way: though the effect itself is largely a result of the bare fact, of what happens, it is not sufficient merely to attain an effect; the effect must be justified. We must acquiesce in the conclusion.

We acquiesce out of a feeling of inevitability: what will be will be. But what is the source of this feeling? A conclusion is inevitable *within the closed system of a work of art* when it satisfies a pattern or principle of order acceptable to the audience. Such patterns are of different kinds, some larger, some smaller. They may be external, as, for example, the full circuit of Fortune's wheel, the fulfilment of the retributive justice of

God, or the progression from order to disorder, concluding sadly in deaths. The pattern may exhibit the causal sequence of realistic fiction, which consists in an exemplification of a syllogistic conclusion (more precisely, an enthymeme) made persuasive. For a causal sequence shows a probable course of action, and by probability we mean a conformity to some accepted commonplace about how men of a certain type will behave under certain conditions. This is persuasive when sharply and compellingly presented so that we do not explicitly recognize the syllogistic nature of the conclusion. We merely believe it, speak of it as if it were really determined, and hence inevitable. We say the conclusion was logical.

The pattern may, however, be internal and involve artistic foreshadowing and completion, suggestion and fulfilment. Artistic devices of this nature are usually referred to and grounded on the personality of the characters, and so exhibit that adjustment of feeling which comprises the ethics of sensibility. Or, and this is quite different, the pattern may be internal and involve the structure of character. In this case it will exhibit responsibility and moral choice, and will exemplify the ethics of character. Of this sort is the pattern or principle of order which is the subject of this essay. It is only one among many, but it will serve to illustrate the kinds of principles I have in mind and the relationship of these to the emotional effect of the conclusion.

The basic text for this principle of order in Renaissance tragedy is the definition of tragedy in Averroës' paraphrase of Aristotle's *Poetics*, which was current throughout the later Middle Ages and was probably more widely reprinted in the Renaissance than the work of any other commentator. The definition reads:

> Tragedy is the imitative representation of a notable action, brought to completion by a voluntary decision, and having in it a certain force of generalization with respect to matters of

some import, as distinguished from a particular proposition about some individual fact. By means of this imitative representation there is induced in the minds of the audience a rightness of feeling which springs from the pity and terror which the representation begets in them.[1]

The final effect of tragedy according to this definition is ethical: it results in an ordering of the irrational by means of a presentation which evokes specific emotional effects. The internal spring of the plot is a willed act, or moral choice. The final cause is right feeling, which is obviously the correlative of the ethical principle of right reason. This rightness of feeling comes through the tragic emotions, but apparently the effective cause of ordered feeling is the force of generalization in the plot. The universal here is an immanent power, not explicit or allegorical, and not singular or particular.[2]

Some of the greater tragedies of Shakespeare correspond well enough to this definition, which supplements the Donatan tradition with, among other principles, the principle of action involving moral choice. But choice in tragedy is usually a choice of evil, and hence the question in Renaissance terms is one of sin. How does a man sin? There are two main views in the Renaissance, the intellectualist view of the Aristotelian and Thomistic tradition, and the voluntarist view whose tradition is more complex. In the former the act of sin is primarily intellectual so that the process involves erroneous reasoning: action follows on reasoned deliberation as the conclusion of a syllogism follows on its premises. The will is considered to be subservient to reason and to embrace almost necessarily what reason proposes. Erroneous choice, then, from this position will be ascribed primarily to sophistry. Practical reason in the possession of the immutable principles of right action fails in the particular application, and so sins. In Duns Scotus' phrase, "We sin by paralogism." For the will never moves except "under the show of goodness," as Thomas says,[3] or, as Iago puts it in *Othello*:

> Divinity of hell!
> When devils will the blackest sins put on,
> They do suggest at first with heavenly shows,
> As I do now.
>
> 2. 3. 356-9

We may account for sin, then, by saying that it is the result of a logical confusion, a failure to discriminate between *a* good and *the* good. Thus in the case of Macbeth it will be granted that the kingship is *a* good, but it was not for Macbeth *the* good. The irrational part of the soul, the passions and perturbations, will affect man, so long as he remains man and is in the possession of his faculties, only to the extent that his reason may be sophisticated so that he accepts invalid for valid argument. For, "if the passions of the mind be strong," Hooker relates, "they easily sophisticate the understanding; they make it apt to believe upon very slender warrant, and to imagine infallible truth where scarcely any probable show appeareth" (*EP*, 5. Dedication). In brief, reason is not dethroned or suspended, but is perverted, commits an error in logic, and is actively enlisted on the side of false desire. The process is one of reasonable choice though the reasonableness be unreasonable. It is briefly summed up in a phrase in *Hamlet:* "reason panders will."

The phrase occurs in the closet scene. It is in its context the last and most violent in a series of illustrations of the perversion of the natural order of things. Hamlet says to his mother:

> Rebellious hell,
> If thou canst mutine in a matron's bones,
> To flaming youth let virtue be as wax
> And melt in her own fire. Proclaim no shame
> When the compulsive ardour gives the charge,
> Since frost itself as actively does burn,
> And reason panders will.
>
> 3. 4. 82-8

235

Rhetorically, this is a very curious passage. It is a series of adynata, of impossibilities. As such, it employs the tritest device of classical and Renaissance rhetoric. We are accustomed to sigh when we meet it. But these are adynata in an ethical context; they are impossibilities only to right reason and uncorrupted nature. To be sure, frost from the point of view of Renaissance science cannot burn as if it were active. But every observer of Renaissance and fallen man knew that lust not only could but regularly did break out, even in those in whom by age and station it was especially indecorous. And every Christian knew that man was inherently sinful, and that the state of sin was that in which reason pandered will. Yet he knew that these perversions of the due order were not right, and he would feel the moral horror that Hamlet, and Shakespeare, expresses by this rhetorical device: the horror that these impossibilities, repugnant to Reason and true Nature, should be not merely possible but actual and in our sense almost natural.

The phrase, then, expresses nothing new in the history of thought. The idea is at least as old as Aristotle; it is, in fact, a compendious statement of the Aristotelian analysis of the act of erroneous moral choice which had been taken up, developed, and rendered almost conventional by a long line of medieval and Renaissance philosophers. In this tradition when reason panders will the due and proper subordination of the irrational to the rational is overturned, and overturned the more grievously in that reason is not merely suspended or dethroned but is actively enlisted in the service of desire. The man who is swept away by emotion acts unreasonably and wrongly but not perversely; the man whose reason is bent to further his unreasonable desires is in that measure diabolical.

As idea, then, it was available and in a sense trite. It had already been employed by Shakespeare, most clearly in one passage which may be regarded as the direct ancestor of this. The passage is in the reply of Adonis to the arguments of

Venus in *Venus and Adonis,* for it was the quaint device of the Elizabethans to believe in discourse of reason, and they would seem, if we may accept the testimony of their literature, even to have attempted seduction by the method of disputation, and by the same method to have repelled it. Such is the case with Comus and the Lady in Milton's poem. And as the Lady in *Comus* extricates herself from the designs of the villain by opposing true reason to false reasoning, true love to earthly lust:

> I had not thought to have unlockt my lips
> In this unhallowed air but that this juggler
> Would think to charm my judgement as mine eyes,
> Obtruding false rules pranked in reason's garb.
>
> 756-9

so Adonis answers Venus' arguments and defines in context the nature of sin:

> What have you urg'd that I cannot reprove?
> The path is smooth that leadeth on to danger.
> I hate not love, but your device in love,
> That lends embracements unto every stranger.
> You do it for increase. O strange excuse,
> When reason is the bawd to lust's abuse!
>
> 787-92

Here the idea is more fully and more analytically presented than in the phrase in *Hamlet,* though less fully and less analytically than in Thomas or Aristotle. To achieve the later phrase there remained only to subject this passage to the Shakespearean transmutation: to turn idea into intuition, to condense it to three words, and by the metaphorical *panders,* a violent and sensuous word, to exhibit reason and will as sinful and shabby figures in a disreputable world.

But though this was the orthodox view, resting on the long Aristotelian tradition, it was not the only view at that time. Erroneous action was often presented in Elizabethan drama as the result of the dethroning of reason. This latter possibility is allowed for in the Scholastic scheme, for it is an

237

obvious fact of experience, but it is minimized. Thomas says, for example, that in cases of sudden and violent emotion, when reason cannot come to the opposition, mortal sin is not involved. But this is only a limiting case. For if the passion, say of love or anger, were in its origin voluntary the consequences would involve sin even though the passion took away the use of reason entirely. The critical point of decision is simply moved further back. Only if the cause were not voluntary but natural, as for example some bodily sickness, would the consequences be excused of sin (*ST*, 1-2. 77. 7).

Nevertheless, interest in the limiting case grew in the Renaissance. The full history of this development is somewhat obscure but the principal lines are clear. In the first place, there was the development of a mechanistic psychology, the Galenic psychology of humors, with its emphasis on the involuntariness of strong passion; the most famous text in English is Burton's *Anatomy of Melancholy.* In the second place, there was the development of a voluntaristic metaphysics in the Franciscan school associated with the name of Duns Scotus, and the subsequent extension of this point of view to ethics. The issue of this movement was the predestinarianism of the Reformation with its emphasis on the helplessness of man, and particularly of his reason, and the corollary interest in Stoic Fate, which was supported by the prestige of Seneca's tragedies. Here, especially in the *Phaedra,* as also in Ovid's Medea, were classic exemplars of tragic characters swept away by an overmastering passion: "I see the better course, and approve of it; I follow the worse."[4] It is curious that this view of human action which ascribes to the will, the faculty of inner motion in man, the ultimate control of his destiny should in practice have issued often in an extreme determinism. Perhaps this is a sign of the thoroughgoing rationalism of the period; the more the will was considered to be irresponsible to the dictates of reason and free to act arbitrarily, the more some principle of compulsion must be invoked to account for the irresponsible arbitrariness

238

of the will.

But whatever the reasons, there are at least four sorts of compulsion to be found in Elizabethan drama. There is, first, the compulsion which is accounted for by a mechanistic physiology and psychology, a type that has been studied a good deal in recent years, notably by Mr. Hardin Craig. He points out, for example, that the sudden and apparently unmotivated jealousy of Leontes in the *Winter's Tale* is explainable in such terms:[5]

> Too hot, too hot!
> To mingle friendship far, is mingling bloods.
> I have tremor cordis on me; my heart dances,
> But not for joy; not joy.
>
> 1. 2. 108-10

I have tremor cordis on me. But Leontes' jealousy is conceived also as voluntaristic, as involving the primacy of feeling. This is explicit in the key line of the speech in which Leontes embraces his unjustified jealousy:

> Can thy dam—may't be?
> Affection! thy intention stabs the centre.
>
> 1. 2. 137-8

Affection denotes the passions, emotions, and feelings which are associated with the will in the moving faculty of the soul, as distinguished from the rational faculty to which the will is attached as the rational appetite. *Intention* denotes the directed movement of a faculty of the soul toward realizing a possibility. It is that which is required to raise the potentiality of knowledge to act, and it is also the movement by which the rational will tends toward and embraces the end of action proposed by reason.[6] The passage means, then, that affection directing its own movement, penetrates to the knowledge of the fact which gives the grounds for being jealous, and at the same time embraces the decision to be jealous. Hence we may translate Leontes' speech into modern terms: "Feeling rather

239

than reason hits the mark and furnishes the decision." This is explicit voluntarism.

The third type of compulsion is that exercised by the Stoic Fate, and operating often through the influence of the stars. The fourth is the theological compulsion of grace and predestination. The two are conjoined and offered as alternative explanations of the tragic action in Heywood's *A Woman Killed with Kindness*. The tragic villain speaks:

> I am a villian if I apprehend
> But such a thought! Then, to attempt the deed,
> Slave, thou art damn'd without redemption.—
> I'll drive away this passion with a song.
> A song! Ha, ha! A song! As if, fond man,
> Thy eyes could swim in laughter, when thy soul
> Lies drench'd and drowned in red tears of blood!
> I'll pray, and see if God within my heart
> Plant better thoughts. Why, prayers are meditations,
> And when I meditate (oh, God forgive me!)
> It is on her divine perfections.
> I will forget her; I will arm myself
> Not t'entertain a thought of love to her;
> And, when I come by chance into her presence,
> I'll hale these balls until my eye-strings crack,
> From being pull'd and drawn to look that way.
> > *Enter, over the Stage, Frankford, his Wife,*
> > *and Nick*
> O God, O God! With what a violence
> I'm hurried to mine own destruction!
> > 2. 3. 1-18

And again:

> I will not; zounds! I will not. I may choose,
> And I will choose. Shall I be so misled,
> Or shall I purchase to my father's crest
> The motto of a villain? If I say
> I will not do it, what thing can enforce me?
> What can compel me? What sad destiny

240

Hath such command upon my yielding thoughts?
I will not;—ha! Some fury pricks me on;
The swift fates drag me at their chariot wheel,
And hurry me to mischief.

                                        2. 3. 96-105

The tragic action follows. And since the first citation above is a soliloquy and the second an aside, they may be taken as representing the view of tragic motivation which the author himself proffers. This is one of sheer fatalism. The character attempts to distract his thoughts, as Thomas for example suggests he should (*ST*, 1-2. *77*. 2: "Whether reason can be overcome by passion against its knowledge"), but the divine sensuality of love overpowers him. He attempts to exercise rational choice, but fury and Fate hurry him to mischief, and with him the other characters. He sees the better course and approves it, but follows the worse. Yet an alternative explanation, which could be regarded as the same explanation under another aspect, is given at the end of the play. Here the leading character, a good man, sums up the whole:

> God, that hath laid this cross upon our heads,
> Might (had He pleas'd) have made our cause of meeting
> On a more fair and more contented ground;
> But He that made us made us to this woe.[7]

For what seems to man to be a result of Fate or fury is but the concealed operation of the Providence of God.

The contrast between the intellectual and voluntarist positions can be made clear by comparing Sextus Tarquin's soliloquy before committing the rape in Heywood's play *The Rape of Lucrece* with the similar soliloquy in Shakespeare's poem of the same title. In the former Tarquin enters Lucrece's bedchamber carrying a drawn sword and a lighted taper. He speaks:

> I am bound
> Upon a black adventure, on a deed
> That must wound virtue and make beauty bleed.

Pause, Sextus, and, before thou runnst thyself
Into this violent danger, weigh thy sin. . .
    Back! yet thy fame
Is free from hazard and thy style from shame.
O Fate! thou hast usurped such power o'er man
That where thou pleadst thy will no mortal can. . .
    Forward still!
To make thy lust live, all thy virtues kill.

                                              4. 3[8]

Certainly reasonable deliberation in the sense of rational awareness is involved here as it was in the previous citation from *A
Woman Killed with Kindness*. But it does not enter into the
decision. The character in the grip of strong emotion must act
contrary to the dictates of reason: Fate sweeps him on. He
makes no attempt to justify his sin; the end is not presented
under the show of goodness.

But in Shakespeare's poem the poet himself explains the
course of Tarquin's soliloquy:

Thus, graceless, holds he disputation
'Tween frozen conscience and hot burning will,
And with good thoughts makes dispensation,
Urging the worser sense for vantage still;
Which in a moment doth confound and kill
    All pure effects, and doth so far proceed
    That what is vile shows like a virtuous deed.

                                              246-52

God for his own inscrutable reasons does not assist Tarquin on
this occasion with his grace *(Thus, graceless)*. Hence Tarquin
must reach this moral decision on a human and ethical plane.
And how is the process described? It is described in medieval
terms as the holding of a disputation. In this disputation
Tarquin urges the worser sense for vantage still; reason is
actively enlisted in the service of desire. When the process
reaches the point of decision it doth in a moment confound all

pure effects, for Tarquin by the decision has sinned mortally. Consequently, the undoing—not of his character, really, in the modern sense, but of his moral principle—doth so far proceed that what is vile shows like a virtuous deed. He sins by paralogism under the show of goodness.

II

The act of decision in the intellectualist tradition has as a further characteristic mark that it is divided into two steps: the choice of the end *(intentio)* and the choice of means *(electio)*. The steps are distinct, though the second is dependent on the first (*ST*, 1-2. 8. 3). I shall now analyze two scenes in Shakespearean tragedy, one in *Othello* and one in *Macbeth*, each of which portrays an act of moral choice that leads to the catastrophe; and I shall conclude with a discussion of the whole scope of *Hamlet*.

The scene in *Othello* concerns the choice of the end, for there is here no serious question of means. Othello has it in his power to kill Desdemona at any time, and presuming his grounds are correct the killing is justified. "Cassio did top her," he says to Emilia:

> Oh, I were damn'd beneath all depth in hell
> But that I did proceed upon just grounds
> To this extremity.
>
> 5. 2. 136-9

As for the death of Cassio, Iago promises to take care of that. The only question, then, is the question of fact; for it is assumed in the play, and made more plausible by locating the action in Venice and Cyprus, that if Desdemona has been unfaithful she must die.

The action of the play, so far as it concerns the moral act, is roughly this: Iago plants in Othello's mind the idea that his wife may be unfaithful, and he does it so skilfully that he is not himself open to attack. The mere idea is sufficient to upset most men:

> Dangerous conceits are in their nature poisons
> Which at the first are scarce found to distaste,
> But with a little act upon the blood
> Burn like the mines of sulphur.
>
> 3. 3. 326-9

But Iago does more than plant the idea; he insinuates a number of fairly vivid and violent images; he raises an efficient head of passion. More than this, he brings to bear on the question a number of commonplaces which make the fact more credible: women are weak; most husbands are cuckolds. He shows that in this special situation infidelity is even more likely, for as Desdemona has deceived her father so she may deceive him. Besides, there is the fact of their disproportion in race, in age, and in social position. Any man would be almost convinced of his wife's infidelity after such insinuation.

But its effect on Othello is only to get him into a passion in which he may do anything. He may even, as he threatens, kill Iago. At this point Iago intervenes with an appeal to reason:

> Are you a man? have you a soul? or sense?[9]
>
> 3. 3. 374

That is, "Are you a man or beast? Have you a rational soul, since reason is the distinguishing characteristic of man? or merely sense, the sensitive soul, the distinguishing characteristic of animals?" He appeals to reason because he does not want to put Othello merely in a passion; there can be no directed action without a reasoned conclusion. And Othello answers this appeal by stating the disjunctive syllogism upon which the play turns:

> I think my wife be honest, and think she is not;
> I think that thou art just, and think thou art not.
> I'll have some proof.
>
> 3. 3. 384-6

244

But he has prefaced this with the statement, "Nay, stay. Thou shouldst be honest." And it has been reiterated throughout the play, not without purpose, that Iago is honest. So when the disjunction is presented almost in technical form: Either Iago is honest or Desdemona is honest, the conclusion that: Iago is honest, therefore Desdemona is not, is almost guaranteed by the assumption that Iago is. Hence Othello goes on:

> Her name, that was as fresh
> As Dian's visage, is now begrim'd and black
> As mine own face.

Nevertheless, Othello's feeling is so strong he does not yet assent; he demands some proof. If he cannot see his wife strumpeted before his eyes, let him at least have some circumstantial sign. However, as Iago has confided to the audience (3. 3. 321-4), Othello, in the distraught state of mind in which he is prepared to assent to the syllogism proposed, will accept as proof the flimsiest trifle of a sign, a mere handkerchief which he saw really but a moment ago. When to this is added Iago's account of Cassio's remarks in his sleep, which is accepted substantially as testimony to a confession on Cassio's part, the cause is finished. Othello consents. "Patience, I say," Iago interposes, "your mind perhaps may change." "Never, Iago" (3. 3. 452-3). The choice is made and solemnly ratified by oath. The following scene (3. 4 together with 4. 1 and 2) supports the decision but is subsequent to it. The play moves on to the catastrophe.

No one cares to see such things happen. Nevertheless, we can acquiesce since we can see "How these things came about." A man "not easily jealous" is operated on by a skilful insinuator and becomes so "perplex'd in the extreme" that his passions easily sophisticate his understanding: "they make it apt to believe upon very slender warrant, and to imagine infallible truth where scarcely any probable show appeareth." Othello is perplexed both intellectually and emotionally, but primarily intellectually. For, as Francis Bacon relates in the *Advancement of Learning*, there is a seducement that works by the subtlety of the illaqueation and another by the strength of the impression. The latter overmasters the reason by power of sense and imagination; the former works by perplexing the reason.[10] The process is described more fully in a sermon by Bishop Andrewes with reference to the fall of Eve:

> For this is not the least policy of the Devil, not to set upon her bluntly, but like a serpent slily and slowly to creep in her little by little, until he has espied some vantage. Therefore his order is: to bring her from questioning in talk to a doubt in opinion, and from that to an error in judgement, and so at last to a corrupt action in practice. And to corrupt her mind within, first he useth this order, to tickle her ears with curiosity, and by that to cause her to have a giddiness and swimming in the brain by fantastical imaginations and surmises; and then to make her secure and careless of the truth, and so at last maketh her somewhat inclinable to error and falsehood.[11]

But Othello's transition to jealousy and sin has not seemed plausible to every reader. It is not true to life, we are told, and the theatrical convention of the calumniator credited has been invented to solve the difficulty.[12] But the crediting of calumny is no mere convention of the theatre; it is a fact of daily life The truth is, the modern critic is concerned to defend the niceness of life, to maintain that successful hypocrisy is unlikely, that no one omits speaking up when he should, that no decent husband suspects his precious wife, and that if he does they just talk it over like civilized people. Anyway, no woman of character will sleep with a man's best friend.

Such critics make the optimistic assumption that men are not likely to go wrong unless there is sufficient cause. But this is modern, and not too well founded in fact. The general assumption of the Renaissance was that men were not likely to go right unless there was a supernatural cause. "Such is the propensity of all creatures unto evil," Bishop Jewel says, "and the readiness of all men to suspect, that the things which neither have been done, nor once meant to be done, yet may be easily both heard and credited for true."[13] The modern critic feels that women do not tend to be unfaithful; the Renaissance man, who was still smarting under Eve's transgression, felt that women were pretty likely to be unfaithful if they only had a chance. He would take Othello's remarks on cuckoldry as hardly exaggerated:

> 'Tis destiny unshunnable, like death.
> Even then this forked plague is fated to us
> When we do quicken.
>
> 3. 3. 275-7

Furthermore, the appeal of Desdemona's innocency is much greater for the reader than it was for Othello; he knows she is innocent, which is precisely what Othello does not know.

Anyone who is willing to believe in evil, and personally I do not find this difficult to do, will not find Othello's jealousy implausible. He may be worried, however, that it all seems to happen in so short a time, and he may wonder just how it is that Othello seems to be convinced that his wife is unfaithful —not how Iago persuades him, for that is clear enough, but by what process he comes to accept the proposition himself. I have held that the process is the traditional one of moral choice and intellectualist in character. For all his passion Othello is not swept away; he is presented with a disjunctive syllogism, draws what seems to him a proper conclusion, confirms the conclusion with a sign, and proceeds upon what he thinks are just grounds to this extremity. The process of choice, itself, takes place in a point of time and is properly represented as occurring within a single scene.

The restriction of the process of choice to a point of time and a single scene contributes to the feeling of implausibility. Our natural tendency, as can be seen in the novel, is to consider the process of choice as distributed through a number of scenes and as in large measure unconscious. We tend to find the condensed incredible and the diffused plausible. We regard decision as so implicated in the circumstances that condition it that neither can profitably be distinguished from the other. We can believe anything if only it be an indistinct compound of environment and heredity, and if we can be persuaded that it has evolved. For what is perhaps the greatest single difference between our habits of thought and those of the Middle Ages and Renaissance is located in the problem of continuity. We believe in the continuous. We believe that contraries shade off into each other. We believe a character is real when he is neither good nor bad but a middling gray. We disbelieve in, though we have not yet disproved, the law of the excluded middle. But the Renaissance believed firmly in Aristotelian logic: for them, B was either A or Not-A.

They also believed firmly in sin and repentance, each of which takes place in a point of time. Sin and grace were precise contraries that could not shade off into each other. Hence their view of the moral life was radically different from ours; it was essentially theological. Man's destiny hung on each decisive act, a life of grace could be cancelled by one mortal sin, and conversely the departing soul of an old and confirmed sinner could, though it was not likely, at the furthest margin of life repent of his sins and so pass joyously into the company of the elect. Such a view was held by both the great parties in the theological wars of the sixteenth century; it was proclaimed openly by those who emphasized man's free choice, but it was also maintained, if paradoxically maintained, by many of the fieriest proponents of predestination. For though a man be predestined to Hell, still he must wilfully embrace that act by which he is eternally condemned, for the responsibility must be his and not the predestinating God's. So likewise, if he be predestined to Heaven, though he make an ungodly life his profession, still at the predestined moment he shall have grace to repent and his will must embrace that repentance. It is clear, then, that the restriction of the process of choice in Elizabethan drama to a single scene is not the result merely of foreshortening and condensation for dramatic purposes, but is a result of the Elizabethan view of the moral life. At the same time, of course, it is more dramatic.

The process of the decisive choice of evil can be seen more clearly, and this time with respect to the choice of means, in one scene in *Macbeth*.[14] It is the seventh of the first act. Macbeth enters and announces in a soliloquy that he has already fallen from the state of grace, that he has preferred the show of goodness in things temporal to the solid goodness of things eternal:

> If it were done when 'tis done, then 'twere well
> It were done quickly. If th' assassination
> Could trammel up the consequence, and catch,
> With his surcease, success; that but this blow
> Might be the be-all and the end-all here,
> But here, upon this bank and shoal of time,
> We'ld jump the life to come.
>
> 1. 7. 1-7

His will has already moved to embrace the end, the kingship, but he is disturbed. He does not see how to accomplish it; he does not see how he can get away with the murder of Duncan:

> But in these cases
> We still have judgement here, that we but teach
> Bloody instructions, which, being taught, return
> To plague th' inventor.
>
> 1. 7. 7-10

Thus there is a consequent weakening of the will:

> I have no spur
> To prick the sides of my intent, but only
> Vaulting ambition, which o'erleaps itself
> And falls on th' other side.
>
> 1. 7. 25-8

Enter Lady Macbeth.

To understand what follows it will be well to recapitulate the requirements for a moral act. Reason must propose an end as good, and when the end is proposed the will moves naturally to embrace it. This has already happened in Macbeth, but it is not sufficient to constitute moral choice. The practical reason must discover means by which to accomplish the end *(consilium)*, and not until the means are available is the choice finally made. There must follow sufficient emotion *(consensus)* so that the choice is actually put into operation *(usus)*. This emotion precedes, accompanies, and follows the act of choice. It is the steam pressure that makes the engine move; there must be a certain excitement in the will to account for the step to choice and from choice to action. It is the office of rhetoric to supply this excitement; its function is to persuade. So Bacon defines it in a passage that has often been quoted but usually not properly understood: "The duty and office of rhetoric is to apply reason to imagination for the better moving of the will."[15] By *apply* here is meant "to put into practical contact with," so that if one were to use these words in a modern context he would rather say that imagination is applied to reason.

The traditional analysis, popularized and lacking the complication of multiplied distinctions, is expounded by the character of Tragedy himself in a play which was presented by Shakespeare's company (ca. 1598) a few years before *Hamlet*. *A Warning to Fair Women* begins with an argument between Tragedy, Comedy, and History. Later in the play, at the moment of moral choice, Tragedy steps forward and explains the process:

> Prevailing sin having by three degrees
> Made his ascension to forbidden deeds,
> At first, alluring their unwary minds
> To like what she proposed, then practising
> To draw them to consent; and, last of all,
> Ministering fit means and opportunity

To execute what she approved good;
Now she unveils their sight, and lets them see
The horror of their foul immanity.

                                    2. 865-74[16]

But to return to *Macbeth*. He has embraced the end, and
now falters in resolution because he does not see how the end
can be accomplished. There is required now fit means and
opportunity to execute what he approved good, together with
a concurrent sustaining and heightening of resolution, the
maintaining of an efficient head of passion. To fulfill this last
requirement, the Ghost had appeared to Hamlet in the closet
scene, and for the same reason Hamlet was made to observe
Fortinbras and his army marching across "a plain in Denmark."
For the same reason in this scene Lady Macbeth speaks in such
shockingly violent terms:

> I have given suck, and know
> How tender 'tis to love the babe that milks me.
> I would, while it was smiling in my face,
> Have pluck'd my nipple from his boneless gums
> And dash'd the brains out, had I so sworn as you
> Have done to this.
>
>   1. 7. 54-9

So also, to Macbeth's assertion:

> I dare do all that may become a man.
> Who dares do more is none.

which is sound doctrine, implying the notion of decorum and
the mean, Lady Macbeth answers with the old commonplace
that Iago had used, of soul and sense, distinguishing man from
beast through the characteristic of willed action:

> What beast was't then
> That made you break this enterprise to me?
> When you durst do it, then you were a man;
> And to be more than what you were, you would
> Be so much more the man.
>
>   1. 7. 46-51

This is obvious sophistry. It makes the will and not reason the distinguishing characteristic of man; it opposes rashness to timidity, excluding from consideration the reasonable mean of right courage. But it takes Macbeth in. His only question now is as to the means: "If we should fail?" Lady Macbeth outlines the way in which the murder can be accomplished and suspicion diverted. As soon as the means are proposed Macbeth assents and the moral choice is complete:

> I am settled and bend up
> Each corporal agent to this terrible feat.
> 1. 7. 79-80

This final decision of the soul, accompanied of course by disordered emotion, persists unaltered through the catastrophe.

But in *Hamlet* the process of moral choice extends throughout the play. The first half is concerned with the choice of end, which rests here as in *Othello* on a question of fact: did Claudius really kill the old King, Hamlet's father? or, what is the same question, is the Ghost a true ghost or a diabolical apparition? To resolve this question of fact Hamlet devises the play scene as an *experimentum crucis*: "If he but blench," Hamlet says in a soliloquy, "I know my course" (2. 2. 625-6). At the close of the play scene, when the King does blench, Hamlet turns to Horatio and says, "I'll take the ghost's word for a thousand pound! Didst perceive?" (3. 2. 297-8). The question of fact is now resolved and Hamlet embraces the end which the Ghost had proposed in an early scene of the play: "Revenge his foul and most unnatural murther" (1. 5. 25). The rest of the play concerns the choice of means, but the means in this case is not easy to find. The King cannot be killed at his prayers and so dispatched to Heaven: "Why, this is hire and salary, not revenge!" (3. 3. 79). He does kill him in the Queen's closet, or so he thinks, but it turns out to be only Polonius, that "wretched, rash, intruding fool." And so on to the close of the play. The proper means to accomplish the end is never discovered until it is too late, until Hamlet when he knows that he is dying stabs the King with the envenomed sword. It is too late, now, for a successful plot.

Hamlet, of course, is a touchy subject. I do not wish to imply that his character is equivalent to this analysis; he is something more and something other. He is an imitation of a person, and thus has an imputed reality. He has a name, which is a chief instrument of individualization. He is implicated in circumstances of some particularity. He does and says much that is not reducible to the central choice. He is presented in a specific body of writing. Nevertheless, a fictional character is not a given, a brute fact of existence. He is a construction, a fiction, and hence he must be constructed according to a scheme and must have a scheme to be intelligible. I am maintaining only that both the play and the character of Hamlet are in part constructed according to the scheme of moral choice as it was analyzed in the scholastic tradition.

It would follow that those who interpret Hamlet's character in terms of irresolution are in a way right, for here the process of choice is extended over the whole play. But they are wrong when they see in this a trait of character. Hamlet delays, not because he is irresolute, but because he is reasonable. His reason must be satisfied as to the end before his will moves to embrace it; his reason must discover the appropriate means before the moral choice can be ratified and action move on to the conclusion. He is irresolute because, as Hooker says, "the Will notwithstanding does not incline to have or do that which Reason teacheth to be good, unless the same do also teach it to be possible" (*EP*, 1.7.5). Hamlet could quote in his defense against his detractors, who perhaps like Coleridge are mightier with the pen than with the sword, the apology of the old counsellor in the *Winter's Tale*:

> if ever fearful
> To do a thing where I the issue doubted,
> Whereof the execution did cry out

Against the non-performance, 'twas a fear
That oft infects the wisest.
1. 2. 258-62

Yet in a sense the resolution of the plot is apprehended
partly in terms of moral action. Everyone knows the famous
line in Hamlet's soliloquy, "Thus conscience," that is, knowledge
and awareness, "does make cowards of us all":

And enterprises of great pith and moment
With this regard their current turn awry
And lose the name of action.
3. 1. 83, 86-8

and the later speech prompted by the sight of Fortinbras' exploits:

What is a man,
If his chief good and market of his time
Be but to sleep and feed? A beast, no more.

Here again is the commonplace of soul or sense.

Sure he that made us with such large discourse,
Looking before and after, gave us not
That capability and godlike reason
To fust in us unus'd. Now, whether it be
Bestial oblivion, or some craven scruple
Of thinking too precisely on th' event,—

in which *event*, of course, means "outcome" or "upshot." The
problem here involves a choice between no action, rational
action with a view to consequences, and action at any cost.
The contrast between the latter two resembles that between the
chivalric rashness of Hotspur and the staid courage of Prince
Hal. In this case it is solved in favor of Hotspur. Hamlet
decides:

Rightly to be great
Is not to stir without great argument
But greatly to find quarrel in a straw
When honour's at the stake.

254

and concludes:

> O, from this time forth,
> My thoughts be bloody, or be nothing worth!
> 4. 4. 33-41, 53-6, 65-6

From this time forth his actions as well as his thoughts are as bloody as anyone could wish. To the earlier death of Polonius he adds the deaths of Rosencrantz and Guildenstern, of Laertes by accident, and the King by design. He acts now partly from "perfect conscience," in the ethical sense of that which incites or binds us either to do or not to do something, and partly in the rashness of honor. Reasonable action has proved inadequate in the circumstances, and is abandoned:

> Being thus benetted round with villanies,
> Or I could make a prologue to my brains,
> They had begun the play.
> 5. 2. 29-31

Deliberation is fatal; only rashness has a chance of success:

> Rashly—
> And prais'd be rashness for it; let us know,
> Our indiscretion sometime serves us well
> When our deep plots do pall; and that should learn us
> There's a divinity that shapes our ends,
> Rough-hew them how we will—
> 5. 2. 6-11

Man proposes, and God disposes. Indeed, Heaven is ordinant even in the accidental details. And so Hamlet gives up the human attempt to achieve justice by rational action, by the calculation of means, abandons himself to the tide of circumstance which is the Special Providence of God, and proceeds to the catastrophe despite his misgivings. He is resigned to destiny, which is God's will; "the readiness is all." The play whose plot had displayed the scheme of moral action ends with the renunciation of it.

Notes

This book was completed in 1945. I have since cut, rearranged, and rephrased parts of it but have made no substantial alterations. I have cited Shakespeare throughout from *The Complete Works,* ed. George Lyman Kittredge (Boston, 1936). I have generally modernized texts.

I. *Introduction: Ripeness is All*

1. G. B. Harrison, *Shakespeare: 23 Plays and the Sonnets* (New York, 1948), p. 3. Similarly O. J. Campbell, *The Living Shakespeare* (New York, 1949), p. 1: "In his plays we constantly meet our own experiences; in his poetry we constantly find our inmost thoughts and feelings expressed with an eloquence and a precision far beyond our reach."
2. T. S. Eliot, *Selected Essays* (New York, 1932), p. 231.
3. Robert Bechtold Heilman, *This Great Stage* (Baton Rouge, 1948), p. 112. The correct interpretation is given in passing by Alfred Harbage, *As They Liked It* (New York, 1947), p. 56.
4. Hugh Latimer, *Sermons* ("Everyman's Library": London, 1906), pp. 352-3.
5. G. H. Mair, ed. (Oxford, 1909), p. 83.

John Bruce, ed., Diary of John Manningham ("Camden Society," XCIX: Westminster, 1868), under March 24, 1603: "This morning about three at clock her Majesty departed this life, mildly like a lamb, like a ripe apple from the tree."

II. *Aught of Woe or Wonder*

1. "De ratione studii," *Opera Omnia* (Leyden, 1703), I, 528 C-D. There is a paraphrastic translation of the treatise in William Harrison Woodward, *Desiderius Erasmus concerning the Aim and Method of Education* (Cambridge, 1904), pp. 162-78.
2. *If This be not a Good Play, the Devil is in It* in *Dramatic Works* (Pearson: London, 1873), III, 264.
3. *Opera,* ed. John Burnet (Oxford, 1903), III.

4. *Aristotle on the Art of Poetry*, ed., tr., Ingram Bywater (Oxford, 1909), *ad* 1452a4; 60a11; 60a18.

5. The classic formulation, cited from the index, *s.v.*, *casus*, of the Vives edition (Paris, 1862 and 1861) of Thomas Aquinas, *Summa Theologica.*

6. 2. Prol., 16-7: *The Shakespeare Apocrypha*, ed. C. F. Tucker Brooke (Oxford, 1908), p. 44.

7. "tristitia namque tragoediae proprium." Diomedes *Ars Grammatica* in *Grammatici Latini*, ed. Heinrich Keil (Leipzig, 1857), I, 488.

8. *ST* denotes *Summa Theologica.*

9. Thomas Dekker, "The Magnificent Entertainment . . ." (London, 1604) in *Dramatic Works*, I, 269. Sidney, *Works*, ed. Albert Feuillerat (Cambridge, 1923), III, 23.

10. Hardin Craig, *The Enchanted Glass* (New York, 1936), p. 27; *Shakespeare* (Chicago, 1932), p. 804.

11. *Works*, ed. Keble, 7th ed. (Oxford, 1888). Hereafter referred to as *EP.*

12. However, for a generalized argument see Marston's *Sophonisba.*

13. Julius Caesar Scaliger, *Poetice*, 3. 96; tr., F. M. Padelford, *Select Translations from Scaliger's Poetics* (New York, 1905), p. 57. John Jewel, *The Defense of the Apology* ("Publications of the Parker Society," XXV: Cambridge, 1848), pp. 249-50.

III. *The Donatan Tradition*

1. The material in the following pages is vulgate: Wilhelm Cloetta, *Beiträge zur Literaturgeschichte des Mittelalters und der Renaissance* (Halle, 1890-2); J. E. Spingarn, *A History of Literary Criticism in the Renaissance* (2nd ed., New York, 1908); John W. Cunliffe, ed., *Early English Classical Tragedies* (Oxford, 1912); L. E. Kastner and H. B. Charlton, edd., *The Poetical Works of Sir William Alexander* (Manchester, 1921); A. Philip McMahon, "Seven Questions on Aristotelian Definitions of Tragedy and Comedy," *Harvard Studies in Classical Philology*, XL (1929), 97-198.

2. "Inter tragoediam autem et comoediam cum multa tum inprimis hoc distat, quod in comoedia mediocres fortunae hominum, parvi impetus periculorum, laetique sunt exitus actionum, at in tragoedia

omnia contra, ingentes personae, magni timores, exitus funesti haben-
tur; et illic prima turbulenta, tranquilla ultima, in tragoedia contrario
ordine res aguntur; tum quod in tragoedia fugienda vita, in comoedia
capessenda exprimitur; postremo quod omnis comoedia de fictis est
argumentis, tragoedia saepe de historia fide petitur." Cited from
McMahon, pp. 128-9. The text is apparently by Evanthius, whose
treatise on comedy is included in the Donatan commentary.

3. A Renaissance commonplace: see Justus Lipsius, *Two Bookes of
Constancie*, tr. Sir John Stradling, ed. Rudolf Kirk (New Brunswick,
N. J., 1939), pp. 85-6.

4. Jacobus Zabarella, *Opera Logica* (Venice, 1586), p. 81: "Quod
Rhetorica et Poetica solius civilis disclipinae instrumenta sint, et
quomodo."

5. *Works*, III, 23.

6. McMahon, *op. cit.*, and "On the Second Book of Aristotle's Poetics
and the Source of Theophrastus' Definition of Tragedy," *Harvard
Studies in Classical Philology*, XXVIII (1917), 1-46.

7. "Tragoedia est heroicae fortunae in adversis conprehensio. a Theo-
phrasto ita definita est, *tragoidia estin eroikes tuches peristasis*. . .
Comoedia est privatae civilisque fortunae sine periculo vitae conprehensio, apud Graecos ita definita, *komoidia estin idiotikon pragmaton
akindunos perioche*. . . in ea viculorum, id est humilium domuum,
fortunae conprehendantur, non ut in tragoedia publicarum regiarum-
que . . . comoedia a tragoedia differt, quod in tragoedia introduc-
untur heroes duces reges, in comoedia humiles atque privatae personae;
in illa luctus exilia caedes, in hac amores, virginum raptus: deinde
quod in illa frequenter et paene semper laetis rebus exitus tristes et
liberorum fortunarumque priorum in peius adgnitio. quare varia
definitione discretae sunt. altera enim *akindunos perioche*, altera
tuches peristasis dicta est. tristitia namque tragoediae proprium."
Keil, *loc. cit.*

8. Cited from Cunliffe, pp. xvi ff.

9. *The Works of Thomas Kyd*, ed. Frederick S. Boas (Oxford, 1901),
p. 164.

10. *The School of Shakespeare*, ed. Richard Simpson (London, 1878),
II, 241ff.

11. *The Shakespeare Apocrypha*, p. 35.

259

IV. Wonder

1. *Works*, III, 23.

2. For fuller discussion and citation with respect to the history of wonder as an aestheic term see the author's "Tragic Effect and Tragic Process . . . ," unpublished Stanford dissertation, 1945; Richard Heinze, *Virgils Epische Technik* (Leipzig, 1903), pp. 454ff.; Marvin Herrick, "Some Neglected Sources of *Admiratio*," *MLN*. LXII (1947), 222-6. The historians of Renaissance criticism, until Herrick's note, had regarded the concept as introduced in the middle of the sixteenth century by Minturno and without effective influence on the drama until Corneille: Gregory Smith, *Elizabethan Critical Essays* (Oxford, 1904), I, 392; Joel Spingarn, *op. cit.*, 52-3, 72, 78-9, 285; René Bray, *La Formation de la Doctrine Classique en France* (Paris, 1927), 213ff and 319; Allan H. Gilbert, *Literary Criticism: Plato to Dryden* (New York, 1940), 461 and index, *s. v. admiration*.

3. The Bywater translation. For the relationship of wonder *(to thaumaston)* and astonishment *(ekplexis)* see Aristotle, *Topics*, 4. 5. 126b13ff.

4. Gorgias, *Helena*, 9 (ed. Otto Immisch, 1927, though the text seems untrustworthy); E. E. Sikes, *The Greek View of Poetry* (London, 1931); Max Pohlenz, "Die Anfänge der griechischen Poetik," *Nachr. d. Gott. Ges. d. Wiss.*, 1920, pp. 167ff.

5. Tr. Allan H. Gilbert, *op. cit.*, p. 15.

6. Ed. Leonhard Spengel, *Rhetores Graeci* (Leipzig, 1853-6), II, 455.

7. Ed. Émile Bréhier ("Collection Budé": Paris, 1924); translation revised from Stephen McKenna, *The Ethical Treatises* (London, 1926).

8. Ed., tr., Horace Leonard Jones, *The Geography of Strabo* ("Loeb Library": London, 1917).

9. Ed., tr., W. R. Paton, *The Histories* ("Loeb Library": London, 1922).

10. Ed., tr., Frank Cole Babbitt, *Moralia* ("Loeb Library": London, 1927).

11. Cited by Sikes, *op. cit.*, 112.

12. The Oxford translation, as before, but I have revised the second sentence.

13. Cited and translated by G. L. Hendrickson, "The origin and

Meaning of the Ancient Characters of Style," *AJP*, XXVI (1905), 255-6. I have substituted "astonished" for "moved" toward the end of the next to last sentence. Text, Augustus Mayer, ed., *Theophrasti Peri Lexeos Libri Fragmenta* (Leipzig, 1910), pp. 14-5.

14. Tr., T. H. Moxon, *Aristotle's Poetics, Demetrius on Style* (London, 1934); I have made some revisions. Text, W. Rhys Roberts, ed. (Cambridge, 1902).

15. Ed., W. Rhys Roberts (Cambridge, 1907). There is an excellent translation by Benedict Einarson (Chicago, 1945).

16. Ed., H. Rackham ("Loeb Library": London, 1942).

17. Tr., John Selby Watson, *Institutes of Oratory*, 2 vols. (London, 1909-10). I have substituted "wonder" for "admiration" in the last two sentences. Ed., L. Rademacher (Leipzig, 1935).

18. *Patrologia Latina*, XLII, 90.

19. *Opera Omnia*, ed. Augustus Borgnet (Paris, 1890), VI, 30a-31a.

20. My translation.

21. The relevant passages are reprinted and translated by Ruth Kelso, "Girolamo Fracastoro, *Naugerius sive De Poetica Dialogus*," *Univ. of Illinois Studies in Language and Literature*, IX (1924), 75ff.

22. *Ibid.*, pp. 58-9.

23. My translation. The texts are cited in Bernard Weinberg, "The Poetic Theories of Minturno," *Studies in Honor of Frederick W. Shipley* (St. Louis, 1942), pp. 104, n. 6(1), and 110, n. 17.

24. E. K. Chambers, *William Shakespeare* (Oxford, 1930), I, 412 and II, 188.

25. *The Shakespeare Apocrypha.*

26. *The Plays and Poems*, ed. J. Churton Collins (Oxford, 1905).

27. Ed. H. Harvey Wood (Edinburgh, 1934-9).

28. *The Shakespeare Apocrypha.*

29. *Works*, edd. C. H. Herford, Percy and Evelyn Simpson (Oxford, 1925—).

30. *Works*, ed. A. H. Bullen (Boston, 1885-6), VI, 370-1.

V. *Reason Panders Will*

I am deeply indebted to Lily B. Campbell's *Shakespeare's Tragic Heroes* (Cambridge, 1930), p. 146, for the interpretation of Hamlet's phrase, "reason panders will."

1. "Definitio . . . est imitatio actionis illustris, voluntarie perfectae, cui inest vis universalis circa res praestantiores, non autem particularis

261

de singula re praestanti: qua quidem imitatione animi recta afficiuntur affectione per misericordiam atque terrorem in eis orta." *Voluntarie* can also be construed as an adjective without significant change of meaning. "Paraphrasis in librum Poeticae Aristotelis," tr. Jacobus Mantinus, ed. Fridericus Heidenhain, *Jahrbücher für classische Philologie,* 17th Supplementband (1890), 359. For Renaissance editions see Lane Cooper and Alfred Gudeman, *A Bibliography of the Poetics of Aristotle* ("Cornell Studies in English" XI: New Haven, 1928), *s.n.* Averroes.

2. A medieval commonplace: see Alexander of Hales, *Summa,* 1. 1. 1. ad 1 and ad 2. (Quaracchi, 1924), I.

3. Chas. R. S. Harris, *Duns Scotus* (Oxford, 1927), II, 288ff; see also Arthur C. McGiffert, *History of Christian Thought* (New York, 1932-5), II, 299ff.; D. E. Sharp, *Franciscan Philosophy at Oxford* (Oxford, 1930), pp. 336-41. *ST,* 1-2. 8. 1. For Thomas's doctrine, see Michael Wittmann, *Die Ethik des Hl. Thomas von Aquin* (Munich, 1933); Etienne Gilson, *Moral Values and the Moral Life,* tr. Leo R. Ward (London, 1931).

4. *Phaedra,* 177ff.; *Metamorphoses,* 7. 20-1. These passages are cited by Melanchthon in his refutation of Stoic fatalism, *Corpus Reformatorm* XVI, 42-50, 189-201, and 336-46.

5. *The Enchanted Glass,* 116.

6. Ludwig Schutz, *Thomas-Lexicon* (Paderborn, 1895), *s. vv.*

7. C. F. Tucker Brooke and Nathaniel Burton Paradise, edd., *English Drama: 1580-1642* (Boston, 1933).

8. Ed. A. W. Verity (London, n.d.).

9. The punctuation is from Q1.

10. Ed., G. W. Kitchin ("Everyman's Library": London, 1930), 132.

11. Lancelot Andrewes, *Lectures* (London, 1657), 256.

12. E. E. Stoll, *Othello* (Minneapolis, 1915); *Art and Artifice in Shakespeare* (Cambridge, 1933), p. 6ff.; Hardin Craig, *Shakespeare,* 715-6.

13. John Jewel, *Defence of the Apology,* 70.

14. In the following analysis I obviously owe a good deal to Walter Clyde Curry's *Shakespeare's Philosophical Patterns* (Baton Rouge, 1937).

15. *Advancement of Learning,* p. 146.

16. *The School of Shakespeare.*

The Ancient Quarrel
Between History and Poetry

A work of art is the embodiment of an intention. To realize an intention in language is the function of the writer. To realize from language the intention of the author is the function of the reader or the critic, and his method is historical or philological interpretation. For Philology, in the older sense of the term, is concerned with the relationship of expression and intention; it revivifies the letter by ascertaining its spirit. And when Philology has accomplished this task, there remains not even the appreciation of the spirit, since the task cannot be accomplished without this.

This premise resolves the quarrel between the historical and the aesthetic approach to literature and to other branches of art. Everyone is familiar with the distinction, and apparently everyone agrees that there is a distinction. Even those who have defended the historical attitude against the onslaughts of the aesthetes have maintained the dualism of the two approaches. For they have held either that the historical is an independent discipline with its own rights to existence, or, more commonly, that though the historical is subordinate, it is a necessary handmaid to the aesthetic: we need historical knowledge to remove the hindrances to appreciation.

The two positions are, of course, compatible: one can hold that the discipline of literary history has independent validity and at the same time hold that it furnishes useful aids to literary appreciation. Furthermore, it is true enough that there is a body of knowledge associated with literature that is in itself worth knowing: not only literary history proper, but also history in the ordinary sense of the term, and indeed many other fields of learning. What is more, all these are useful; in fact, it is doubtful if there be any kind of knowledge that will not at some point or other prove useful in the study of literature. Furthermore, the ways of understanding and the habits of attention which are developed by some of these disciplines are of the greatest value, both in themselves and for the study of literature, and there is much to be said for the old argument that a thorough grounding in Anglo-Saxon and textual criticism form a good preparation for the study of the English essay or the poetry of T. S. Eliot. But the general habits formed in this way can be acquired without these disciplines; the information needed to understand a given work can be picked up from those who have it; and as to the associated learnings, the aesthetic critic can grant them validity and properly ignore them on the grounds that a man can only do so much and that his business is appreciation. Let the historian write history, let the aesthetic critic appreciate—or let the one man alternately do both.

Such is the common resolution of the problem, and the only argument is over the spoils: which shall have the greater prestige or make the more money. But the dualism is not only unnecessary, it is pernicious.

It rests apparently upon an empirical basis. We are told that works of art take on new color with each succeeding generation if not with each succeeding reader, that they are complexes of symbols that seem to offer an almost inexhaustible variety of interpretations. They are all things to all men and all ages. And the living greatness of a work of art is often thought to reside in this chameleon character. It is this, we are told, which distinguishes the major from the minor work, which marks the difference between *Hamlet* and *The Spanish Tragedy,* or the work of living interest from the work of mere historical interest.

But is this really the case? The difference is obviously in part one of merit, or of imputed merit. The case is not that the one is

264

better because it is more living, but simply that it is more living because it is better. The argument, then, mistakes an effect for the cause, or is naively circular. There is, moreover, a second consideration which is usually unnoticed in these discussions. The work that is thought to be more alive and more universal usually turns out to be simply more familiar, for the familiar is that with which we feel we can take liberties. Donne, for instance, achieved universality by becoming fashionable, and so with Gerard Hopkins. Thus the contemplative spirit becomes fashion or custom.

But the position rests in truth, as a distinguished scholar tells us, not so much upon an empirical basis as upon an assumed distinction between the work of art "as artistic phenomenon and historical fact," a distinction which leads logically to the disappearance of the work of art itself. The distinction is made clear by Curry in the following passage:

> But as historical fact it [the work of literature] must inevitably bear upon it, in both form and content, the stamp of historical associations which influenced its production and from which it emerged. Criticism, we may say, attempts to report faithfully upon the efficacy of an artistic construction as a stimulus of aesthetic experience; historical interpretation, on the other hand, is concerned with orienting the historical fact in relation to the historical events—traditional or otherwise—which urged the dramatist to create it. But wherever these scattered events originally focussed upon the drama have been forgotten, it is evident that criticism cannot exercise its function properly and completely without relying upon the findings of historical interpretation.

Although in the last sentence the scholar suggests that historical interpretation is the handmaid of criticism or appreciation, the dualism he erects does not leave room even for this. For the distinguishing mark of literature, in so far as it is true art, he asserts, is its universality, and by this is meant that "as art-work it may be immediately possessed by the contemplative spirit of men in any age and under any circumstances; as a stimulus to aesthetic experience it is timeless, self-sufficient, and free."

From this account it is not at all evident how criticism and historical interpretation can have anything to do with each other. On the one hand, the historian is concerned with the origin of the stimulus, with what urged the writer to create it. On the other hand, criticism reports on the "timeless" response to the stimulus—any response, and the only question is, Does it get a response? So the multiplicity of wild and inconsistent interpretations of *Macbeth*, as Curry hastens to explain, testify to the virility of the Macbeth-stimulus, and not at all to the stupidity, confusion, and selfishness of the interpreters. But who is going to look at the stimulus itself? Here are ancestors and descendents, but where is the man? Who is going to look at *Macbeth?* And if the scholar himself looks very closely and very accurately at *Macbeth,* this only refutes his theory by his practice, for his practice exhibits that fusion of accuracy and feeling which we have defined as genuine historical interpretation.

But, according to the theory, appreciation is the actual response to the work of art, though usually it is the response of certain selected persons. For it is not held to be, except by some cultural anarchists, any response of any person, but rather that of what is generally called the man of sensibility who appreciates in the light of universal aesthetic values. Now, few will deny that there are men of sensibility and men of insensibility, that there are those who are capable of responding to works of art and those who should not be allowed to try, though there may be some disagreement as to who belongs in what category. But when we have settled on the elect, what have we? We have contemplative spirits who immediately possess the aesthetic experience, which is timeless, self-sufficient, and free. There is apparently a kind of Oversoul of Culture in which are absorbed all the aesthetic monuments of the past, which have put off the body of this death and the material clothing of their particular expressions, and in which the elect participate by a parody of the Beatific Vision.

The more cautious will bring this heaven down to earth, and will allow the work of art its material embodiment. But they will

266

regard the historical nature of the work only as a hindrance to the universality of the artist's vision, or as an accident to be disengaged from the substance. They will maintain that historical interpretation is necessary, but that its purpose is to remove the ignorance or misapprehensions which hinder our direct appreciation of the text.

On the contrary, the accidents are integral to the substance. Hindrances are not merely hindrances: they are in themselves important. They are the points at which we become conscious that the text cannot be understood on our own terms. We are reading another, not ourselves. This fact should provoke us to look with some skepticism on what is meant by the universal in the context of aesthetic appreciation. By the universal is usually meant that which concerns you; hence as a principle of aesthetic importance, it is the principle of selfishness and ignorance. For what you immediately understand you regard as essential; what you do not, as accidental.

However, we need not deny that the appreciation of a work of art on one's own terms and even in defiance of the known historical intention of the work is more valuable than a dry and desiccated antiquarianism. For the one has life and the other has not. And such appreciation is especially valuable to the man who would integrate in his own experience the monuments of the past. But the man who does this should remember that he is not integrating in his experience the experience of the past. By being unhistorical he has abjured that experience; he is abusing the monuments of history to inform them with his own life. At the best, if he is himself a competent artist and if the material is tractable, he may produce a new and different work, and this may in itself have value.

This is sometimes accomplished, for example, in the transcription and arrangement of old music, as in Bach's transcription of Vivaldi or Chavez' of Buxtehude. In literature the best and most obvious examples are to be found in the seventeenth and eighteenth century adaptations of the classics. Today, it is usually done in critical essays for the reviews. But in such cases we are dealing with a new, though derived, work. The new work may throw some light upon its source, and an understanding of the source may be an important element in the understanding of the work. But the point is: an adaptation is an independent work and not primarily an interpretation.

On the other hand, translation and interpretation are essentially alike. For, although a translation is manifestly other than its original, nevertheless we can designate a translation as correct or incorrect, as more or less adequate to the original. Now, it is that understanding of the original which enables us to say that a given translation is more or less adequate, which is the aim of historical interpretation. Furthermore, this understanding of the original is the work of art. Hence, the work of interpretation consists precisely in the recovery, so far as is possible, of the original; that is, of the author's intentions as realized in the particular text under consideration.

For this is the way in which the genuinely sensitive man approaches a work of literature. It is a method that, as a matter of fact, does have close analogies with the method of religious surrender. It consists in yielding as completely as possible to the experience of the work, with the intention of formulating afterwards the alterations which this surrender has wrought. As such, it is not only unobjectionable but necessary, both in art and in life. It is the initial act of abandonment, of faith and sympathy, without which we will never penetrate any human experience.

But, unless it is protected by the constant awareness that the experience we are penetrating is that of another, such aesthetic surrender can only be an elaborate game by which we discover with surprise that the attitudes and preconceptions with which we view the object are really here, although in fact we put them there in a somnambulistic trance. Thus the aesthetic experience proves often enough to be only an affirmation of solipsism, and the aesthetic soul a parody of the Neo-Platonic God whose spirit infuses all things, which are but degradations of Itself. However, if the act

268

of faith and sympathy with which we surrender ourselves to an object be one which involves a scrupulous responsibility towards the object in all its specificity, this is nothing other than historical interpretation.

It is in fact nothing other than morality, if it is not too out of fashion to connect morality with such pursuits as poetry and scholarship. For the understanding of an author in the scholarly sense involves the exercise under defined conditions of the two fundamental principles of morality in the Western tradition: 1) the principle of dignity, or of responsibility to the external fact, in the special form of respect for another person as revealed in his works; and 2) the principle of love, the exercise of sympathetic insight, or of imaginative transformation.

For (to sum up) the premise of historical interpretation is that a piece of writing is an historical document, and by this is meant that it is to be interpreted, understood, and experienced as nearly as possible in the way in which it was originally intended to be interpreted, understood, and experienced. Hence, in historical interpretation our allegiance is to the external, to the historical experience implicated in the system of signs which is the work under consideration.

For whatever be the case with the other arts, the arts of language consist of statements, and a statement means what it says. We look at what a work says to find out what it means, and the apprehension of its meaning is the work of art. Insofar as the meaning is not expressed in or not recoverable from the statements, the work is deficient. Furthermore, it is a simple principle of ethics, provable in daily conversation, that the meaning of a statement is not what anyone chances to attribute to it—how hurt we are when we are misconstrued—, but what it was intended to convey. The intention is the intention of the author as expressed in the language which he used and qualified by the circumstances under which he expressed it. Hence every statement is an historical statement, and it is properly understood only by historical interpretation.

Thus, since a work of literature is precisely the apprehension of its proper meaning, the appreciation of literature resides in historical interpretation. There are not two approaches to the study of literature, but only one: historical interpretation is aesthetic appreciation. If the two are distinguishable, they are distinguishable only as aspects of one another. The historical is that act of respect by which we recognize otherness: to this the various historical disciplines are subsidiary. The aesthetic is that act of sympathy by which we realize the other and make it our own.

NOTE: There is a distinction to be made in the use of the term *historical*. In the wider sense, it denotes that interpretation which takes into account the time, place, and conditions of an utterance. But there is a fundamental difference in methodology between the literary approach to a text and the approach of the historian in the narrower sense of the term. The literary interpreter is interested solely in understanding what the text was intended to say, neither more nor less. The historian, in the narrower sense, is interested primarily in the reality supposed to lie behind the text. He is as interested in what the text does not say as in what it does. His method consists in breaking down the text, in destroying its literary finish in order to penetrate to the reality which the words conceal. In brief, the historian treats a text as evidence, the literary interpreter treats it as a composition whose surface is inviolate. The historian's allegiance is to the facts which the text enables him to conjecture, to infer, or to establish. The allegiance of the literary interpreter is to the text itself.

Perhaps a trivial example will make the distinction clear. The notorious sea-coasts of Bohemia in the *Winter's Tale* are evidence to the historian of a certain casualness and vagueness about geographical matters on Shakespeare's part. To the literary interpreter this is irrelevant. Bohemia to him is precisely what it was to Shakespeare, a remote kingdom which may as well have a sea-coast as not.

APPENDIX II

Tragedy as Essence

The humanist in areas that are of special concern to him, as in the case of tragedy, tends to be an uncritical Realist, a simple-minded believer in a realm of essences. Let us take the case of tragedy and see what this belief entails. The asumption that there is a stable and external reality corresponding to the idea of tragedy, the assumption, indeed, that there is an Idea of tragedy, and the subsequent inquiry into its definition always presupposes at least that there is a given and prior body of material associated with a common name in common use. Otherwise, one could never begin. Furthermore, the name itself, being a term in common use, has associated with it a group of notions whose content and relationship is only partly fixed and defined. A certain vagueness and slipperiness is part of their meaning. The process of investigation, then, consists in introducing a more explicit structure into the notions associated with the term and a more limited reference into the term itself. In this way the element of slipperiness and vagueness, if not eliminated, is considerably reduced. The term in its more closely defined sense is then re-introduced into the body of the material so that some items are excluded from consideration, while others are arrayed in degrees of importance on the basis of their approximation to the definition. The *Spanish Tragedy* is not really a tragedy but a melodrama, and *King Lear* is more tragic than *Richard III*.

The result of such an investigation is a definition which cannot be regarded as merely arbitrary, as simply stipulated. It refers to reality and proposes to get to the heart of it. And the heart of it is an essence. But if what one arrives at by this process be an

271

essence, in any of the normal senses of this term, we must suppose that the terms of ordinary language, or at least some of them, derive their content and reference from some source other than the historical process of usage, and that this source is to a sufficient extent controlled by a realm of essences. We must further suppose that the methods by which we clarify the definition of the word and thing is the reverse of that by which the word in the historical process of actual usage became corrupted by vagueness of content and slipperiness of reference, and we must assume that the process is reversible. These assumptions seem to me to entail a Platonism that is denied by my experience and by what historical knowledge I have of, for example, the notions of tragedy in various literatures and various times.

I should prefer to define such a notion as tragedy in terms of those principles of order that enter into the intention of a given work or given body of works in so far as the explicit recognition by the author of those principles as the principles of what he calls tragedy and their intended recognition by the reader is guaranteed by historical evidence. There may thus be a relationship between tragedies of various authors, groups, and periods so far as similar principles of order can be defined in different traditions. There is in this sense a continuity in the tradition of tragedy between Classical Antiquity and the English Renaissance. In this the chief mediating source was not Aristotle's *Poetics*, but the definition of tragedy gathered by the grammarians of later Antiquity out of Classical theory and practice and transmitted as a scheme to be realized to the writers of the Renaissance. Consequently it is possible to construct a history of tragedy from Aeschylus to John Ford that would be a genuine history without presupposing that any such entity as tragedy really exists except in the notions of tragedy which writers and readers have entertained.

Notes

Appendix I. *The Ancient Quarrel Between History and Poetry*

[1] Walter Clyde Curry, *Shakespeare's Philosophical Patterns* (Baton Rouge, 1937), pp. xi-xii.